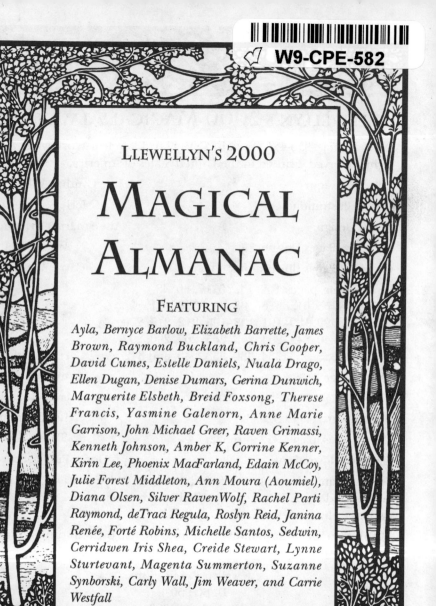

LLEWELLYN'S 2000

MAGICAL ALMANAC

FEATURING

Ayla, Bernyce Barlow, Elizabeth Barrette, James Brown, Raymond Buckland, Chris Cooper, David Cumes, Estelle Daniels, Nuala Drago, Ellen Dugan, Denise Dumars, Gerina Dunwich, Marguerite Elsbeth, Breid Foxsong, Therese Francis, Yasmine Galenorn, Anne Marie Garrison, John Michael Greer, Raven Grimassi, Kenneth Johnson, Amber K, Corrine Kenner, Kirin Lee, Phoenix MacFarland, Edain McCoy, Julie Forest Middleton, Ann Moura (Aoumiel), Diana Olsen, Silver RavenWolf, Rachel Parti Raymond, deTraci Regula, Roslyn Reid, Janina Renée, Forté Robins, Michelle Santos, Sedwin, Cerridwen Iris Shea, Creide Stewart, Lynne Sturtevant, Magenta Summerton, Suzanne Synborski, Carly Wall, Jim Weaver, and Carrie Westfall

LLEWELLYN'S 2000 MAGICAL ALMANAC

ISBN 1-56718-950-4. Copyright © 1999 by Llewellyn Worldwide. All rights reserved. Printed in the United States of America.

Editor/Designer:	Cynthia Ahlquist
Cover Illustration:	Merle S. Insinga
Cover Design:	Anne Marie Garrison
Calendar Pages Design:	Andrea Neff
Calendar Pages Illustrations:	Carrie Westfall
Illustrations, pages 1, 2, 14, 16, 17, 36, 38, 46, 48, 54, 55, 61, 63, 66, 68, 84, 85, 90, 91, 93, 94, 96, 99, 189–191, 193–195, 212, 213, 220, 222, 238–240, 242, 254, 263, 265, 267, 290, 292, 306, 307, 328, 333, 334, 336, 338, 340, and 342:	Carrie Westfall
Photo, page 310:	Bernyce Barlow
Photos, pages 81–83:	deTraci Regula
Illustrations, pages 320, 321:	Bill Cannon
Illustrations, pages 313 and 322:	Tom Grewe
Clip Art Illustrations:	Dover Publications

Special thanks to Amber Wolfe for the use of daily color and incense correspondences. For more detailed information, please see *Personal Alchemy* by Amber Wolfe.

Moon sign and phase data computed by Astro Communications Services (ACS).

Llewellyn Publications
Dept. 950-4
P.O. Box 64383
St. Paul, MN 55164-0838

ABOUT THE AUTHORS

AYLA is a solitary Wiccan and mother of a four-year-old. She holds a B.S. in mathematics, but spends her time writing poems and children's stories. She loves crystal work and divination, reading, and hatha yoga. She is a member of several earth-conscious organizations and loves getting letters from fellow Wiccans.

BERNYCE BARLOW is the author of *Sacred Sites of the West,* from Llewellyn. She researches and leads seminars on sacred sites of the ten western states. Bernyce is currently working on a CD of music for the sacred sites. She is also an elder of the Boot-to-the-Head tradition of spiritual enlightenment.

ELIZABETH BARRETTE is a regular contriubutor to *SageWoman, PanGaia, Circle Network News, PagaNet News,* and *Moonbeams Journal.* Much of her involvement with the wider Pagan community takes place online, where she has helped build netwoking resources such as the Pagan Leaders Mailing List and the Pagan/NeoPagan sections of the NWS Theology Website. Visit her website at http://www.worthlink. net/~ysabet/index.html.

JAMES BROWN is a practicing Witch from Scotland.

RAYMOND BUCKLAND is the author of several best-selling books, including *Buckland's Complete Book of Witchcraft; Practical Candleburning Rituals; Practial Color Magick; Scottish Witchcraft; Secrets of Gypsy Fortune Telling; Secrets of Gypsy Love Magic; Doors to Other Worlds; Advanced Candle Magick; The Buckland Gypsies Domino Divination Deck; The Gypsy Dream Dictionary,* and the novels *The Committee* and *Cardinal's Sin.*

CHRIS COOPER is a solitary and unafilliated Pagan whose writing credits include the *Star Trek: Starfleet Academy* comic books and *Queer Nation: The Online Comic* on the worldwide web. He is continuing to work on a myth cycle of his own invention, since none of the existing pantheons would return his phone calls.

DAVID CUMES, M.D. has a private medical practice in California. He was born and raised in South Africa, where for a time he lived with the Kalahari Bushmen. Dr. Cumes was trained as a wilderness guide and has traveled extensively in the wild, leading groups on healing journeys to Peru, South Africa, and the Sini Desert. He is the author of *Inner Passages, Outer Journeys* and *The Spirit of Healing*.

ESTELLE DANIELS is a professional part-time astrologer, author of *Astrologickal Magick*, a guide to using astrology and magic, and co-author of *Pocket Guide to Wicca*. Estelle has a small select private astrological practice and travels to festivals, bookstores, and conferences in the U.S. lecturing and teaching. She is a High Priestess of Eclectic Wicca and teaches the Craft to students of varying interests and levels.

NUALA DRAGO is a folklorist, musician, and Wittan. She is currently working on a book-length tale of the Otherworld, a Celtic fantasy in which she hopes to impart the awesome, often horrifying, beauty of the ancient Celtic culture in the mythic style. She enjoys the study and use of herbal medicine and is passionate about animal rights.

ELLEN DUGAN is a practicing Witch and a psychic-clairvoyant. She has lectured on various topics such as psychic development, the tarot, magical gardening, and Wiccan families.

DENISE DUMARS is a widely-published poet, critic, and author of science fiction, fantasy, and horror stories. Her articles on strange phenomena have appeared in *The Gate,* and she is the author of the section on Santería in Merrimack Books' writers' guide to religions called *A New Age*.

GERINA DUNWICH is a Wiccan High Priestess, professional astrologer, and author of numerous books, including *Wicca Craft; The Wicca Spellbook; Candlelight Spells; A Wiccan's Guide to Prophecy and Divination; Everyday Wicca;* and *Wicca A to Z*.

MARGUERITE ELSBETH (Raven Hawk) is a professional diviner and a student of Native American and European folk healing. She is co-author of *The Grail Castle: Male Myths and Mysteries in the Celtic Tradition* and *The Silver Wheel: Women's Myths and Mysteries in the Celtic Tradition* with Kenneth Johnson, and author of *Crystal Medicine: Working with Crystals, Gems, and Minerals*.

BREID FOXSONG is a British Traditional Wiccan who has been practicing for more than twenty years. She is the former editor of *Sacred Hart Magazine* and has had articles published in other magazines, ranging from *Green Egg* to *Craft/Crafts*. She is also active in her community, hosting open circles and introductory classes in Wicca.

THERESE FRANCIS, PH.D. is a third degree Wiccan (Turquoise Path), astrologer, teacher, shaman, and author. She teaches personal sovereignity, self-defense, and cross-cultural understanding to the general public through the Whole Life Expo and similar events. She is the designer of the *Age of Aquarius Astrology Game* and author of numerous books, including *Bless This House and All* and *101 Things to Do During a Retrograde Mercury.*

YASMINE GALENORN has practiced in the Craft since 1980. She teaches classes on natural magic, leads public and private rituals, and is a professional tarot reader with a loyal clientele. She has written *Embracing the Moon, Dancing with the Sun, Tarot Journeys,* and *Trancing the Witch's Wheel.*

ANNE MARIE GARRISON is the Senior Creative Designer at Llewellyn Publications, author of *Gods and Goddess of the Zodiac: A Coloring Book* (from Crossquarter Breeze of Santa Fe, NM), and co-owner/founder of Witches Stitches: Cross-stitch Patterns for Crafty Pagans. She has been active in the Pagan community for over ten years. Currently, Anne Marie is working on her Gardnerian second degree, an eclectic Wiccan third, and exploring her Germanic roots.

JOHN MICHAEL GREER has been a student of the Western esoteric tradition since 1975 and teaches Cabalistic magic in the Golden Dawn tradition. He is presently an active member of five fraternal and two magical lodges. He is the author of *Circles of Power: Ritual Magic in the Western Tradition, Inside a Magical Lodge, Earth Divination, Earth Magic,* and *Paths of Wisdom: The Magical Cabala in the Western Tradition.*

RAVEN GRIMASSI is a hereditary Italian Witch practicing a family tradition of Stregheria. He is also an Initiate of Pictish-Gaelic Wicca, Gardnerian Wicca, and Brittic Witchcraft. Raven is the author of *Ways of the Strega; The Wiccan Mysteries;* and *Wiccan Magick.*

KENNETH JOHNSON obtained his degree in the study of comparative religions. He has been a practitioner of astrology since 1974 and is the author of six books. Some of them are *Mythic Astrology: Archetypal Powers in the Horoscope, Jaguar Wisdom: An Introduction to the Mayan Calendar, Slavic Sorcery,* and *Witchcraft and the Shamanic Journey.*

AMBER K has been an ordained High Priestess of Wicca for almost twenty years. She is the author of *CovenCraft* and the bestseller *True Magick.* She has served as National First Officer of the Covenant of the Goddess, a federation of more than 100 covens and many solitaries. Amber has been a guest speaker at Pagan festivals nationwide.

CORRINE KENNER is a tarot card reader, speaker, and professional communicator. She is a member of both the American Tarot Association and the International Tarot Society. She is also the creator of *Llewellyn's Tarot Calendar* and the editor of *The Reader*, a quarterly tarot newsletter. Find her website at http://www.TwoOfCups.com.

KIRIN LEE writes and does graphic design for a science fiction magazine and is the managing editor for a rock and roll magazine. She writes science fiction as well, and she is currently working on a *Star Trek* novel. She is also beginning a Pagan parents' handbook.

PHOENIX MACFARLAND is the author of the *Complete Book of Magical Names*. She is also one of the authors included in Dr. Lonnie Barbach's book, *Seductions,* from Dutton Press. Her erotica has appeared in *All Acts of Love and Pleasure*. She is married to Kerr Cuhulain, the famous Pagan cop who wrote *The Law Enforcement Guide to Wicca*.

EDAIN MCCOY is part of the Wittan Irish Pagan Tradition and is the author of *Witta: An Irish Pagan Tradition: A Witch's Guide to Faery Folk; The Sabbats; How To Do Automatic Writing; Celtic Myth and Magick; Mountain Magick; Lady of the Night; Entering the Summerland; Inside A Witches' Coven; Making Magick; Celtic Women's Spirituality; Astral Projection for Beginners;* and the forthcoming title on the magic of romance, *Bewitchments*.

JULIE FOREST MIDDLETON is the compiler, editor, and publisher of *Songs For Earthlings: A Green Spirituality Songbook* ($27+$4 shipping to Emerald Earth Publishing, P.O. Box 4326-L, Philadelphia, PA 19118). She is a Priestess of Ge and a member of Mom's Janitors, an elite corps that understands that picking up trash is both a spiritual and political act.

ANN MOURA (AOUMIEL) has been a solitary Witch for more than thirty-five years. She is the author of the books *Dancing Shadows, Green Witchcraft,* and *Green Witchcraft II: Working With the Dark Powers*. She has been preparing a handbook for coursework in Green Witchcraft based on the classes she teaches, and she is also writing a fiction book.

DIANA OLSEN maintains an herb garden in her tiny apartment and performs "discount tarot readings" to earn extra money for school. She has practiced magic throughout her life and Wicca for the last three years. If anyone has a decent-paying job for a college graduate, let her know.

SILVER RAVENWOLF is director of the Wiccan/Pagan Press Alliance, a third-degree Craft initiate, and a HexCraft (Pow-Wow) instructor. She also runs a healing circle for people of all religions. She is the author of many popular books, including *To Ride a Silver Broomstick; To Stir a Magick Cauldron; Angels; American Folk Magick; Teen Witch;* and the forthcoming *Silver's Spells for Prosperity* and *Halloween.*

RACHEL PARTI RAYMOND is a writer, glassblower, Pagan priestess, and mom living in Northern California.

DETRACI REGULA is the author of *The Mysteries of Isis* and co-author of *Whispers of the Moon,* a biography of Scott Cunningham.

ROSLYN REID is a Druid and a member of the Moonshadow Institute. She is a regular contributor of art and articles to Llewellyn, as well as to Pagan-oriented publications such as *SageWoman* and *Dalriada,* a Scottish magazine of Celtic spirituality. She has also published pieces in consumer magazines like *Tightwad Living* and *Thrifty Times* and was a contributor to Susun Weed's book *Breast Cancer? Breast Health!*

JANINA RENÉE is the author of *Tarot Spells* and *Playful Magick.* She is currently studying herbs on the theory that healing results from the soul-spirits of human beings establishing connections with the soul-spirit of nature. Her primary goal is learning to "affect the outcome of the day;" in other words, making choices that create harmony with the universe's flow.

FORTÉ ROBINS and her husband practice as a duality (as opposed to either being a solitary). They are eclectic in nature, though heavily influenced by shamanism. They own a business and have the privilege of being the caretakers of four very selective felines.

MICHELLE SANTOS is an enthusiastic amateur astrologer and believer in fairies from an early age. She writes short stories, historical novels, and feature-length articles. Her articles can be seen in *Bride's Magazine, SageWoman, Renaissance Magazine,* and *Victorian Decorating and Lifestyle Magazine.*

SEDWIN is an artist and explorer of the ancient Goddess spirituality. She has created and teaches the "Speaking the Language of the Goddess" workshop, and writes "The Wheel of the Year" column in *The Light Network Newsletter. The Light Network Newsletter* is available online at www.photon.net/lightnet.

CERRIDWEN IRIS SHEA is an urban Witch who writes in many genres under several different names. Her play *Roadkill* had successful runs in London, Edinburgh, and Australia. *Scrying* received four-star reviews in Edinburgh. *Plateau* is being adapted for the screen. She is currently working on a play based on the Iphigenia myth.

CREIDE STEWART, ESQUIRE is a Solitary Wiccan and Pennsylvania attorney, practicing primarily in the areas of criminal defense, family law litigation, and constitutional rights. She is the national Vice President of the Witches' Anti-Discrimination League and the Founder and President of the Coalition for Religious Freedom.

LYNNE STURTEVANT is a solitary pagan practitioner. She has a B.A. in philosophy and has had a life-long fascination with ancient cultures, mystery cults, myths, fairy tales, and folk traditions. She is an accomplished craftswoman and an avid collector of folk art.

MAGENTA SUMMERTON has been a Witch for more than twenty-five years, a priestess for over twenty years, and is a one of the founders of the coven Prodea, which has been practicing for more than eighteen years. She frequently presents workshops at a variety of festivals, gatherings, and conferences in the Upper Midwest.

SUZANNE SYNBORSKI is a freelance writer and novelist. Her current projects include research on the history and practices of the Traiteur and plans for a novel that will feature a Traiteur as the protagonist.

CARLY WALL is author of *Flower Secrets Revealed: Using Flowers to Heal, Beautify and Energize Your Life!* from A.R.E. Press, as well as *Naturally Healing Herbs, Setting the Mood with Aromatherapy,* and *The Little Encyclopedia of Olde Thyme Home Remedies,* from Sterling Publishing. A regular article contributor for Llewellyn's annual publications for the last seven years, she holds a certificate in aromatherapy.

JIM WEAVER is a writer and collector of American folk art. Working in his herb and flower gardens helps him stay close to nature while celebrating the changing seasons.

CARRIE WESTFALL is a professional artist and self-proclaimed "nocturnal vegetarian compulsive green Witch of chaos." When she is not creating lovely interior illustrations and articles for the *Magical Almanac* and other publications, she enjoys horticulture, recycling roadkill, and explosives. She loves her mother and her wonderful cat Weh-weh.

TABLE OF CONTENTS

THE SINGER AND THE DRAGON: A CREATION MYTH

BY CHRIS COOPER

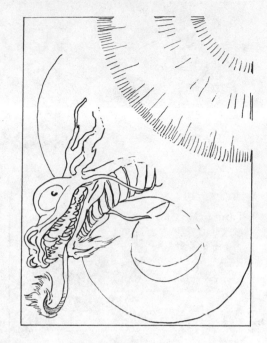

One of the more disturbing revelations of modern physics is the law of entropy, which predicts that the destiny of the universe and everything in it is total chaos. Yet despite this inexorable trend, our restless universe persistently blossoms with order, from the structure of DNA to the human body to the shape of galaxies—all of it transient, doomed to break down and die. In the face of such gloom, reassurance can be found in the oldest of sources: creation myths, both Wiccan and those of ancient mythologies. Or better yet, a synthesis of the two...

In the beginning, there is Unu, and Unu is All; from its harmony and its discord all things flow, and to its ever-shifting pattern all things return, for in truth they have never left. But in the end, beyond Unu, the dragon waits: the all-consuming nameless, whose shapeless form is chaos, whose hunger knows no bounds, whose gaping maw forever strives to swallow all sound and to extinguish all light.

Feeling the cold breath of the dragon as it drew near, the great goddess Unu raised her voice and began to sing; and this song of diversity, intolerable to the dragon, became the Goddess's sole weapon in her struggle against the beast. The magic of the song set to work instantly, changing one into many, so that the Goddess now has three faces and wears three different forms, the better to fight the dragon with. The first face, shining with the fearsome light of his flaming eyes, is that of Cosmos, Lord of the Stars; the second face is that of gray-haired Chronos, Father Time; and the

third face remains forever hidden in shadow, for it belongs to the dark lord, Night, the Master of the Mind and the Lord of Things Unseen. Together, the Three Who Are One struggle against the dragon to this very day.

But the great song had only just begun...

The Three Who Are One looked out into the void and saw their own reflection, knowing themselves at last for who they truly were: Unu in her fullness, beckoning her other selves as suitors. Through the power of her song, she shattered all boundaries so that reflection and self could momentarily touch. Seeing the beautiful goddess made manifest before him, the bright lord Cosmos could not contain the fiery lust within him; his powerful body surged toward her, rashly pushing his two brethren aside. Night too was smitten, falling in love with the goddess for her fathomless complexity; but he courteously stepped aside and, with a knowing smile that on his shadowed face none could see, he let the physically superior Cosmos lie with the goddess first. Aged Chronos, meanwhile, had absolutely no carnal interest in the Goddess; the twilight lord was well beyond such desires and focused his attention with infinite patience on his sole task: shepherding the passage of time.

And indeed, a long time passed before Cosmos, in ecstasy with Unu, had finally spent himself. But once he had, it was time for Night's long-awaited union with the Great Goddess. She was already pregnant with billions upon billions of children from Cosmos's potent seed, so virile was he; but now Night set his plan in motion, for as he lay with the Goddess he used his magie to change the nature of all that was in Unu's womb, so that the countless children that would have been Cosmos's would now be his, Night's.

Learning of this after the fact, Cosmos was beside himself. He raged, and wept fiery tears from his flaming eyes, and, finally, sought help from Chronos. With a heavy sigh, the graybeard intervened, joining with the Great Goddess himself. Though he could not undo Night's spell, Chronos added his own magic to it, so that although all things born of Unu would fall to Night's domain, they would do so only at their appointed hour.

And so from the Great Goddess were born the children of Cosmos, the celestial gods—trillions of worlds and stars, beautiful daughters and radiant sons whose dance forms the whirling heavens and whom Cosmos lovingly embraces in the folds of his cloak of space. To Chronos the Goddess bore a single child, their son Doom—alone, save for his father, as a temporal god. From Night's seed, Unu gave birth to the nocturnal goddesses, the twin sisters Death and Sleep. With all these new melodies, the universe was born, reverberating with Unu's song.

And still the song unfolds, in infinite complexity...

Cosmos, his lust irrepressible, took all the trillions of celestial gods as his own lovers, shapeshifting into myriad wondrous forms to pleasure them. But though Cosmos found each coupling exquisite and unique, none could rival that first joy of his union with the Great Goddess, a joy he vainly strives to re-create, finding her everywhere and yet nowhere until the end of time. Still, of all the celestials, the twin goddesses Maia and Luna were his favorites; his passion for them was matched only by their passion for each other. Thanks to Cosmos's potent seed, soon Maia gave birth to earthly life— millions of species, from the lowliest microbe to the commonest weeds to the mightiest dinosaurs to humankind itself. Each was a new note, shifting in combinations harmonious and dissonant, of concordance and conflict, but all contributing to Unu's song.

Even now the Great Goddess sings her song of diversity, turning one into many, who dance to her spiraling tune. We are born of Unu and that song, the children of a fertile earth and a starry sky, fated to return to her through Night's embrace at our appointed hour. Until then we sing, each of us and everything, creating all anew every day, holding the dragon at bay.

PROSPERITY MAGIC

BY SILVER RAVENWOLF

There are five main types of magic as they relate to the human condition: love, money, health, protection, and spirituality. I would like to meet the idiot who, eons ago, declared that to be spiritual you are not allowed to have money, good sex, a safe house, and good health. I would like to tell that person how much pain, suffering, and sorrow he or she has caused the future generations of "the faithful" because he or she chose to be a poor, starving, sexually-repressed, spiritual wretch. Indeed, we would have a long conversation where I would be doing most of the talking.

Although we've pretty much gotten over the taboos on health, love, sex, and safety (well, most of us), magical people still seem to have a problem with those good old American greenbacks, and how this money relates to our spiritual growth, if at all. It took me many years to realize that prosperity is nothing more than energy and we, as a society, place far too many riders on the contract for universal abundance than we should. Due to negative programming as a child, I carried with me the burden that only the poor are deserving of spiritual rewards, and therefore I should just stick to my lot in life and be thankful that I would enjoy better times in the hereafter. I brought this idea with me into the Craft, never realizing that nowhere within witchcraft teachings is there such a philosophy. If someone manages to find such a philosophy, tell them their magic hat is dented.

Our prosperity is linked to our spiritual well-being. If you are not prosperous and your body suffers because of lack of food or shelter, you are directly attacking your mental and physical stability, which results in the weakening of your spirituality. You cannot be a kind, compassionate, loving person all the time if you are cold, hungry, or sick. You are also in no position to assist others under these circumstances, as this could result in cloudy judgement that may cause more harm than good. Prosperity energy, then, is just as important as the need for love, health, protection, and spirituality, and whether we like it or not, links the other four categories together. We are a part of the earth plane, and abundance is the gift from Spirit that helps us to attain our spiritual and physical missions in life.

"That's all well and good," you say, "but how do I become more prosperous? I'm $50,000 in debt and I can hardly make my house payments, let alone send the oldest kid off to college next year." First, we learn that prosperity is an energy that can be manipulated. Then we proceed with learning how to manifest abundance and banish poverty. The easiest way to do this is to concentrate on working our prosperity magic with the phases of the Moon. The dark and waning Moons are for banishing poverty and rebuilding our financial affairs. The New and waxing Moons relate to manifesting abundance. The Full Moon gives us the power to manifest important changes that lead to our personal transformation. For most of us this is a systematic process that may take several months (or years) to accomplish, depending upon how much negative programming you've stored up in that magical brain of yours over your lifetime, and how much damage you've managed to do to your financial security in the meantime.

Once you begin a concerted effort toward working prosperity magic, I'm sure you'll be pleasantly surprised. It's quite possible that your results may be small at first. Mine were. Just keep going. The key to prosperity magic is endurance. Learn to manifest. Learn to banish. Yes, you will have setbacks. Pick yourself back up and continue where you stopped. Believe me, you won't be sorry. Once you know you are headed in the right direction, and things are going smoothly, don't back off. That's the biggest mistake I've seen magical people make in reference to prosperity magics. They think, okay, things are cool, I can slack off now. Horse piddle! Keep going. Add new goals, celebrate your successes, and enjoy your newfound prosperity—you absolutely deserve it!

BRINGING HOME THE BACON

BE YOUR OWN BOSS THE MAGICAL WAY

BY ANNE MARIE GARRISON

A good friend has often told me that Wicca will not be a true religion until our holidays are known not by the rituals we perform, but by the foods we eat, the songs we sing, and the silly activities that are cherished and passed down from generation to generation, even if their original religious significance should be forgotten along the way. Why? Because those are the things that identify us and show where our hearts and roots lie. In other words, those are the things that make our culture.

Building a Pagan culture based on our love of the earth and our gods is a huge undertaking. The Pagan community has made enormous progress in this direction in the last couple of decades, and it will probably take centuries more. Finding Paganistan starts with each of us living a life that allows magic to touch everything from what we believe to what we eat, where we work, what we purchase, and how we interact with our fellow beings. If all of this is true, then there are countless opportunities available for you, the magical person who is ready to be your own boss in service to the community, to make a living in harmony with your Pagan lifestyle. Are you up to the challenge? Great! Now, where to begin?

Well, in any business, the key to making money (and let's face it, it's darn hard to live any lifestyle, magical or otherwise, without money) is to fulfill an unmet need in the community. In other words, provide goods or services that people want. So before diving in, take the time to think about what talents you have to offer. Do you love to cook? Are you a computer wiz? Can you take care of plants, pets, or children? Do you make beautiful art? Are you psychic? Are you musical? Can you build or fix things? Ideally, something should spring to mind that you have a real passion for. Do not underestimate the power of passion. Starting up a business takes lots and lots of hard work for little or no pay before anything will start to show promise. Don't get trapped work-ing at something that you won't be willing to give up your social life for. Otherwise you might as well stay at your day job, right?

Now then, have you decided what you're burning with desire to do? Super! Think about how you can take all that energy and raw talent and put it to use. Channel your skills and experience into something there is a market for. Better yet, come up with an idea for something that doesn't have a market yet, but could. What does the local (or national) Pagan community need? Here's a hint: Successful businesses offer one or more of the following: something cheaper than anybody else, something more convenient than anybody else, or something that is unique or is of better quality than anybody else's.

While price and convenience are essential parts of a business plan (and I'm sorry, but you will need to write a business plan), I personally believe uniqueness and quality are where a small business can really shine. For example, if you want to make hand-crafted clothes with magical designs, don't try to price yourself to compete with clothes at WalMart. There is no way you will survive! Instead, go look at other artisans who make and sell hand-made clothes. Go visit all of the competition that you can! Ask lots and lots of questions. Most people will be happy to help—honest. See how they do things, how they package what they do, where they sell their things, and what kind of people buy from them. Find out how much money you will need to get started, and how many hours per product or service you will have to invest. Do some divination to check if this is the right path for you. Then, if you are still determined to proceed, go and make your own clothes (or whatever) to sell at a similar price range, but with better quality and better designs. Then you will have something that folks will gladly give you money for.

All right, now we're off to a great start. Next, you have to make several prototype items (magical clothes, web-pages, hand-dipped candles, Moon-shaped cookies, beautifully land-scaped herb gardens, whatever it is you plan to do). Be sure that you have worked out what supplies you will need, and set aside some time to give them and your workspace a ritual blessing. Then, practice your craft until you can get consistently good results. Remember, you're a professional now. Work toward having clients or customers who will give you a good endorsement, even if you have to work for free at first. (You won't mind, will you, after all—you have a passion for this!)

Once you have gotten that far, you should be ready to go public. Whoopie! This is where it gets fun. Think up a catchy name for yourself (my company is called Witches Stitches: Cross-Stitch Patterns for Crafty Pagans) and register with your secretary of state to do business under an assumed name. Follow any laws and advice the government sees fit to send your way. Then get a tax ID number from the IRS. And, oh yeah, don't forget to keep EVERY receipt for each business-related expense you incur. Be sure to clearly label each receipt with a date, what you purchased, and why. Keep them in a clearly-labeled safe place. That way your accountant will be able to sort it all out at the end of the year. Oh, did I mention getting an accountant? The one I go to only charges fifty dollars to do my business taxes once a year, and it's worth every penny! If you get enough business income to justify paying quarterly taxes, then good for you, and be doubly sure to get a good accountant. I told you this would be fun.

Now you need to let the universe know you are ready. I highly recommend hiring a professional designer to create a corporate identity for you. This should include: a logo, business cards, letterhead, product packaging or store sign, and a web page. A good corporate image will let the world know that you mean business. Let your designer know exactly what you need and don't need, what sort of image you want to present, and set a reasonable budget. You can always have additional materials designed and printed later as your business grows.

Finally, with your cool new corporate identity in hand, get out there and advertise, advertise, advertise! In the Pagan community there are lots of good ways to do this. Word-of-mouth is obviously a first-rate place to start, but it may not get you very far. I recommend starting with the really cheap display or classified ads available in most Pagan newsletters or magazines. Check on the worldwide web for other places to advertise with, clubs or groups that might be willing to endorse you, and trade organizations you can join. Get your website into some Pagan web rings such as Avatar (www.avatar.com). Say hello to any chat rooms that would have an interest in what you do. Send out free samples to anyone who does Pagan-friendly product reviews: *Green Egg, SageWoman, PanGaia,* and *Circle Network News* are good places to start. Write articles for anybody who will take them. Most periodicals or newsletters will gladly give you a free ad space or a blurb mentioning your business in exchange for a free article or artwork. Register with the *Pagan Yellow Pages.* It's a quarterly listing of hundreds of Pagan groups, organizations, and businesses nation-wide. (It's a great resource to keep handy, too!)

Once your business is off the ground, kick that old broomstick into high gear. In other words, get out into the community and promote yourself as a leader. Offer to teach classes in whatever it is you do (most local new age or metaphysical bookstores are looking for people like you to offer seminars). Sell your stuff at Pagan gatherings and conferences. (See *Llewellyn's New Worlds of Mind and Spirit Yearly Festival Guide* for more information). Be sure to host your own events or workshops as often as is practical. Later, if your business can afford it, look into getting booth space at local New Age Conventions or the International New Age Trade Show in Denver each summer.

If your business involves making any gift items or books, then you will want to look into finding some distributors to sell your stuff directly to bookstores. New Leaf Distributing Company and White Light Pentacles are two businesses that specialize in getting Wiccan/Pagan/New Age products into metaphysical bookstores. I have found the people at New Leaf wonderful to work with. Another possible direction to explore is finding an agent to handle the promotion/distribution end of things for you. Don't forget about selling to mail-order catalogs such as the Pyramid Collection, JBL, and the hundreds of other Pagan-friendly mail-order businesses out there.

Soon you will find yourself pointy-hat deep in a whole new exciting life. Just think, you could soon be a full-time Pagan and your own boss! May prosperity and success be your constant companions on this journey!

RESOURCES

New Leaf Distributing Company, 401 Thornton Road, Lithia Springs, GA 30057-1557. 1-800-326-2665.

White Light Pentacles, Sacred Spirit Product Distributors, P.O. Box 8163, Salem MA 01971-8163. 1-800-MASTERY.

New Age Retailer (Trade Magazine), 1300 North State Street #105, Bellingham, WA 98225. 1-800-463-9243.

Wholelife News-UK, Carl Sims, Publisher. P.O. Box 127 Shewsbury, England SY3 7WS. Telephone: (44) (0) 1743-341303.

Witches:
Fact and Fantasy

By Marguerite Elsbeth

Witches have been around for hundreds of years, and continue to live among us in indigenous cultures as well as in the contemporary Wiccan movement. Still, there are questions regarding the seemingly extra-ordinary spiritual, traditional, and practical aspects of the Craft. What is fantasy and what is fact?

FANTASY: All Witches choose their calling to practice the Craft.

FACT: Some individuals are born with a special gift to perceive and interact with the subtle forces of nature, and so are drawn into the deeper mysteries of life. Eventually, they may choose to be initiated into the Craft in order to have fellowship and be active participants in the Wiccan religion. However, not all Witches belong to a coven or group; some are solitary practitioners who prefer to work in private.

Hereditary Witches receive their knowledge as a result of family bloodline, or through a Witch who recognizes their potential and passes the skill onto them. Sometimes these individuals are not consciously aware of their spiritual endowment. Consequently, they may or may not develop their gift or practice the Old Religion.

FANTASY: Witches worship a horned god who is actually the Devil.

FACT: The Horned God worshiped by Witches is symbolized by an antlered being, a deer or elk spirit who represents the masculine aspects of nature. He is the great Gaulish god of European lore: Slavic Bog (god), English Herne, Nick, or Neck (spirit), Welsh Boucca, and Indo-European Cernunnos. Moreover, Witches acknowledge the feminine side of nature in the Goddess, the Horned God's female counterpart.

FANTASY: Witches make a pact, denounce their families, and make living sacrificial offerings to the gods.

FACT: The pact made by Witches suggests obedience to natural laws, and may be summed up by a tenet of the Witches' Rede, which states, "Do as you will, and it harm none." Witches do not denounce their families, but vow to expand their recognition of the ideas related to father and mother toward a more spiritual perspective.

Human and/or animal sacrifice is not a part of the Wiccan religion. Witches see the living spirit of the Great God/ess in all creatures and things.

FANTASY: The Witches' sabbat is a woodland frolic in the buff for the sole purpose of obtaining sensual pleasure.

FACT: These ideas associated with the word "sabbat" may originate from the French *s'ébattre,* meaning "to frolic," or from the name of the Thracian god Sabazius, who was worshiped with frantic debauchery. However, the sabbat is not merely a woodland party.

The Sabbat occurs both in and out of doors, and most are as benign as a church social. When in attendance, many Witches keep their clothes on, unless a particular ceremony indicates a need to work in the nude. The focus is on ritual, not sex.

FANTASY: Witches can fly and shape-shift into animal forms.

FACT: The popular mystique around the contemporary witches' flight may be attributed to astral travel or out-of-body experience (OBE). Once upon a time, unless the Witch was unusually gifted, this phenomenon of creative imagination was generally trance-induced with the help of hallucinogenic herbs such as henbane, belladonna, cannabis, or fly agaric mushrooms. Witches and shamans of indigenous cultures may still rely on these herbs to fly without the proverbial broom, but modern Witches prefer to use meditation techniques

Shape-shifting, or changing from human to animal form, is a very real event in shamanic cultures today; for example, Navajo Witches, called Skinwalkers, can change into wolves (but use this ability for nefarious purposes). Generally, Witches do not actually become the animal, but either project an astral thought-form, or imagine that they are one with a particular animal consciousness.

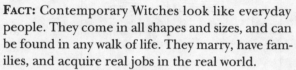

FANTASY: Witches have a special appearance, and live in a supernatural world.

FACT: Contemporary Witches look like everyday people. They come in all shapes and sizes, and can be found in any walk of life. They marry, have families, and acquire real jobs in the real world.

Hereditary Witches may have some special mark or feature that distinguishes them from others—they may be born with a tiny prehensile tail, caul (a thin veil of skin over the face), a prominent birthmark, or a physical deformity, such as a harelip, club foot, or knocked knees. This distinction may also be a physical, emotional, or mental condition with which the person must contend over the course of his or her life.

FANTASY: Children who are raised in or around the Craft grow up with mental and emotional problems, or are maladjusted.

FACT: Children of the Craft are raised in household environments not unlike what one might find in an indigenous society or among country folks. The home is clean, though maybe in a state of disarray. Kids and pets are often free to roam. The entire home atmosphere is generally loose, loving, creative, protective, and invitingly comfortable.

Kids who paint their rooms black, use addictive substances, and immerse themselves in black magic tomes usually grow up in an atmosphere based on religious fundamentalism and/or emotional repression. Considering the contrary nature of children in general, Witches' kids are just as likely to become doctors, lawyers, certified public accounts, or preachers! This is because Wiccan children are given freedom of choice and a well-rounded, home-style education that prepares them for life in both worlds, ordinary and extra-ordinary.

Tarot Meditation for
Overcoming Creative Blocks

By Kirin Lee

Creative blocks are the plague of talented people everywhere. They hold up important projects and drive otherwise sane people to do strange things. Here's a great way to break through those blocks and generate ideas without forfeiting your sanity.

Banishing the Block

Creative blocks are caused by built-up negativity from various other sources in your life. Stress is a major culprit, and will stonewall any inner creative urge before it starts.

You must begin by banishing the cloud of negativity hanging over your head. To do this, take a black candle and place it on the left side of your altar. Follow it with a blue one to boost creativity, a yellow one for imagination, and an orange one for success and stimulation of ideas. Arrange the candles in a half-circle across your altar. Your dining room table will work if you have nothing else.

Select a tarot card or cards from your set according to the list below. This card represents the area in which you wish to release your block.

Card List

Page of Wands: band member, instructor, "garage" inventor.

Queen of Wands: actor, artist, entertainer, designer, musician.

King of Wands: drafting, computer-aided design.

Page of Cups: poet, dancer.

Queen of Cups: dramatic actor.

Page of Swords: singer, architect.

Queen of Swords: editor, computer program designer.

King of Swords: interior decorator, public relations specialist.

Page of Pentacles: producer, photographer.

Queen of Pentacles: nonfiction writer, painter, inventor.

King of Pentacles: fiction writer, director, lecturer, fashion designer, scriptwriter, radio writer, sculptor.

Place your card(s) in a row before the candles. At this point you may cast a circle if you wish.

Light the candles and sit before your altar. Concentrate on each candle in turn, and visualize its purpose. Take your time, and don't rush it.

Next, concentrate on the card(s). Visualize yourself as successful in your field. Picture yourself with an endless stream of ideas. All you need to do is summon them. Don't let any negative thoughts intrude. Visualize your ideas bringing you success. You can be more specific when visualizing ideas, such as "hard science fiction stories," or an "action adventure screenplay." Don't be afraid to tailor this meditation to fit your needs at any given time.

When finished, extinguish the candles in reverse order and close your circle. Repeat the meditation as often as necessary.

TAROT TO GO

BY CORRINE KENNER

Sometimes, a good tarot reading depends as much on atmosphere as it does on the cards. Granted, we don't really need any props. One nice thing about tarot as a hobby is that it's possible to simply throw a deck of cards into your purse or your pocket, and go. Like most tarot afficionados, I've spread my share of cards on cloth napkins, paper placemats, kitchen towels, wet bars, and kid's plastic tabletops, all without hampering my style a bit.

Sometimes, though, I've found that a few subtle touches can transform a mundane reading into a deeply moving experience. It's like the difference between eating dinner over the kitchen sink and setting the table with fine china and linens. Both meals are equally nourishing to the body, but those extra touches also nourish the soul.

Rather than be caught unprepared for moments that transcend the everyday, I finally put together a traveling "tarot to go" kit that I can simply grab on the way out of the house, no

matter where I'm headed, and even if
I don't plan to read for anyone.
Feel free to adapt these
ideas any way you like.

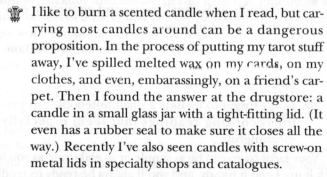

First, and this is prob-
ably the most important
part, find a small traveling tarot bag or box that
you think is absolutely
stunning. I use a tapes-
try cosmetics bag that I
picked up on clearance
at a discount store. It's
about six inches wide,
six inches tall, and four
inches deep. It opens and
closes with a tassled zipper, and
it's got a handle sewn into the lid. It fits nicely in my totebag,
and it cost less than five dollars.

A friend of mine uses a similarly-sized wooden purse from
the late 1960s that she found at Goodwill. It's got a hinged lid,
a matching wooden handle, and it's decorated with jewels and
the word "love" in lime green and orange paint. Totally groovy.

Once you have your bag in hand, gather your favorite
tarotphernalia.

- I like to burn a scented candle when I read, but carrying most candles around can be a dangerous
proposition. In the process of putting my tarot stuff
away, I've spilled melted wax on my cards, on my
clothes, and even, embarassingly, on a friend's car-
pet. Then I found the answer at the drugstore: a
candle in a small glass jar with a tight-fitting lid. (It
even has a rubber seal to make sure it closes all the
way.) Recently I've also seen candles with screw-on
metal lids in specialty shops and catalogues.

- Candles need to be lit, so I keep a small box of
wooden kitchen matches in my bag, too.

nothing. All the totems, helpers, and guides—the spirits, animals, and ancestors—are very real friends and allies that the healer may call upon for guidance, but it's not really all that necessary.

HEALING CUSTOMS

Tribal and rural village people take the healing process very seriously. Among many traditions, there is usually much discussion by the patient with family, friends, and elders. Everything and everyone involved—the healer, the illness or issue demanding treatment, as well as the suggested therapy—must all be synchronistically correct and in its proper place according to custom before the healer is called upon to perform the work. It may require several sojourns between the healer, the patient, and his or her relations before the patient accepts the healer and the healer accepts the patient. Then there may also be certain preliminary activities before the actual medicine work takes place, such as fasting, seeking a vision, sweating or purification, prayers, offerings, and feasting. The concept behind shamanic medicine work is to alter the patient's consciousness because a glimpse into non-ordinary reality may bring about spontaneous healing, and thus affect a cure. Nor will the healer ever seek to help a person who does not formally ask, as this would be considered a violation of natural principles and laws.

Faith is a most necessary ingredient for successful healing. This spiritual virtue forms an emotional connection between the healer and the patient, allowing the healer to transmit vital life-giving energy via the methods selected for healing. The patient should expect to be healed, for if there is any doubt in the healer or his or her abilities, the results may be unstable. A healer must be ready to compensate for any physical, emotional, mental, or spiritual inbalance within the patient. This makes the healer a spiritual go-between due to his or her ability to speak with the spirits, animals, plants, and stones, and receive an answer as to how to achieve wholeness.

DO YOU HAVE THE HEALING GIFT?
A QUIZ

Answer yes or no to the following questions and statements:

1. Are you knowledgeable, bright, and productive?
2. Are you humorous, cheerful, and compassionate?

3. Are you forebearing, strong, and disciplined?

4. Are you bold and imaginative?

5. Are you fair, mindful, and alert?

6. Are you wholesome, calm, and clear?

7. Are you aware of the spirit world and well-grounded in this world?

8. Were you born with the gift, is it hereditary, or was it willed to you?

9. Do you have the calling, which may come in the form of a dream, vision, accident, illness, near-death experience, or even actual death?

10. Can you and communicate with spirits, dead people, animals, birds, insects, rocks, monsters, space aliens, and/or elemental beings?

11. Did you receive your guardian spirit, healing and spiritual knowledge, power objects, and doctoring tools through your dreams and visions?

12. Are you often lonely and misunderstood by others?

13. Have you sought spiritual aid, courage, and training through vision-seeking and power quests in sacred natural spaces, such as by the ocean, beneath a waterfall, on a mountain, in the deep desert, or in a remote forest?

14. Have you been led to an older healer or medicine person who acknowledged your gift and became your mentor?

If you have a majority of yes answers to the questions and statements above, your personality type, along with your unique qualities and experiences, may indicate that you indeed have the healing gift.

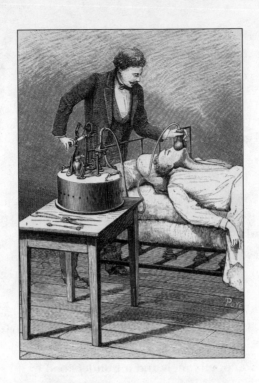

Slavic Folk Healing

By Kenneth Johnson

The village folk healers of Eastern Europe have survived for centuries, with many aspects of their art virtually unchanged since Pagan times. They survived the efforts of the Orthodox Church to turn them into good Christians, and they survived the attempt of Peter the Great and other rulers to "modernize" them. Finally, they survived the years of Communist rule when their healing practices were branded as "superstition." In many cases, they were locked away in mental institutions labeled as schizophrenic.

Now the Communists are gone and the folk healers are still there. Although the collapse of the old agricultural lifeway in Eastern Europe has sent many of them in search of new homes in the cities, their ancient arts remain essentially the same.

Slavic folk healers diagnose a client by using their psychic senses. They focus their consciousness somewhere in their diaphragm or belly, which they call their center of power. Using the "eyes" that rest in that center of power, they gaze out from that vantage point and examine the client's inner body. They often believe that evil spirits are the cause of diseases, and their eyes of power are used to reveal the presence of such spirits.

Having identified the problem, they may use several different forms of healing. For example, they may:

- ๛ Chant a spell or incantation designed to frighten the spirit away from the patient's body

- ๛ Lead the patient to a special rock, tree, or forest glade, a magical "place of power" in which the nature spirits themselves help to heal the client

- ๛ They may simply place their hands over the client and heal her or him with pure energy alone

Although all these methods are common amongst the healers, perhaps the most popular method of all is the use of magical water.

Slavic healers believe that water is the greatest healer, although the water must be cold in order to be at its greatest apex of power. When you see pictures of Russians bathing in ice water "for the sake of their health," try to realize that this tradition has its roots in ancient sorcery. Besides that, the water must be made sacred. The best way to endow water with sacred power is to use techniques of meditation to build up the energy of the water. Sometimes there are special traditions about the water itself: I know of one healer who only uses water taken from a westward-flowing stream. I have known others who simply sprinkled holy water from the nearest church into the water they intended to use for healing.

When a bowl of water is properly prepared, the healer generally melts a cake of pure beeswax over the stove. The melted wax is poured into the bowl of water. As it begins to congeal, the healer passes the bowl of water slowly over the patient's body, paying special attention to the seat or center of the illness.

The illness—or, perhaps, the evil spirit— is believed to be charmed out of the patient's body and into the wax. Some healers actually exercise their psychic powers by "reading" the ball of congealed wax in much the same way as one might read tea leaves.

CEREMONIAL MAGIC AND THE AVERAGE PERSON

BY ESTELLE DANIELS

When they get into magic, many people come into contact with the magical system known as Ceremonial Magic. Perhaps it is cloaked in other guises, like Enochian, Thelema, Kabbalah, Thaumaturgy, or Geomancy, but it's out there and quite widespread. Much of Ceremonial Magic is quite formula oriented. It demands a thorough knowledge of astrology, Kabbalah, and other disciplines, and a knowledge of Hebrew would be very useful also. This is more than the average person is willing to take on just to see if that system is right for them.

There are, however, a couple of rituals used in Ceremonial Magic that are easily done and very accessible to all. The Lesser Banishing Ritual of the Pentagram (LBRP for short) and the Rose Cross are fairly simple and work well with most any tradition or style. They can be used by themselves, together, or be adapted to work with other types of circles and magical techniques. In our classes we make the students learn and memorize these rituals so they are available to them at all times. The reason is that they are simple, effective, and when done correctly, they always produce results. No matter what state of mind you are in, no matter where you are, if you say the correct words and go through the motions, these rituals will produce a result. If you put energy into them and add the proper visualizations, the results are more effective.

This is because since these rituals were developed they have been in continuous use by magicians. This has built up a cosmic energy bank on the astral, so that anyone who uses them can tap into that vast magical reservoir and benefit thereby. These rituals are also ones that cannot cause harm if done incorrectly. In other words, if you accidentally say the wrong word or visualize an incorrect color, you will not blow up, get an energy backlash, or be harmed. The worst that can happen is that nothing will happen. This is important because people can be apprehensive if they have heard some of the legends and folklore built up around ceremonial magic.

These two rituals are both magical circles. They create a sacred space that is cleansed and consecrated and can also provide a measure of insulation and protection to those within the circle. They are also automatic circles, and dissipate on their own. They do not need to be taken down. They are quite good for divination. Divination within a circle is more effective, for you are screening out all the everyday static and noise. You can concentrate better and can tap into the fountains of inspiration more easily.

Ceremonial magic is quite old, though it has been growing, changing, and evolving since ancient times. Most of the ceremonial magical rituals and spells are based upon Kabbalah and Hermeticism, with liberal doses of other occult disciplines thrown in. These can be argued to be the descendants of the ancient mystery schools—the ancient Greek and Egyptian rites as they were handed down through the ages—with doses of Kabbalah and Christian mysticism thrown in. Ceremonial Magic is a system, not a theology. The practitioner is calling on certain God-forms, but these are not exclusively Jewish, Christian, Greek, or Egyptian. They are an amalgam.

Perhaps the god-forms would best be described as archetypes rather than specific deities.

Most of what is published today about Ceremonial Magic descends from the Golden Dawn, a magical group formed in the late 1880s. During the years when the Golden Dawn was active and flourishing, most of the Western mystical tradition was reviewed, revised, corrected, codified, explained, and updated by members of the group, and then written down and passed on to their successors.

Ceremonial Magic is the main foundation of the Western magical tradition. Much energy has gone into it, and therefore it becomes a sort of "black box" technology. You do not need any psychic ability to use Ceremonial Magic, though that can help.

The Lesser Banishing Ritual of the Pentagram, or LBRP, is a grounding, centering, and cleansing ritual. I use it a lot when traveling. Once I am in my hotel room for the night, I do an LBRP and this psychically seals the room from outside psychic influences. By morning, when I am ready to leave, it has dissipated and the room is back to "normal."

The Rose Cross is another circle, but it is also useful for healing. There is a warning: do not use this ritual on anyone with an unstable heart or cardiovascular condition. The extra energy can cause problems. In any case, when doing this ritual, you can call down the energy, but let the person take as much or as little as they want. Do not force it on them.

No matter what one's tradition or training, these two rituals are useful tools in a person's magical repertoire.

ROMANCE: NOT JUST FOR VALENTINE'S DAY ANYMORE

BY EDAIN MCCOY

High on the list of the most romantic days of the year is St. Valentine's Day, named for a canonized third century Christian martyr. Like many holidays in the Christian calendar, this high holy day of love and romance has roots in the Pagan past. The Roman feast of Lupercalia, celebrated on February 15, honored the mating of young men and women who chose each other as life partners by lottery on this day. Though this sounds decidedly unromantic, the day was chosen because it was believed that wolves, creatures who mate for life, choose their mates on this day.

Lupercalia is not the only romantic holiday founding the Pagan calendar, but one of many honoring love, romance, and sexuality. The following is a list of a few of the great excuses for having a special romantic day that are to be found in modern Paganism.

GERIENT DAY (WELSH)

January 10

The famous Welsh myth collection known as the *Mabinogion* tells the story of the Arthurian warrior Gerient, who fights a battle to avenge the honor of Queen Guinevere. While involved in this intrigue he falls in love with Enid, a lady in waiting to the queen. At their marriage the White Hart appears to them. This white stag, with roots in the most ancient of Celtic mythology, is deeply linked with the Otherworld, and with messages brought to earth from divine realms. His appearance to the earthly

lovers symbolizes the fact that their union is of a sacred nature, one that not only links the male and female, but also the mundane realm with the Otherworld. If one reads the myth of Gerient closely, and reads between the lines, a picture emerges of not just a minor warrior, but of a young man poised on the union of sacred marriage.

St. Agnes Eve (English)
January 20

Like many Christian saints, this one had her origins in a now-forgotten goddess of fire. It is traditional on this night for young women to sit before the fire and divine their romantic future. It is also believed that if a young woman eats an apple in front of a mirror on this night, the image of her future mate will appear.

Beltane (Anglo-Celtic)
May 1

As one of the major festivals of the Wiccan year, Beltane hardly needs explaining to modern practitioners of natural magic. This was a time for honoring the sacred marriage of the God and Goddess, whose union would produce the coming harvest. It was also a time when young men and women chose a sexual partner whom they may or may not marry. In contrast to the puritanical view of sex and marriage, the Celts believed in sexual freedom, and celebrated the joyous mating of two individuals as images of the God and Goddess.

The Night of Venus (Roman)
Waxing Moon nearest Autumn Equinox

The early blending of attributes of the Greek goddess of sex and love, Aphrodite, with Rome's earthy goddess Venus resulted in the Night of Venus, festival of fertility and mating similar to Beltane.

MAKARA (INDIAN)
Fifth day after the New Moon after the Sun enters Capricorn

Makara is the Indian New Year, which begins on the fifth day after the first New Moon after the Sun enters the sign of Capricorn. The goddesses of fertility are honored at this time, and it is considered an excellent date for producing children with spiritual gifts.

FEAST OF DIANA (ROMAN)
April and September

The Goddess of love and the hunt had so many festivals throughout the year that many dates are given. Diana as a huntress has often been used as a metaphor for seeking a mate.

BINDING OF THE WREATHS (LITHUANIAN)
First Full Moon after the Summer Solstice

This ancient Slavic spring festival has preserved many of the old Pagan marriage customs from Slavic culture. It is a time for weaving wreaths out of flowers and greenery, under which the couples will dance. Later in the evening, engaged couples are crowned with the wreaths, reminiscent of the way in which the man and woman who represent the God and Goddess at other Pagan spring festivals are crowned. Often weddings will be held on the same day.

Think Pink Love Magic

By Marguerite Elsbeth

Most of you will agree—there is nothing worse than a good love gone bad. Perhaps those of you who are magically inclined may want to do something, well, magical, to rectify the situation. Not. Witches, seers, diviners, and astrologers all have the unfair advantage of being able to cast a bewitchment, interpret a chart, or read the cards to determine how to get their lover to come back, while the wayward mate may not have the same capability or disposition. It's tempting, especially when you know he or she is a soul mate, but the other person doesn't necessarily know that. Anyway, no matter how much you hurt inside, it just isn't ethical.

Why Two Wrongs Don't Make a Rite

Cosmic ethics determine how far we can go with our magical knowledge. These are not quite the same as moral standards, which vary from culture to culture. Natural principles are founded on karmic consequence and spiritual conscience.

Karma, translated from Sanscrit, literally means "action-work" and indicates that we are cosmically bound by what we do and how we go about doing it. What we do will affect the farthest reaches of heaven and earth, and how we do it will come back to haunt or help us in threefold measure.

Spiritual conscience can be summed up nicely by the Wiccan credo: "Do what you will, and it harm none." This means that your actions must be set in motion with the consideration that no one, not even you, will be negatively affected by your performance. Easier said than done.

When we are in an overly emotional state, such as feeling angry, jealous, desolate, and hopeless, our intentions may be muddled because we are not thinking very clearly. Feelings of this nature are usually unsettled, irregular, wandering, even devious, because they are based on primal fear.

Emotionally-charged thoughts are ensouled by one's motivations. Once they're sent out over the ethers, they've got to land somewhere, and that's usually in one's ex-partner's heart-center, especially when we've been visualizing them while stewing in our own juices over real or imagined slights. Essentially, we are hurting them because we are hurting.

So, while we may want to believe that casting a love spell to bring our lover back is ultimately in his or her best interest, often it's *our* best interest that we are really concerned with at the time, and we are just acting out of selfishness and denial. This is the time to think pink.

THINKING PINK

Did you know that pink has some very interesting connotations? A radical person is sometimes called a pink, and we have all heard of "being in the pink," which is an overall condition of physical, emotional, mental, and spiritual good health.

These two ideas are exactly where we want to go when it comes to nurturing a broken heart. We want to be radical enough in our thinking to overcome feeling fearful, and we want to heal, or become whole again. We can do this by thinking pink—returning our thoughts to honor, higher love, and a cosmic sense of morality.

Pink thoughts may enhance self-purification, forgiveness, and all the exalted virtues of romance. Thinking pink will not forever bind a lover to you, but will allow you to open your heart to loving this person unconditionally even though he or she has chosen freedom over you. If you think pink often enough, eventually it will dawn on you that your love served its purpose in teaching you something about yourself, and that the love you once shared can never be taken away from you because it lives forever in your heart.

PINK CANDLE LOVE MAGIC

The following love spell is twofold. First, you need to heal your emotions by getting your aura back in the pink. Then you need to change the energy around the entire situation for the better by bringing about resolution.

Gather together two tall pink candles; a flat plate with a mound of damp sand on it; one pink rose in a water-filled vase; two images (photos or mental) reflecting happier times (one of you alone, and one of you and your ex-partner together); and a small, low table on which to place the above items.

Set aside a quiet place that will remain undisturbed for several hours after you have completed the magic, as well as a period of time when you can work uninterrupted. When you are ready to begin, plant the candles (symbolizing you and your ex-partner) in the sand on the plate, arranging them so that their stems are touching from the base to the tips. Place the rose in front of the plate holding the candles. If you are using photos, lean the one of you against the vase, and position the other one behind it so that you cannot see it. Light the candles. Sit before your altar, relax, and begin breathing deeply. Gaze at the pink candles and the pink rose, and start to pull the color into yourself until it fills every cell. Imagine that you are so full of pink light that it seeps through the pores of your skin and forms a protective oval of pink light all around you.

Look to your image and bring up feelings of joy, happiness, peace, calm, and self-forgiveness. Move the image of the two of you to the foreground, surround it with pink energy, and bless the union that was with all your heart. Mentally embrace and release your lover, then watch and wave "good-bye" as he or she "flies" away.

Finally, place the image of you alone in the forefront again, removing the image of you as a couple entirely. Reflect again on the pink light within and without you. Draw this light deep into your heart center, and vow to keep it there. Allow the candles to melt down until the flames extinguish, taking your emotional ties to the relationship along with them.

Joining a Magical Lodge

By John Michael Greer

Back before today's magical renaissance, most magicians in the Western world learned their art by joining a lodge. Lodges were the most common type of organization in the magical community of those times, and lodges nearly had a stranglehold on magical knowledge. It's hard to imagine from today's perspective, but between 1700 and 1900, fewer than a hundred books on practical magic were published in English, and most of them were very hard to obtain. At a time when being openly involved in magic was a shortcut to social ostracism, too, the secrecy of magical lodges had a definite appeal.

Times have changed. Teachings that were once jealously guarded can now be found in shopping mall bookstores, and covens, circles, and other less formal groups play a much larger role in the magical community than magical lodges. The lodge system itself is poorly understood these days, and not all of those who run magical lodges have a solid grasp of how and why the system works.

Despite these changes, though, there are still good magical lodges to be found, and good reasons to consider joining them. Many lodges offer a solid education in magic, based on a tested curriculum and taught by experienced magicians. Belonging to a magical lodge

also offers the chance to take part in intensive group rituals, to experience a series of initiations, and to become part of a community dedicated to serious magical work.

WHAT IS A MAGICAL LODGE?

Few people know much about lodges these days, however, and inaccurate notions about the lodge system are common. Many of these are simple confusions between lodges and other ritual groups. A lodge is not just a coven with fancier robes and titles. Nor is it a circle, a church, a cult, or an encounter group. It's a distinct kind of organization, with its own ways of carrying out the various tasks of group work.

Perhaps the most important factor that sets lodges apart from other occult groups is the role of structure. Lodge work follows a framework of rules and procedures; each lodge officer has specific duties, and ceremonial work follows texts that are changed only in special circumstances. There's a point to this—setting up a structure and sticking to it shifts the focus of attention from management to the magical work of the lodge.

Lodge structure has another dimension. With few exceptions, lodges have a series of levels of membership—"grades" or "degrees" in lodge jargon—and magical lodge members have to earn their way up, normally by meeting the requirements of a curriculum of training. Many lodges require members to reach a certain grade before they can hold office or take other active roles in lodge; some require members to reach a certain grade before they can attend lodge meetings at all. This may grate on modern sensibilities, but once again there's a point to it. Advanced magical work requires a fair degree of skill to carry off successfully, and lodge members need to demonstrate that they know what they're doing before they take part.

Obviously, then, joining a magical lodge is not for everyone. To be comfortable in a lodge, it's necessary to have some tolerance for structure and an interest in serious magical work. If these things appeal to you, though, you may find a magical lodge well worth the time and effort.

Joining A Magical Lodge

Like the old recipe for rabbit pie that begins, "First catch your rabbit," the first step in joining a magical lodge is finding one. This isn't always easy. There are active magical lodges in most North American cities of any size, but few advertise their presence. Getting in touch with one may take time and patience. If you make contacts in your local magical community and ask around, you're likely to turn up lodge connections, although those connections may want to know more about you before they start answering questions.

This brings up an important point: magical lodges are usually selective about potential members. This is partly a matter of tradition, and partly one of hard experience. Not everyone who wants to join a lodge does so for good reasons, and a lodge that opens its doors to all comers may find itself saddled with members who are more interested in playing politics or sitting on the sidelines pretending to be magicians than in doing real magical work. You may be certain that a magical lodge has much to offer you, but you need to remember that the members will be asking themselves what you have to offer the lodge.

What they will be looking for, if the lodge in question is worth anything, is evidence that your interest in magic is serious, and that you are willing to commit time and energy to the lodge and its work. If they are looking for anything else, for example, money, sexual favors, or the promotion of some pet cause, you're better off working on your own. Most lodges do ask for dues to meet hall rental and other expenses, but anything more than fifteen to twenty dollars a month is probably lining someone's pocket.

The first stage of becoming a lodge member, then, is usually a matter of coming to the notice of people who belong to the lodge, or finding information that allows you to make contact. Then a more formal process begins, in most cases with a written application followed by an interview. After the interview, the lodge will vote on your application, and if you pass the vote the next thing you'll receive is a phone call or letter letting you know when to show up for your initiation. At that point, you'll stand at the beginning of a profound, transformative, and, in every sense of the word, magical journey.

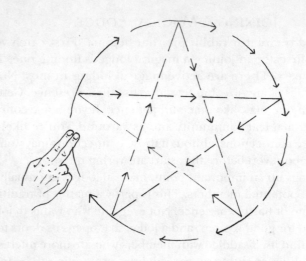

The Lesser Banishing Ritual of the Pentagram (LBRP)

By Estelle Daniels

Before starting, take three deep cleansing breaths and let each out slowly. Let all the tension and outside distractions fade away.

Part One: The Kabbalistic Cross

Stand facing east, feet shoulder-width apart, solidly and comfortably. Take your right hand hold it above your head, and grab a golden energy beam from above and pull it down to mid-chest. As you do this intone AH-TAY (ATEH in Hebrew).

Next, take your right hand and grab the golden energy beam from below and pull it up to mid-chest height (same place as before—the two beams should meet and join), and say: MAL-KOOTH (MALKUTH in Hebrew).

Take your right hand and reach to the right and pull the golden energy beam from the horizon to mid chest, meeting the other two, and say: VAY-GEH-BOO-RAH (VGBRH in Hebrew).

Take your right hand and reach across your body to the left and pull the golden energy beam from the horizon to mid chest, where all four beams should meet, and say: VAY-GEH-DOO-LAH (VGDLH in Hebrew).

Then take both arms and cross them at chest level, hands touching shoulders, bow head and say: LAY-OH-LAHM as you seal the four beams together and feel the energy.

This roughly translates as "The Kingdom, and the power and the Glory for ever and ever." This part can be done alone. It is a grounding and centering ritual that can help clear the mind.

PART TWO

Facing east, take the first two fingers of your right hand extended together (the universal athame) and make a high magic banishing pentagram in yellow—starting lower left and going clockwise. (See diagram.) When you finish the pentagram, point your fingers in the center of the pentagram. As you point say: YOHD-HAY-VAVH-HAY (YHVH in Hebrew—the tetragrammaton). The window opened by the pentagram will then draw out all the negative air energy from the circle.

Taking your fingers/athame, move to the south, make a pentagram in red, and say: AH-DOH-NAI-EE (ADNH in Hebrew, translated "the great and powerful lords"). You are now removing the negative fire energy.

Move to the west, make a pentagram in blue and say: AY-HAY-EE-AY (EHIH in Hebrew, translated "I am what I am"). You are now removing the negative water energy.

Move to the north, make a pentagram in green, and say: AH-GAH-LAH-AAH (AGLH in Hebrew, translated "Thou are great forever oh Lord"). You are now removing the negative earth energy.

Return to the east. Stand with your feet shoulder width apart, arms extended out to the sides, right hand pointing up, left hand pointing down.

Say, "Before me RAAF-AYE-EL," and visualize either the Archangel Raphael in yellow robes, or picture a yellow caduceus.

Then say, "Behind me GAB-RYE-EL," and visualize the Archangel Gabriel in blue robes or a blue trumpet.

Then say, "At my right hand MIKH-AYE-EL," and visualize the Archangel Michael in red robes or a red flaming sword.

Then say, "At my left hand AUR-AYE-EL," and picture the Archangel Auriel in green robes or a green lantern.

The next part is more complicated. First say the words, "Around me flame the pentagrams, above me shines the six-rayed star." There are three simultaneous visualizations that go with this. It takes practice

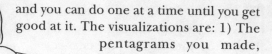

and you can do one at a time until you get good at it. The visualizations are: 1) The pentagrams you made, which are hanging in space, and are connected by a thread of bright silvery-blue as the circle seals itself. 2) Above your head appears a star of David, which is two interlocking triangles, a white one pointed upward and a black one pointed downward. 3) Through your body, shaped and directed by your hands and arms, will appear a cosmic lemniscate, better known as the infinity sign (like a figure eight on its side), in gold. Feel the energy flowing around and around through your arms and body.

All this is occurring as you are saying the phrase. If you need to, take your time, stabilize the energies, and wait until it is all there. With practice it comes quickly.

Part Three

Repeat part one. You can bring the energy beams through your body this time if you want. You can also end with "amen" to seal it.

All the words should be intoned—almost sung. Be loud. The first few times you do it you will feel conspicuous. That's normal. You will eventually get over it. We make our students do this every morning and evening for at least three weeks, and we do it in a group at the start of each class to get us into class mode.

This is an effective grounding and centering exercise. It can be done audibly or silently, with or without the actual motion, visualizing only, and it still works. Technically this will also work if you just say the words and go through the motions without doing the visualizations.

This creates a circle specifically for banishing, cleansing, and warding. It should be allowed to dissipate, not be taken down. You do not have to cut yourself out when exiting or entering. I use it to seal hotel rooms when traveling. I also use it when I cannot sleep at night. It grounds, centers, and shields you from all the noise (both audible and psychic), allowing you to relax and sleep. It also helps cut out extraneous noise when life gets hectic.

Sea Priestess Bath

By deTraci Regula

E ven when we are far from the ocean, the rhythms of the sea influence our lives. Many people who are drawn to the worship of the ancient gods and goddesses feel a particular call from the sea. If landlocked, it can be hard to get to the ocean and feel the pulse of the great waves. In summer, when tourists crowd the beaches late into the night, it can be unpleasant to visit the ocean, but by avoiding it because of the tourists we neglect sensing the great heart of the world.

It's especially fortunate that there is a relaxing, spiritually refreshing way of attuning with the sea. In these time-starved days, it's also a powerful way of reclaiming spiritual time for oneself. While I've called this the "Sea Priestess Bath," please note: would-be Poseidons can also benefit from this wonderful soak.

If you live in a non-polluted area by the sea, gather some of the seaweed from the shore yourself, if possible. For others, however, a trip to the local health food or herb store will provide some of the ingredients. While this bath is designed as a method of meditation, be aware that seaweed tends to remove toxins from the body, and this may manifest itself as increased sweating during or after the bath. For most people, this is an additional benefit, but if you suffer from heart trouble or high blood pressure, use caution.

Types of Seaweed

Dulse: This delicate maroon seaweed expands in water to resemble waving swatches of frayed silk. Slightly grainy when rubbed between the fingertips, it's beautiful to watch.

Bladderwrack: This seaweed takes its name from the small air-holding vesicles found in its fronds. Under water, they keep the plant upright. To provide yourself with a bathtub forest of

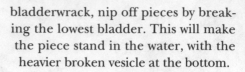

bladderwrack, nip off pieces by breaking the lowest bladder. This will make the piece stand in the water, with the heavier broken vesicle at the bottom.

KELP: Possibly the most beneficial sea weed, the broad-leaf forms of kelp release a purifying gel into the water from between their leaves. To maximize this release, make sure the water is very hot initially. You don't have to enter the tub until it has begun to cool a little. Bits of kelp can be placed against the body to enhance the healing effect. Kelp is very rich in iodine.

SEA PALM: The long, buoyant, ribbed fronds of the sea palm resemble their counterpart on land. Stringy, long pieces can be tied loosely around the body and playfully woven through fingers and toes.

ALARIA: This edible seaweed can be used in sea baths, and is similar to Japanese wakame. It's a soft, broad-leafed seaweed with a strong central midrib. It works very well for plastering against the moist skin, laying over shoulders, or just using it as a seaweed washcloth.

SALTS

What salt you use is a personal choice that enhances the total bath experience. You can use a scented mix—I like "green tea" bath salts, which also impart a lovely color to the water. Use whatever you prefer, including epsom salts or plain or iodized table salt.

OIL

Any energizing, purifying bath oil will be useful in giving a wonderful feel to the water, and helping the sea minerals contained in the seaweed to coat your skin. It should be of a scent that is compatible with the

ocean. At present, I'm enjoying using ginseng oil or flax seed oil.

How to Take a Sea Priestess Bath

To release the healing properties of the seaweed, very hot water is needed. Run hot water for a few minutes, add the seaweed, wait for a few minutes, and then bring the temperature down by adding cold water. Slip into the water and soak, meditating on the little sea that you have created around you.

Some commercial "sea bath" packages include watercress, which can be a problem for plumbing. At the end of your bath, take a moment to "gather ye seaweed while ye may" and prevent it from clogging your drain. The used seaweed can be left to dry and added to another bath, though most of the therapeutic benefits will have been removed in the first soak. This is similar to re-using a teabag. Some people prefer to make an actual tea of the seaweeds and then add that to the bath. While most of the therapeutic benefits will remain, the psychological ones will not be so strong. Part of the pleasure of the bath is playing with the seaweed. It's a very strange feeling to climb into a tub of gently floating weeds, and simply watching their motion induces a calm, meditative state perfect for a temporary visit with the divine kings and queens of the sea.

The effect of this bath is not entirely psychological. Seaweeds will help to draw toxins from the body, and do this very effectively. Some people experience dizziness or light-headedness from the combination of the seaweed and the warm bath water. Keep a sponge moistened with cold water within reach. Be careful getting out of the tub, and let yourself relax afterward. If you stay in the water too long, dehydration, ironically enough, can occur, so drink some water, or keep a plastic bottle with you in the bath.

Breathe slowly and relax in the warm waters, so like the inner sea that held us all before birth.

SACRED SHOWER RITUAL

By Ayla

Greetings! Do you often feel grumpy and irritable in the morning or wish you had more time to spend caring for yourself? Of course! We all do. Sometimes, with all the responsibilities we have, we forget our most important responsibility— to love and care for ourselves! Many people do not have enough time each day for solitude and quiet contemplation. Luckily, one thing we usually do have a few minutes for is a quick shower before our day officially begins. Here is a self-nurturing ritual that can be performed every day, or just when you feel you may need a bit of a boost. Try it and enjoy yourself. Remember that you are important, too!

First, assemble shower and ritual tools: a big, fluffy, white towel; three white votives or pillar candles; your favorite incense, and a great bar of soap. Splurge and get a bar of soap that you've had your eye (and nose!) on. Pick out a relaxing CD and something to carve with, like a bolline or other small knife.

Arrange the candles and light the incense. Hang your towel nearby, put the soap in its holder, and turn on the music. Take five deep breaths, center, and ground yourself before beginning. Next, take the soap and carve a pentacle on both sides. Ask for and sense the presence of the Goddess and God. Hold the bar in the air while saying these words:

O Mother Goddess
O Father God
Bless this soap that you
have seen
Soap to make me pure
and clean.
Clear away all dirt
and grime
Protect my body all the time.
Blessed Be

Place it back in the holder in the shower. Lastly, take each candle and carve a pentacle or protective rune on its side. Grasp all three candles in your hands and repeat these words:

Candles that I light this day,
Keep all evil thoughts away.
As the water washes me,
Burn out all negativity.
Blessed Be

Kiss each candle then light it. You are now ready to take your shower. While the water runs down your body, try to imagine it rinsing away all your stress, sadness, and worries. Visualize the soap bubbles cleaning off dirt and leaving your skin glowing with a radiant white glow all around you. This will keep you feeling strong and protected all through the day. Thank the Goddess and God for their presence and put all tools away for next time. Always be good to your mind, body, and soul. Love and Blessings to all!

SUGGESTIONS FOR INCENSE: frankincense, sandalwood, patchouli, cinnamon, or rosemary.

MUSIC: nature sounds like babbling brooks, crackling fires, chirping birds, or roaring ocean waves.

SOAP: cedar, patchouli, sandalwood, lavender, or rose.

DOGS

BY RACHEL
PARTI RAYMOND

Human beings and dogs have a relationship that extends back into antiquity. Dogs have been companions to humans for so long that they have a seemingly infinite number of associations and a huge body of lore. Dogs provide protection and assistance with hunting, thanks to their enhanced sense of smell and hearing. In return, human beings provide a warm place by the fire and all the bones you can chew. Domesticated dogs easily adopt human beings as members of their pack. There is definitely a difference between wild canines and domesticated ones, yet who can really say who has domesticated whom? How much have we as a species learned from observing the pack behavior of dogs? Perhaps they have been domesticating us all along.

Hounds are sacred to several gods and goddesses. The Egyptian dog-headed god Anubis was a psychopomp. It was his job to accompany the recently deceased before the goddess of truth, Maat, in the throne room of the Underworld god Osiris. Hounds of all kinds were associated with death deities and were considered to be agents of the Underworld. This was due to their habits as scavengers who routinely buried and then dug up bones. Dogs, unlike cats, are just as happy to find their dinner already dead; in addition, dogs were thought to be able to see ghosts. The triple goddess, Hecate, who sees the past, present, and future simultaneously, resides in a cave at the entrance to the underworld that is guarded by Her three-headed dog Cerebus.

When the Welsh goddess Cerridwen pursued Her errant assistant Gwion in his form as a fleet-footed hare, She turned Herself into a greyhound, the fastest hunter known to the ancient Celts. Greyhounds were known for their swiftness even in ancient Egypt, where they were employed to hunt antelope. To the Hindus, dawn was personified as the greyhound, Sarama. In China, it was a dog of the heavens, and the eleventh sign in the Chinese zodiac. As a heraldic device, greyhounds symbolized vigilance, courage, and loyalty.

Dogs were also associated with the Moon, thanks to their tendency to howl when it was Full. The lunar goddess Artemis always traveled with a pack of hounds. She had an affinity with dogs that did not bode well for Acteon, the rash hunter who spied on Artemis while she was bathing. She turned him into a stag and had him hunted by his own hounds. This is probably a Hellenic revision of a much earlier goddess rite. The consorts of Lunar Goddesses (in this case Acteon) were often depicted as stags, the horned ones who roamed the woods at will during spring and summer, but who shed their antlers with the first winter snows.

Female dogs were considered to be especially fierce and effective hunters because of their desire to feed and protect their young. Because of this, the word "bitch" was once a title of respect and admiration. One might say "She's quite the bitch," much as one might say today "he's a bear of a man."

The dog days of summer are so named because it was thought that the dog star, Sirius, brought them. The dog star accompanies the hunter constellation, Orion. "Hair of the dog that bit you" is a phrase that came from the idea that placing a hair from the dog that had attacked you would heal the wound. I wish I could think of some quasi-scientific reason why that superstition might have developed, but I am cynical. I can't see how putting dog hair on an open wound would help anybody. The word "cynic" comes from Latin, meaning dog-like, and implying one who is suspicious and skeptical. In Semitic lore, dogs were considered unclean and harbingers of disease, which may well have been true, especially in the that climate, which was, no doubt, abundant with fleas. However, dogs are also associated with healing, and were shown as the companions and guides to several mythic healers including the Babylonian goddess Gula, the Celtic god Gulens, and the Greek Aesclepius.

The true magic of canines is their unflagging loyalty and devotion. If you are fortunate enough to have the love of a good dog, then you know what it is to be cared for by one of the Goddess' most magical of creatures.

The following deities are associated with dogs: Artemis, Hecate, Gula, Gwydion, Kambel, Kaulu, Legba, Manannnan, Maui, Nuada, Thoth, Wuni, and Zorya.

A Charm of Isis

By deTraci Regula

Isis is perhaps the most multi-faceted of all the goddesses known to us. Earth mother and star spirit, sacred healer and Amazon warrior goddess, passionate lover and pure holy priestess of the divine, She can be approached to answer any human need. As the divine spell-maker and compounder of mystical medicines, she is also known as the "one who hears," who responds to the devotions and rites of Her followers and even to those who merely call on Her out of curiosity or indefinable need. Her responsiveness is legendary, but don't ever invite Her with disrespect or in a desire to dominate a deity. It won't work out the way you expect. Enough said.

How to Make an Isis Charm

Go to a sacred space, at your home altar or out in nature. Draw one of Isis' symbols on a piece of paper or in a spot of clear ground.

Take a strip of white cloth long enough to tie around your wrist, ankle, or waist. Smooth out the strip and anoint the cloth with a sweet-smelling oil, such as amber, kyphi, or a blend named for Isis. It should be a scent that you enjoy. As you anoint the cloth, say these or similar words:

> Great Isis, Lady of the Universe,
> Let your divine nature flow into this band of cloth.
> I ask for your protection in difficult times
> I ask for your help and assistance with difficult people
> Let me have knowledge of my own power
> And enlightenment to guide me
> In your name, Isis, divine protectoress,
> Who guards all those who call upon Your name.

As you write on the cloth, say:

> As I inscribe this cloth
> so let me be also inscribed
> with the enduring mark of your protection.
> Holy Isis, Lady of the Words of Power
> Hear my words and may they be pleasing to you.
> Grant to me your divine protection
> as I bind to me with the divine knot of Isis
> Your Holy name.

Tie the cloth around you. It should be left loose enough that it can be slid off again without untying it.

> I glory in the light, I share in the sacred and eternal life.
> Thank you, Great Isis, Lady of the Universe!

Wear the cloth through the difficult situation, or until you feel that the power it represents is present within you.

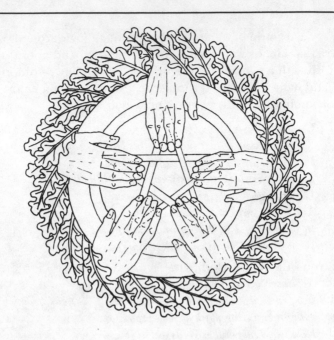

Covens, Circles, and Groves

By Amber K

When Pagans gather, they often do so under the banner of organized small groups with colorful names like the Grove of the Ancient Forest, Crescent Moon Coven, or the Circle of Cerridwen. How does one tell the difference between covens and circles, inner circles and outer circles, groves and study groups? If you decide to organize a group, what should you call it?

To begin with, none of these terms are copyrighted, and you can legally call your group anything you want; but if you use certain terms inappropriately, it will cause misunderstandings in the community. Don't call your group a coven unless your members are Witches/Wiccans, and if you use the word "grove," be aware that some will assume you are Druids.

For most Pagan groups that are neither Druids nor Wiccans, "circle" is a fairly safe and non-specific term. (Even here there could be confusion with the organization Circle, based in Wisconsin, which is a large network of subscribers, festival-goers, and friends of Circle Sanctuary. To complicate matters further, some Wiccan covens use "circle" as part of their names instead of "coven," as in "Circle of the Summer Sun.") "Temple" is another term that could refer to a coven or almost any Pagan church.

Many people begin with the idea of a study group, which could be you and a few friends gathering weekly to talk about nature religions and perhaps magic. The focus is on education or information-sharing, and the term "study group" is innocuous enough that most schools, colleges, libraries, and community centers will let you use their facilities for meetings. A study group will probably have weekly presenters or discussion topics, and not much structure or program beyond that.

At some point the study group members, or some of them, may feel the need to become more deeply involved in the practice of Pagan religion. Then you may want to consider starting an independent Pagan circle or, if you have been involved in the Unitarian Church, a chapter of the Covenant of Unitarian Universalist Pagans (CUUPs). The latter is a nationwide organization in the United States for people who consider themselves both Unitarian and Pagan.

If your interests are definitely Witchy, then you may prefer to organize a coven. Now, the most cautious way to do this is to join an existing coven and get solid training and experience before you launch out on your own. Still, there are people who have initiated themselves and founded covens with no more background than reading some good books on the subject. It's a difficult path, but if you're a brilliant organizer you might be able to do it.

What's the difference between a study group and a coven? A study group exists simply so that the members may learn about a subject. A coven is a religious organization of priestesses and priests dedicated to practicing the Old Religion (Witchcraft or Wicca). Witches don't just study: they celebrate the turning of the seasons and phases of the Moon, work magic, heal, lead rites of passage, and seek spiritual growth by connecting with the goddesses and gods of nature. The same is true of other Pagans, except that they may emphasize magic less and do not all consider themselves to be clergy.

According to the tales, Witches' covens were originally small, underground societies created to keep the Craft alive in the face of horrifying persecution by the Inquisition. The Witches of the Middle Ages would meet to celebrate the sabbats or invoke the aid of the Triple Goddess of the Moon and the Horned Lord of the wild places. Some now believe that no covens survived into modern times; others say they did, and initiated people such as Gerald Gardner into an unbroken tradition stretching back centuries.

Whether covens originated a thousand years ago or fifty is a moot question. They are a vital part of the living religion of Witchcraft. Most covens average about seven adult members; few are larger than thirteen. In this small, supportive environment, deep emotional and psychic bonds are formed and intensive spiritual and magical work is carried out.

The word "grove," which originally referred to a sacred place in the woods, has been used at least three different ways among Pagans. Sometimes it is simply a gathering of Pagans of no particular denomination. Often it means a local organization of Druids. Occasionally it refers to a group of Pagans who gather to worship under the guidance of a Witches' coven; this kind of "grove" is also called a "congregation" or "outer circle," as distinct from the "inner circle," which is composed of the priests and priestesses of the coven.

In legal terminology, all these organizations are "churches." If your group chooses to incorporate and even seek federal tax-exempt status, you will be called a "church" or "not-for-profit religious organization" in legal documents.

Witches in a given region may join Local Councils of the Covenant of the Goddess (COG). COG is a federation of Witches and covens, formed to secure religious rights of Witches and foster networking among them. Presently it has about 120 member covens, mostly in the United States, plus many elder solitaries and associates. COG has about fifteen Local Councils throughout the States. Other large networks are the Pagan Federation (headquartered in the United Kingdom) and the Pan-Pacific Pagan Alliance (including Australia, New Zealand, and the Pacific).

From local groups to vast regional networks, Pagans are organizing. What were once the folk religions of villages, tribes, or nations are now recognized legal entities linked by modern telecommunications and the Internet. Paganism may have roots in the distant past, but it has arrived in the age of high technology.

WE ARE STARDUST

BY MARGUERITE ELSBETH

During ancient times, people of various cultures believed that the sky was made of stone. This idea is not as far-fetched as it may seem. The earth itself is a large rock hurtling through space, and we can still see stars, meteorites, comets, and other heavenly bodies falling from the sky to earth. In fact, as the earth is in outer space along with the rest of the luminaries and planets, can't we conclude that we are from outer space too?

STAR DUST

Objects from space fall from the sky and shower the earth with crystal stardust. When meteorites fall from the sky, they take on the appearance of fire. Meteoric iron, or any part of the meteor, manifests the power of lightning, or electrical fire from the sky. Wind and rain shift the earth's covering, helping the stardust, or sky-fire, to seep underground, where it is transformed into the higher mineral forms that go into the making of the elements we call fire, water, air, and earth. These elements gather around the fiery central core of space minerals to create life as we know it. All around us, hidden within all creatures and things, is sky-fire in earth form. The Sun, the Moon, the planets, and the stars, which are always vibrating and moving, are bound together and made to appear static to the naked eye by the sky-fire that lives in all of us—our consciousness.

STAR MAGIC

Star magic, the mind-fire or conscious awareness that enables us to be the intermediaries between earth and sky, is our gift from the heavens, but we cannot live in harmony with nature until we learn to balance our star-borne abilities. This is difficult when we are surrounded by the chaos and flux on our planet—the endless round of war, disease, and death brought about by the unfortunate condition of world affairs today. However, we must remember that sky-fire develops at varying degrees and stages in all of us. When we are awake to the magic of the stars within, we can move beyond the appearance of limitation presented by the wily world of form and our straight-line mental constructs. Our awareness can move mountains if we dare to believe. We have within us the star magic empowerment to heal the earth, but we cannot do this until we are willing to heal ourselves first.

EARTH ALCHEMY

Earth alchemy is a process whereby we can change our bodies and our personalities to reflect the union that exists between the mind-body connection and the cosmos. We can easily recognize this restorative process in ancient myth, such as when the Bone Goddess raises the "dead," a metaphor for those who are asleep or unconscious, in order to recreate the cosmic human, a being who is a re-membered whole. Mexican Indian lore speaks of La Loba, the she-wolf goddess; Sumeria gives us the rejuvenated Ishtar; Russia speaks of Baba Yaga the Witch; and Egypt provides us with Isis, the goddess who restored Osiris to life. All of these earth goddesses are alchemists, shamans, and healers, releasing a magical elixir that is made of medicinal elements from the stars: air, the mind-fire or mediator; fire, the personality or spirit healer; and water, the body or star medicine.

ELEMENTAL HEALERS

Air, fire, and water are synonymous with the alchemical principles of mercury (the mind), sulphur (the spirit), and salt (the body). When it comes to recreating wholeness, all three alchemical principles or elements of the body must work together. The mind should be vital, intelligent, and open to new ideas. The spirit should be passionate, active, and filled with the desire for life. The body should be flexible, mobile, and able to function in its highest capacity.

Sky-fire requires a form to work in and through, so it is up to us to provide our bodies with optimum care, compliments of the stars. When stars explode, they release countless elemental healers, the trace minerals that are necessary to sustain life.

STAR MEDICINE

All the necessary star medicine minerals are found in fresh fruits and vegetables, especially dark, leafy, bitter greens such as kale or arugula. We can also find star medicine in crystals and gemstones, because tissue salts are actually meteoric mineral crystals in a natural chemical matrix.

One particular gemstone that comes as a gift from the stars is moldavite, a silica or salt-based stone. It is colored a beautiful, translucent olive green, reminiscent of deep, verdant earth. Moldavite is empowered with electrical energy, and literally embodies fire from the sky because it is a rare type of meteor formed over fifteen million years ago. We may all benefit from this stone tonic as it quiets the senses and increases our understanding of our relationship as mediators between heaven and earth. Carry moldavite on your person, in a pocket, or a small pouch fashioned from a natural substance, such as leather, silk, or cotton.

Finally, remember to embrace the entire cosmos while re-membering your unique wholeness, for we are stardust.

SHIVA: THE OLDEST OF THE GODS

BY KENNETH JOHNSON

The ancient civilization of the Indus Valley sleeps deep beneath the dust of the present-day nation of Pakistan. Though the people of the early Indus cities are long gone, their ideas and beliefs gave birth to the great spiritual traditions of India that remain powerful and strong to this very day.

A wealth of clay seals survives from this ancient culture, many of them depicting gods and rituals long forgotten. One such seal shows a man with horns, seated cross-legged in the "lotus position," which is still practiced by yogis. This seal is perhaps three thousand years old, and although most of the goddesses and gods of the Indus remain mysterious to us, this one is still worshipped by millions of people and is perhaps the oldest deity to still command the devotion of mortals.

The horned god of the Indus is none other than Shiva, the Cosmic Dancer. His name means "the auspicious one," for it is proper to speak only of his benevolence, and not to draw too much attention to his wilder side. One of his many names is Rudra, the Howler, for he is the power of the storm and the howling winds. While his cosmic dance may sometimes bring worlds into being, it may also sweep them away with the power of an atom bomb. As scientist Robert Oppenheimer witnessed the first nuclear test in New Mexico, he chanted the words of an ancient Sanskrit text: "I am become Shiva, destroyer of worlds."

The god of the Indus is crowned with horns because he has a mystical connection with animals, and with wilderness in general. Like Pagan European gods such as Cernunnos, he is sometimes known as Lord of the Animals. Shiva has no patience with cities and civilizations; his energy is vested in the wild places of the world. Those who follow his path frequently forsake all the comforts of home, setting forth to wander through forests and mountains, sleeping on the ground, making friends with the wild beasts, and meditating in caves and by the sides of streams. They turn aside from marriage and child-rearing as well.

Though marriage may be forbidden to the wandering devotee of Shiva, sex is not, for Shiva is the god of Tantra or sacred sexuality. His bride is called Parvati, the Goddess of the Mountains, and their lovemaking is part of the divine play of universal energy. In marriage, this divine sexual play is dedicated to the good of society as embodied in the production of children. To the Tantric adept, whether woman or man, sexuality is pure ecstasy, a free flow of energy that partakes of mystical rapture and has absolutely nothing to do with the bonds of marriage or the limitations of society. In the same way, the stimulants that are forbidden to most Hindus are frequently used by Shiva worshippers to attain mystical communion.

Yet it would be a mistake to imagine that all, or even most, of Shiva's devotees are engaged in an endless party. Shiva is the god of yoga as well, and those who have the mystical strength to turn away from the world, to practice ascetic disciplines requiring complete control over mind and body, are also his devotees. Perhaps it is for this reason that the oldest of the gods is also called Mahadeva, which means "the Great God," for he leads us to a life of magic and self-empowerment as well as inviting us to take part in the dance of ecstasy.

Quick Moon Cakes

By Magenta Summerton

O h no! Your coven is arriving in half an hour, and you were supposed to bake the Moon cakes for tonight. Try telling your boss who gave you extra work to finish, the traffic that insisted on piling up, or your toddler who wants attention *now*. What's a Witch to do?

Most Moon cakes are actually cookies, and many of the best recipes take time, which you may not have available. Rich cookie recipes have to be prepared, rolled out, and cut into rounds to represent the Full Moon, or perhaps cut into crescents. These need to be transferred to a baking sheet, and carefully watched so they won't burn. The horns of the crescents have a tendency to drop off while being moved or to burn if left in the oven a minute too long. Here are alternatives to the traditional recipes.

First, if you plan ahead, and have the money, buy round shortbread cookies. These are available in the fancier supermarkets and specialty food stores. Imported from Scotland, these buttery confections are perfect little Moons. You could also buy a whole wheel of shortbread. Both will keep in your pantry for several months if necessary, but they are expensive.

Better yet, try these two quick recipes. They are based on the idea that the best symbol for the Moon is one large round cake, rather than many small ones.

Full Moon Cornbread

1   cup cornmeal
1   cup flour (this could be all white flour, or half white, half whole wheat)
1   tablespoon baking powder
½   teaspoon salt
½   cup sugar, if desired (can be decreased or omitted)
1   cup milk

1   egg

¼   cup oil

Preheat oven to 425°F. Grease a 9-inch round pan. (It must be 9-inch, 8-inch is too small.) Combine cornmeal, flour, baking powder, salt, and sugar. In another bowl, combine milk, egg, and oil. Add the liquids to the dry ingredients. Mix quickly and pour into pan. Bake 20–25 minutes, and you have a large pale yellow Moon cake for your coven to enjoy.

Brownie Moon

For New Moon, you may wish to use a dark cake. Here is a New Moon cake recipe that is almost as quick and easy.

⅜   cup (¾ of a stick) butter or margarine

⅜   cup cocoa

2   eggs

⅛   teaspoon salt

1   cup sugar

1   teaspoon vanilla

½   cup flour

Preheat oven to 350°F. Grease a 9-inch round pan. Melt butter or margarine in a saucepan. Remove from heat, and add cocoa. Beat eggs and salt until light, about 5 minutes. Gradually add sugar, then vanilla. Fold in the chocolate mixture, mixing only until blended. Fold in flour, mixing only until the flour is no longer visible. Do not overmix. Pour into pan. Bake 25–30 minutes.

Pagans and the Law:
Rights and Responsibilities

By Creide Stewart, Esquire

Everyone knows that being an out-of-the-broom-closet Pagan is a difficult lifestyle. People look at you just a little bit differently. Your pentagram necklace always causes a few stares and whispers of "Satan-worshipper," but since you know that we Pagans do not even believe in the Christian Devil, you think that these people have just bought into the misconceptions that abound about our faith and practice. Our beliefs represent a religion after all, so why is it any of "their" business? In America, we are guaranteed the right to freedom of religion by the Constitution, so we must be allowed to live and present ourselves however we see fit.

There is just one little problem with the scenario above. We are also a minority in this country, and while that status gives us certain rights under the law, fighting for those rights can be a difficult and expensive legal endeavor if someone attempts to take your job, your athame or, worse yet, your children away from you. The law does not always care about the First Amendment when average people in society are presented with beliefs they do not understand. Pagans need to take the responsibility to educate themselves as to their rights before they face a crisis, and then act in accordance with that knowledge.

The Constitution states that the government shall neither establish nor prevent the free exercise of religion. Most people assume that those words mean that one can do almost anything they choose and later justify that behavior in the name of belief. However, that is not what the law on religion in this country is in reality and practice. The Supreme Court Justices of the United States, the final judges of what is and is not allowed, have decided that those words mean that there may not be a "state religion" and that no one may be forced to participate in any spiritual process. They have also decided that there can be limits placed on spiritual practice so long as those limits do not judge the validity of a particular religious path. Any investigation into a religious practice must be performed on religiously-neutral grounds, but limits may be placed on certain activities that are considered harmful either to individuals or to society as a whole.

It was through this sort of reasoning that Native Americans were prohibited from the use of peyote in their rituals. The Supreme Court did not say that the usage was not an acceptable religious practice, but decided that peyote was a controlled drug and could be regulated as such despite the religious implications. To a lesser degree, the same sort of reasoning applies when a Pagan is arrested for carrying an athame. Many jurisdictions have rules about carrying knives, both openly or as concealed weapons, and those laws can apply despite the religious character of a ritual blade. Certain townships and municipalities have rules and regulations about open fires or permits for gatherings. These too must be obeyed, or a Pagan could face valid criminal or misdemeanor charges, which will be upheld regardless of whether there is a perfectly reasonable explanation, based in religious practice, for thirteen people meeting in a meadow at midnight and dancing around a blazing balefire.

Naturally, the worst outrage Pagans can face is the loss of their children because of their religion. There are several ways in which children may be taken from their Earth-centered, polytheistic mothers and fathers. The usual manner in which this happens is the type of case we, as Pagans, hear the least about. A couple divorces or splits up in some way and a custody battle ensues. As a part of the process, the Pagan parent's religion is made an issue by the other parent and the courts, although constitutionally bound to not consider religion in and of itself, must consider the impact that the parent's practices have on the "best interests of the child."

There are no Pagan judges in this country to my knowledge, and the judiciary is not often educated about the truly positive nature of Pagan beliefs. Upon hearing testimony that a mother casts a circle, performs skyclad rituals, and celebrates different holidays than "normal" people, a judge is ethically required to determine whether these practices are harmful to the children. The result

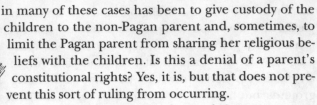

in many of these cases has been to give custody of the children to the non-Pagan parent and, sometimes, to limit the Pagan parent from sharing her religious beliefs with the children. Is this a denial of a parent's constitutional rights? Yes, it is, but that does not prevent this sort of ruling from occurring.

The other type of custody case brings state agencies into the picture. These cases are much uglier from a legal perspective because some branches of children and youth services will create evidence of abuse or neglect using religion as an excuse. That sounds harsh and is patently unfair to the many good people who work in the social services field, but it happens in some areas, and Pagan parents must be aware of the possibility in order to protect themselves. Once again that word "responsibility" rears its ugly head above what should be the free exercise of religion. There is not a single Pagan in this country who cannot take steps to protect him or herself and loved ones from falling victim to religious discrimination.

The best guideline in protecting oneself is to use common sense. The general public does not like to see knives flashed openly, so keep your athame inconspicuous. When traveling with a blade, put it in your trunk (there are certain search and seizure laws that forbid the search of a car's trunk without probable cause) or in a zippered bag far out of your reach. If the police officers ask if you have any weapons, be honest and politely tell them that there is a ritual blade and tell them where in the car it is. As a parent, make sure your children are well groomed, polite, and complete all their school assignments. Do not allow your religion to be made an issue—if you do not give Youth Services or a divorcing spouse a foothold, they will be less likely to use your religion against you.

Most importantly, be aware that you are a representative of the Pagan Community as a whole. How each of us behaves and conducts our lives reflects upon all others who share our faith. Be an honest and upstanding citizen—a person whom people point to and say: "I can't believe s/he is a Witch. S/he is so normal." Normal is good because we are a newly-recognized spiritual path from a legal perspective, and the groundwork is still being laid for how we will be treated in the future. Your actions now will help to form a positive image of Paganism for the next century, when one hopes we can all co-exist with those of other faiths on an equal standing.

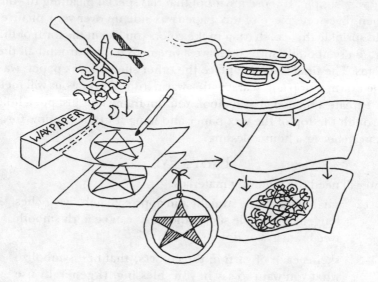

KIDS' CRAFTS: MAKE YOUR OWN STAINED "GLASS" WINDOWS AND LADY'S EYES

BY BREID FOXSONG

Parents, here are a couple of fun projects to do with your kids. Any of these can be done by children over three, as long as there is a little supervision and assistance with the iron for the youngest ones.

STAINED "GLASS" WINDOWS

For the first project, you will need:

Old, broken crayons	Scissors
Wax paper	Newspapers
White paper	Markers
Warm iron	Potato peeler

Place several newspapers on the table to protect it. Separate the crayons by color. Use a knife or a potato peeler to make shavings out of them. A pencil sharpener also works well, but crayons will dull the pencil sharpener.

On the white paper, draw several Pagan symbols (pentagram, tree, chalice, etc.). You can also use printed pictures as long as they are very simple. Choose a symbol that has special meaning to you. Then place one piece of wax paper wax side up over your picture, and sprinkle the wax shaving in the colors you like in the form of the chosen symbol. Be sure you leave a one-inch border around all the edges. The final step is to place the other sheet of wax paper, wax side down, in top and seal it with a warm iron. The crayons will melt and create a stained glass symbol. You can frame it or just put a hole through the top of the wax paper and hang it in the window for a sun catcher or a house blessing.

LADY'S EYE

You will need the following materials:

2   small sticks, fairly straight and approximately five inches long, or 2 popsicle sticks (the sticks can be fairly smooth tree branches or dowels)

1–3   skeins each of yarn in the color(s) that best symbolize what you want to say in your blessing. (I generally use green for prosperity, gold for health, or blue for protection, but choose your own favorites. You can combine more than one color on any piece)

Small bells or beads for decoration (optional)

The third project is a simple weaving that makes a beautiful house blessing to hang on the wall, reminding us that the Lady looks with love on people everywhere. I call these house charms "Lady's eyes." They sound complicated, but are really very easy to make!

STEP 1: Cross the sticks at the center. Tie them together with the end of the strand of yarn, making an X, but don't cut the yarn off its skein. Tie the yarn in back of the two crossed sticks.

STEP 2: Looking at the equal-armed cross formed, number the "arms" in a clockwise manner so you are bringing the yarn to the front between sticks three and four. Pull the yarn over stick three and the next one too (stick two), and bring it to the back between sticks two and one. Wrap it behind stick one and bring it to the front again between sticks two and three. Pull it over stick two and the next one too (stick one), and wrap it behind stick one.

STEP 3: Pull the yarn over stick one and the next one too (stick four) and wrap it behind stick four. Pull it over stick four and the next one too (stick three) and wrap it behind stick three. This is one complete

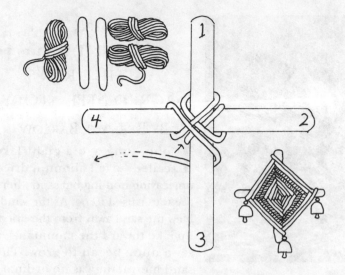

round. Always lay the yarn next to, not on top of, the yarn already in place. As you weave, chant the blessing that you wish to lay upon the charm. I use something like:

> *Money, love, and peace abound, as I weave this charm around*
> *The Lady's eyes will clearly see; as I will so mote it be!*

If you are using multiple colors, you can have one chant for each color. If you started with blue for peace, you could say something like:

> *Harmony and peace be near, banish anger banish fear,*
> *Lady's eye will guard and guide, and peace to all who here abide*

STEP 4: Keep on wrapping the yarn behind each stick, over that stick and the next, and around behind that one, then over that stick and the next and behind that one. As you continue making the rounds, always be sure that the yarn lies next to, but never on top of the yarn in the previous round. After the first few rounds, you will see the woven pattern of the "eye" beginning to form.

STEP 5: When you have an "eye" in one color of yarn, you can cut the yarn and tie on another color, and continue weaving. Make sure that the knot that you joined the two colors with stays in the back.

STEP 6: Keep weaving the Lady's eye until you are about a half inch from the ends of the sticks. Cut the yarn, leaving approximately a seven or eight-inch tail. Tie the tail in a knot in back. If you have bells or beads for decoration, attach one to each of the ends.

The Singing Mountain: A Children's Sacred Site Story

By Bernyce Barlow

Long, long ago a giant lake called Lake Lahonton dried up, leaving nothing but sand where the water used to be. As the winds blew the sand away from the dried-up lake toward the mountains, a sand dune began to grow. The sand mountain was no ordinary sand dune. It was a singing sand dune! Sometimes, when the sand slipped off the tip top of the mountain, it would sound like a pipe organ or cello. At other times, the sand avalanche made flute sounds and drum booms. Sand Mountain was indeed no ordinary sand dune.

Once, when the angels were rejoicing in the heavens, they heard the musical tones of the booming sands and came closer to its source. The angels were so impressed with the mountain's beautiful sounds that they spontaneously burst into a celestial chorus in harmony with the sand dune. The music filled the air. Lizards and coyotes crept out of their homes among the rocks and cliffs to listen to the heavenly concert. The eagles also came to listen. They soared through the atmosphere as if carried by the windtune that the sky danced to. It was a harmonic celebration of heaven and earth. The more the dune boomed and cooed, the more angels joined the choir, until the sky was almost full!

A great wind was aroused as the wings of the angels kept beat to the mountain melody. It got stronger as more angels joined the festivities. It was then that the angel of the wilderness became concerned as the sand mountain was blowing away in the wind. By the time the rest of the angels saw what had happened it was too late. The singing sand dune had disappeared. "Oh dear, what happened?" they asked.

The angel of the wilderness explained the wind from their wings had blown away the sand off the mountain in four directions. So the angels made a plan to restore their beloved musical mountain. First the angels gathered all together, then some went to the east, some to the south, and the others to the west and north. When they had gathered in all four directions they began to sing and beat their wings. Sand began to swirl and dance within a whirlwind that centered itself where the mountain used to be. Bigger and bigger the sand dune grew until it was its original height. The angel of the wilderness was pleased, as were the other angels.

The next time the angels gathered around the mountain they did not sing but listened to its music instead as booms and whistles, drones and deep notes emerged from it. After the concert, each angel blessed a grain of sand. Every grain was blessed because there are many, many angels.

Nowadays, people who live near Sand Mountain say once in a while it mysteriously disappears, but always magically returns a year or two later. Of course, you and I know how this happens, don't we? We know the angels are singing on the mountain, keeping winged rhythm with its heartbeat. From the four directions when the sand is scattered will come a mighty desert wind strong enough to rebuild the singing mountain and carry its sound to the Creator. So, if you ever meet someone who asks what happened to Sand Mountain, you can tell them the angels borrowed it!

AUTHOR'S NOTE: Sand Mountain is located twenty miles east of Fallon, Nevada and is one of three "booming sand dunes" in the U.S. It does disappear and reappear from time to time and it also sings. The last audio recordings of a Sand Mountain sheer avalanche sounded like a didgeridoo.

A River Story

By Carrie Westfall

Look up into the sky and you will see the great river flowing from beyond one horizon to beyond the other. All the power for living our visions is carried to us in that river.

A long time ago, there were two bear cubs who were learning to fish from the river. The older of the two cubs was called Ahimué, and she had learned how to stand up in the river's flow, letting the fish swim into her waiting paws as she stood firmly facing the current.

The younger of the two cubs was called Zhojté, and she was just learning how to find her balance without being swept away. Both cubs had learned that where you stood in the river depended on who you are, and that everyone had a place where they could best find their balance. Once you found your balance, you had to make sure that you faced the way the river came from so you could catch the fish as they swam to you. This part had been difficult for Zhojté to learn, but eventually the cub figured it out, and now she stood with her little bear toes dug into the river bottom at her very own balancing place, waiting for a fish to come within her grasp.

Ahimué, in the meantime, was becoming quite good at catching up only those fish that the river guided directly to her. She had learned that as long as she stood in her balancing place, she would never be sent a fish that was too strong or too tough for her to manage, or a fish too small to give her nourishment.

Being the older of the cubs, Ahimué felt responsible for making sure the less experienced Zhojté managed to survive in the flow of the great river. Sometimes Ahimué would call out encouraging words or instructions to the awkward younger bear, and she felt great pride when Zhojté's balance and fishing skills improved.

All this time, the river continued to send fish to both cubs, but sometimes, distracted by her concern for Zhojté, Ahimué would let a fish slip past her unnoticed. Ahimué was not allowing herself to be properly nourished by the fish sent to her. As Zhojté grew steadier in the river's flow, Ahimué became more certain that the opposite was true. More fish began to slip past Ahimué and her vision became less clear until she became convinced that there were not enough fish. As still more fish slipped by, Ahimué's strength was no longer enough to stand firmly against the current, so she began to lose her balance.

Ahimué was now convinced that the river's current was getting stronger, too strong, she was sure, for little Zhojté. In reality, Zhojté had continued to grow stronger and steadier, all the while following Ahimué's good advice to stand quietly in balance and wait for the fish to come. So quiet had the little bear become that Ahimué, no longer able to see or think clearly, was convinced that Zhojté was drowning. Ahimué reached far out from her place in the great river and caught hold of a very powerful salmon as it swam against the current.

The salmon is a great power in the river. Born at the river's source, it spends its youth swimming within the flow of the river, sometimes providing nourishment for those who stand in the river and wait, sometimes slipping past those who are not attentive and making its way downstream, growing large and powerful and in need of fulfillment. This makes salmon a little crazy and very determined to return to he river's source to fill the void in its purpose. This is such a powerful force that it is a thing way beyond the abilities of a young bear cub, let alone a starving cub, to control.

Ahimué struggled to exert her will upon the great fish, pulling on the salmon's fins to redirect its course and carry her to where she thought Zhojté was drowning. Together the powerful salmon and the desperate little cub made their way in a ragged diagonal across the steady flow of the river until they were close to where Zhojté stood quietly fishing. The salmon, unwilling to be further diverted from its

own purpose, gave a mighty leap out of the water, taking the startled Ahimué yelping into the air. As the salmon reached the height of its leap, it arched its slippery back wildly, sending Ahimué tumbling right down on top of Zhojté.

Fortunately for the bear cubs, Heron, who carries dreams and visions up and down the great river, was nearby. In fact, Heron was returning from an errand downstream just as Salmon made its leap from the water.

Heron had seen and heard a great many things on her journeys, but having never seen a flying bear nor heard a yelping salmon, she decided to investigate. When Heron reached the cubs, the salmon was already far upstream and the two cubs were nearly drowned. As carefully as if they were visions, Heron caught the cubs up and took them to a stone in the river to rest. She listened patiently as Ahimué told her how she had failed in her responsibility to Zhojté. When Ahimué had finished her story, Heron paused a moment, and then, reaching swiftly into the water and pulled out a fish, which she divided between the cubs.

Now rested and with full bellies, the little bears listened as Heron explained that the true responsibility that Ahimué had neglected was the one to herself. By not keeping herself in balance, she had accidentally sent everyone around her out of balance as well. Then Heron asked each little cub if they now understood that by taking responsibility for themselves, they were in fact acting responsibly for everyone in the river, and that part of being balanced meant trusting in the ability of others as well as yourself.

With this last reminder, Heron carried each cub back to her balancing place. Then when Heron could see that both Ahimué and Zhojté were each restored to balance and to the business of being bears, she continued on her journey.

PAGAN PLACE

MAGICAL HOUSE NAMES

BY PHOENIX MACFARLAND

From the treetop nests of apes to high-rise condos of modern humans, one thing remains true. We harbor strong feelings about the places we call home. Home has been called "the place you hang your hat" and "the place where they have to let you in," but home is more than that. Our homes become extensions of ourselves, a repository of our memories and our dreams.

To many Wiccans, home is also a place of worship. Anthropology tells us that the Goddess was evident in the earliest homes, which often included a nitch in the wall bearing a statue of the Goddess, conceivably to bless the home and its inhabitants. This was the first known house magic. As the first Gaia figures evolved into specific deities involved with the home, we saw Goddesses such as Hestia occupying the household altars. Modern Catholics with crucifixes above their beds and statues of Mary guarding their front doors are only a step away from the ancient Pagans and their Gaia figures.

Giving your home a magical name is one way of using magic to protect your house. In Victorian times it was customary to name one's house. It was a much more romantic and creative system than today's dehumanizing addresses. Naming one's home is still a practice so common in England as to be considered conformative. In North America, however, it is still rare enough to be considered a refreshing idea.

My husband and I have named every home we have lived in. First we got to know the house, its quirks and graces. Then we found the perfect name. Finally we hung a carved wooden sign with the new name on it near the front door. When we moved out we left the sign because it belonged to the house, not to us. We were delighted to see that long after we moved out, each new tenant retained the name and the house name signs still swing overhead, welcoming friends.

While the thought of naming one's house is quaint and creative, what practical purpose does it serve? Many. In searching

ELFIN ESTATE

out magical names for our homes, we look inward and explore our own expectations of what we hope this living situation will afford. That helps to fine-tune goals, and sometimes acts as a catalyst for better communication between dwelling partners.

Mostly, in assigning a house a magical name, we can combine that act with protection and blessing rituals to draw good fortune into the lives of its inhabitants.

HOW TO PICK A HOUSE NAME

You can use the following criteria in naming your home:

√ Descriptions of the house: House of Seven Gables, Red Gate Cottage, The White House

√ Location of the house: Bay View House, Gothamview

√ Distinctive vegetation growing near the house: Holly House, Fir Manor, Cedar Cottage

√ Fantastic elements connected with the house: Elfin Estate, Avalon, The Hobbit Hole

√ Mythological aspects: Valhalla Hall, Diana's Den

√ What the house is used for: Covenstead Corner

When you decide to give a magical name to your home, try looking at the house through fresh eyes. Ask yourself some questions:

√ What did the house look like when it was new?

√ What it will look like when it is old, if it's new?

√ What sorts of people have lived in it?

√ When you first saw the house, what made you decide to live there?

√ What is your favorite spot in the house?

Those questions help determine what the house is like now. Next, ask questions to determine what you'd like the house to become:

√ What role do you want the house to play? (Sanctuary, power base, lover's getaway, family nest, animals' den, covenstead, hobby place, office, springboard to a nicer place, retirement home, nursery, etc.)

THE HOBBIT HOLE

√ What element do you want to improve to become the most noticeable about the property?

√ What do you want to attract into your home?

√ What/Who do you want to repel from its doors?

√ What do you want to convey to others in the name?

√ If this is a temporary house, what sort of permanent dwelling do you want to attract into your lives?

This last list is the most important in formulating the basis of a house blessing ritual. Getting these goals and expectations clearly in focus helps you to achieve a clear direction in your house magic. Each person can have a hand in name choosing, perhaps in carving or painting a sign for the front door as part of the ritual. Anointing it with oils or passing it through the elements as you weave a protective spell around it, will make it a talisman that hangs outside your front door attracting and/or warding off energy. You can do this as part of your house cleansing ritual. Cleanse it first, physically and spiritually, ridding it of all past negative energies. Then do the house naming as part of the protection spell that seals it from future negativity. I usually paint a little pentagram on each of the house's windows with clear nail polish during this ritual. The nail polish is mostly invisible except when the light is right, then a crystalline-looking pentagram emerges to shine in the Sun before becoming invisible again. Very good ju-ju. At the end of the ritual, hang the house name sign near the front door. Then you will have more than a charming sign that greets all who come to your door. You'll greet them with magic.

Nature-Dyed Eggs For Ostara

By Annie Redwing (Carly Wall)

The Spring Equinox, occurring between March 19 and 21, marks the first day of true spring—the time when day and night are equal. This also heralds Ostara; the fertility festival celebrated the world over by Wiccans. It is a sacred day full of celebrations, lighting of fires at sunrise, ringing bells, and decorating hard-boiled eggs.

Eggs have been viewed as the symbols of fertility for many, many centuries, and as such, would never be left out of the festivities of the fertility festival. The rituals of dyeing, gathering, and eating the eggs symbolize fertility, prosperity, and protection—powerful amulets on such a special day.

Why eggs? The golden center of the egg came to be viewed as representative of the Sun God, the white shell symbolized the White Goddess, and the whole soon came to be seen as the reawakening of the Mother Earth from the deep winter's sleep.

Usually, the eggs are dyed in bright colors and decorated with wax and other items to make special amulets to hide and find. Dyeing the eggs and decorating them naturally makes for a much more powerful energy. Originally, collecting bird's eggs of many different colors from the wild was the goal. Early ancestors observed how the birds wove their nests, and this is how baskets and eggs came to be connected. Today, it is hard to find wild areas and many species of birds are protected, so natural dyeing would bring us as close to nature as we can come.

I raise my own chickens, and so I get a first-hand look at the changes spring brings. At this time of year, I'm inundated with eggs. Because I choose to go as natural as possible, I've collected many ideas for natural dyeing so that I can share them with you.

Over the years, I've dyed many types of eggs because of all the varieties of chickens I've had. I've found that brown eggs dye just as beautifully as white ones (they take on deeper hues) and the smaller eggs from the miniature breeds (bantams, silkies) are very unusual and remind one of wild bird eggs.

This year, I've even been blessed with five new baby chick silkies in an array of colors—white, black, and a few white/black combos mixed with a little brown, so I'm sure to have an abundance of varied eggs to color.

Here are some tips.

Raspberries and cranberries will make the reds, blueberries and blackberries will make the blues and purples, and turmeric and spinach will make the yellows and greens. All you have to do is take each ingredient and boil it in a stainless steel or enamel pan a few minutes, then simmer for thirty minutes and strain. Splash in some apple cider vinegar (a tablespoon to a quart of liquid to make the dye adhere better) and carefully add boiled eggs to the hot dye. The colors will have a pastel hue, but become darker the longer you leave them in.

What to do after collecting all those eggs? This year, I plan on giving prizes for certain marked eggs. After the hunt, we'll use some of the eggs in a special recipe to make the best egg salad sandwiches ever! They are great with tomato soup, too.

HERBED EGG SALAD

8   hard-boiled eggs, peeled and chopped
4   tablespoons mayonnaise
4   tablespoons plain yogurt
2   tablespoons dried dill weed
2   tablespoons dried parsley
½   cup minced onion
1   tablespoon lemon juice
2   teaspoons spicy mustard

Stir ingredients together, salt and pepper to taste. Makes enough for 8 sandwiches.

The Mysterious Eggplant

By Jim Weaver

Ever since the Arabs brought the eggplant from northern India to the Mediterranean, this attractive member of the nightshade family has become an integral part of Mediterranean cuisine.

As the eggplant's popularity in the kitchen grew, so did the magical folklore surrounding this mysterious-looking vegetable. The beautiful purple-black color and its unusual shapes—some are shaped like an egg, while other varieties are long and slender—no doubt contributed to the belief that eggplants possessed magical powers.

I've seen eggplants tumbling from the vegetable stalls in the grocers of Athens, and wagons of them stacked in pyramid shapes at Istanbul's markets. Their dark, shiny skins are both beautiful and intense at the same time. Beneath the Mediterranean Sun they do indeed make a dramatic sight, and it is easy to see why they have stirred the imaginations of people over the centuries. Here are a few folk beliefs about eggplants:

- At first, eggplants were not eaten because they were thought to be poisonous.

- Due to their dark color, eating eggplant was thought to be a sure way to bring bad luck.

- Some people wouldn't plant eggplants in the garden for fear an evil one would grow, cursing those who came into contact with it.

- An eggplant that grew into an odd shape or became darker than normal was avoided because it was believed to cause infertility.

- As with many foods found in the Middle East, eggplants were thought to sometimes be inhabited by spirits, or even a genie.

Today, cooks around the Mediterranean have about as many recipes for eggplant as Scheherazade had tales to tell. Eggplants may be fried, baked, stuffed, or mashed. I've even had very small eggplants that were made into a delicious sweet preserve.

Eggplants lend themselves easily to many meatless recipes. Here is an easy eggplant and cheese casserole I've made many times. I like to serve it with a tossed salad, garlic bread, and red wine. I guarantee, it will satisfy even the hungriest genie in your house!

Baked Eggplant and Cheese

1   medium eggplant
    Salt
1   egg plus 2 tablespoons water
¾   cup flour
1   teaspoon salt
¼   teaspoon pepper
⅓   cup vegetable oil
1   (8-ounce) can tomato sauce
1   (6-ounce) package shredded mozzarella cheese
1   teaspoon dried oregano

Slice eggplant into slices ¼-inch thick and lay them on a large baking sheet. Sprinkle slices with salt (this will remove any bitter juices) and let sit for about 15 minutes. Rinse off salt with water and pat slices dry with paper towels. In a shallow bowl beat the egg and water together with a fork. In another dish mix together the flour, remaining teaspoon of salt, and pepper. Dip the eggplant slices first into the egg mixture, then coat with flour. Fry coated slices in hot oil until they are golden on both sides. If needed, add 2 more tablespoons of oil until all the slices are fried. Drain slices on paper towels. Spray a 8 x 11-inch shallow baking dish with vegetable cooking spray. On bottom of baking dish, spoon about a third of the tomato sauce. Next, layer half the eggplant slices by overlapping them over the sauce. Drizzle another third of the sauce over the slices, then sprinkle half the cheese and half the oregano over the cheese. Repeat with the rest of the eggplant slices, sauce, and end with remaining cheese and oregano on top. Bake at 350°F for 30–35 minutes, or until cheese is gold and bubbly. Serves 4.

TIPS FOR THE COMMUTING PAGAN

BY MICHELLE SANTOS

So, your car resembles the dumpster in back of a fast food restaurant, your life consists mainly of working, sleeping, and eating, and you have a more intimate relationship with your car than your significant other. Face it. You are a commuter, a person who travels at least one hour, one way, to get to work.

Since many Pagans feel an affinity with nature, they often choose to live in the country and work in the city. This arrangement allows plenty of space for herb gardens, sunrise walks, and outside rituals on the weekends. During the week, however, the blissful countryside turns into a never-ending stretch of highway, a loud cacophony of horns, and a bright twinkling of brake lights as the country-dwelling Pagan treks into the city.

Having commuted an hour and a half into Boston for work or school for many years, I understand the frustration, the anger, and the resentment of the commuter. You need the money, but you have no time for anything meaningful in your life. The following is a compilation of all the tricks I have devised to make my commute more enjoyable.

BREATHE. Taking deep breaths when upset calms the body, slows the heartbeat, and allows you to make more rational decisions. Even when you are not upset, consciously focus on your breathing. Not only will it take your mind off the jerk in front of you who obviously got his license at the local convenience store, but the regular breathing will center you and put you in greater connection with your body. Open the window. If the weather allows, let fresh air filter through your lungs (minus all the carbon monoxide spewing from the tailpipes of various cars and trucks, of course). When your car is stopped next to a clump of trees, listen for the birds. Marvel at the beauty of nature. She's the reason you're in this two-mile back up.

LISTEN TO TAPES. Don't waste your valuable time by listening to the prepubescent babble of the local talk radio disc jockey. Instead, buy or borrow some books on tape. When you want a change of subject, there are several other educational topics to choose from. Learn Spanish.

Understand the periodic table of elements. Any tape you choose allows you to do something constructive with your commuting time.

DECORATE THE INSIDE OF YOUR CAR. People decorate their homes for the holidays. You spend a lot of time in your car. Why not decorate your car for the holidays? Bring a bit of nature inside with ivy and holly for Yule and mini sheaths of wheat and dried flowers for Lughnasadh and Mabon. Welcome spring with dyed eggs for Ostara and brightly-colored ribbons and fresh flowers for Beltane. Hang a mini candle and honor the hearth Goddess of your choice during Imbolc. Put a traditional Witches' hat and a stuffed black cat in your car, along with pictures of your dead loved ones to celebrate Samhain. Remember the little people with a pendant or glossy picture of a gossamer fairy for Midsummer.

CREATE OR BUY A PROTECTIVE TALISMAN. Much of the stress of commuting comes from the other drivers on the road. Give yourself peace of mind and the protection of the Goddess and God with a talisman. Many Pagan books have large craft sections that illustrate how to create a talisman. (My favorite is the God's eye in Edain McCoy's *The Sabbats: A New Approach to Living the Old Ways*.) However, if you have no time or simply no talent, you can buy a talisman at any Pagan or new age store or catalog. (Be sure to cleanse and consecrate your talisman, but not while you're driving.)

SAY A PRAYER. At the end of the day, once you've put the city behind you, at a point where you see and feel the comforting presence of nature, praise the Goddess and God for seeing you safely through another hectic commute. I personally believe that the best prayers are those that come directly from the heart, bypassing the brain, and have no words to them. However, you can chant a rhyme, sing a song, or form a prayer in celebration of nature and deity.

I hope these hard-won tips help to make your commute a more pleasant experience while bringing you closer to the Goddess and God. They certainly helped me. The next time you are stuck in a huge traffic jam, breathe the scent of fresh flowers into your lungs, smile, and remind yourself that it's worth it.

LIGHT IN EXTENSION: THE HERMETIC ORDER OF THE GOLDEN DAWN

BY JOHN MICHAEL GREER

The Hermetic Order of the Golden Dawn, or GD, was founded in 1888 and fell apart in a series of political struggles between 1900 and 1903. At its height, the GD had only about a hundred active members—a small fraction of the size of other occult organizations at the time. Yet within these limits, the GD laid the foundations of today's magical renaissance and put together a body of occult knowledge fundamental to magical groups ever since.

The roots of the GD lie in the magical subculture of Victorian England. Scientific materialism had driven English occultism underground, but never quite eradicated it. This underground was revolutionized by the founding of the Theosophical Society in 1875. A complex mix of Eastern and Western mysticism, Theosophy was the first modern non-Christian spiritual movement to gain a mass following.

One person who saw the possibilities was Dr. William Wynn Westcott. A member of the Theosophical Society's exclusive Esoteric Section, Westcott was a student of Cabala, Hermeticism, and Ceremonial Magic. He was also a Freemason with connections all through the Victorian occult underground. At some point in 1887, he came across a manuscript in an ancient cipher. Decoding it, he found detailed outlines for a set of initiation rituals for an "Order of the Golden Dawn." To expand the outlines into full-scale ritual texts, Westcott turned to his friend Samuel Mathers, a brilliant, if unstable, magician who shared many of Westcott's occult connections. Westcott, Mathers, and another Masonic occultist, Dr. W. R. Woodman, then founded the new Order on February 12, 1888, and began initiating members.

Around this set of events a good deal of mythology sprang up, aided and abetted by Westcott and his associates. It was claimed that, together with the cipher manuscripts, Westcott had found the address of a German adept named Anna Sprengel, and received authorization from her to found the Golden Dawn. Letters in German from Fraulein Sprengel were duly shown to members of the Order. Those letters are obvious forgeries, written by someone whose native language was clearly English. It's a good bet that Westcott himself had them manufactured, and easy enough to see why. At the time, nearly all occult groups claimed connections to "Secret Chiefs," and Westcott no doubt felt the need to give his new Order an equally impressive background.

Fortunately, these dubious matters were not part of the main work of the GD, which was the systematic training of its members in magical theory and practice. Westcott and Mathers assembled papers covering everything from the symbolism and philosophy of magic through basic, intermediate, and advanced ritual work, to alchemy, geomancy, tarot, astrology, and many other occult teachings. Members studied these as they worked their way through a series of different grades.

Newcomers started in the Outer Order—the Golden Dawn proper—with the Neophyte Grade, and advanced through the grades of Zelator, Theoricus, Practicus, and Philosophus before finally reaching the Portal Grade, the threshold of the Inner Order. In these outer grades, the initiate learned magical symbolism, theory, divination, and basic rituals.

The initiate then entered the Inner Order, the Ordo Roseae Rubeae et Aureae Crucis (Order of the Red Rose and Golden Cross). After entering the first inner grade, Adeptus Minor, initiates tackled an intensive curriculum of magical theory and practice. Those who mastered this went on to the next grade, Adeptus Major, and there were plans to add even further grades and more advanced magical studies.

What put an end to these plans was the failure of the order's system of governance. In its early days, the order was managed by Westcott, but in 1896 rumors of his occult activities reached his employers, and he was forced to leave the Golden Dawn to keep his job. That left the order in the hands of Samuel Mathers, who was an incompetent manager and a tyrant to boot. Mathers' pretensions—he insisted that the GD's members swear allegiance to him personally—soon drove the order to open revolt.

In 1900, Mathers was deposed by a council of the Order's adepts, who set out to establish a new constitution. The revolt stirred up a wasp's nest of disagreements, though, and after several years of increasingly bitter politics the GD broke apart. The largest faction, headed by Robert Felkin, renamed itself the Stella Matutina (Morning Star); a second, headed by A. E. Waite, kept the original name, while a third group of Mathers loyalists took the name of Alpha et Omega. The Stella Matutina survived in a few places into the 1970s, while the other two were long dead by that time. Meanwhile, though, the legacy of the GD had entered a new era.

Part of this was the doing of several Golden Dawn alumni who founded new orders of their own based in part on GD material. Dion Fortune and Aleister Crowley, the most important of these figures, also wrote extensively about some elements of the GD system. The most important part, though, was played by one man: Francis Israel Regardie.

Regardie had joined a Stella Matutina lodge in the 1930s in Bristol, and rose quickly through its grades. Appalled by the incompetence and petty politics he found there, he decided that the GD legacy had to be made public if it was to survive at all. His anthology *The Golden Dawn* was published in four volumes in 1937–1940, and has been fundamental to modern magical practice ever since.

In recent years, several dozen new Golden Dawn temples have come into being, drawing on published sources and (in a few cases) on links with the GD's successor orders as well. Many of these new temples have done solid work; some of them, though, have fallen into the same petty politics that wrecked the original order. Still, if the new Golden Dawn revival can learn from the example of its predecessor, the future of the tradition is bright.

THE TEMPLE OF ISE

BY deTRACI REGULA

The Shinto temple of Ise, sacred to the Sun goddess Amaterasu, lies in a beautiful forest, an essential component of major temples in Japan. As at other Japanese sacred sites, the buildings are completely rebuilt with new wood every twenty years, with two sacred platforms. One is in use by the present building, and the other is where the replacement building will be erected in a few years. On the empty site, a small hut holds a single concealed pillar, the *shin-no-mihashira,* which translates to an almost Egyptian-sounding phrase, "the August (or great) column of the heart." This powerful piece of wood will be the heart of the new temple. In some places, there has been an unbroken rotation and rebuilding of the temple for hundreds of years. At Ise, the grove and site have been sacred since forgotten times, but the buildings were first said to be rebuilt in 692 by the Empress Jito, wife of the Emperor Temmu, who first united Japan.

Ise is approached through a giant torii gate, which visitors clap beneath to attract the deity's attention. A bridge passes over the sacred Isuzu river, and visitors begin the walk through the forest, stopping at the purification pavilion to pour water over their hands and to rinse their mouths with water. Then there is a passage under another torii gate, which one also passes under while clapping, and the temple complex comes into view.

Visitors to the temple complex must be appropriately dressed, and this particularly applies to women. Bare arms are considered disrespectful, as are low necklines, and the priestly guardians are perfectly willing to bar someone from entering the temple if their costuming is inappropriate.

In September, the Ise Shrine presents the Kagura festival, with special dances held in the beautiful wooden halls. Observers kneel in the ritual posture of Japan, which can be amazingly difficult after ten or fifteen minutes. The polite Japanese will try not to notice the contortions of inflexible Western guests. If you go to Japan and intend to participate in cultural activities, you may want to give yourself some practice beforehand. After a while, the muscles become used to the position and it becomes very natural and graceful.

The sacred presentations are done to the accompaniment of drums and flute music by musicians wearing traditional clothing. The priests and priestesses, garbed in silk kimonos, bring in the ritual objects, including evergreen branches of the sakaki tree, kegs of sake, and grain, and offer these symbols of food and abundance to the resident goddess.

Outside, the priests do a brisk business in selling amulets for travel, protection, and other needs. These tend to be a bit expensive but are delightful reminders of your journey.

By the temple grounds of Ise is a small, traditional Japanese town, now given over primarily to tourist shops. However, in Japan, even the tourist shops can be graceful, with traditional signs announcing their wares. In Ise, one shop offers nothing but lovely paper goods, an origami artist's dreamworld.

Japanese temples almost always offer the visitor an abundance of things to do. For a small donation, bundles of incense are available for burning in one of the giant bronze vessels. One popular activity is divination by lots, which is accomplished in a variety of ways. Some seldom-visited temples have actually installed coin-operated machines that emit a fortune for the curious. Others have cylindrical containers holding metal sticks. These are shaken so that one stick comes out through the hole in the cap, and then the stick and container are taken to a priest. He matches the markings on  the stick with a cubbyhole in a cabinet holding fortunes and gives you the fortune paper to keep. Most Japanese don't keep their fortunes, but instead tie them onto a nearby bush or a stand strung with wires for the purpose. This is supposed to remove any negative aspects of the fortune by in effect putting it back in the hands of the temple deity.

Probably the most clever revenue-generating custom is the idea that the deity of a temple can be attracted by the clattering sound of coins tossed in special bins. This noise also scatters negative spirits, but it can be jarring for the unsuspecting Western visitor accustomed to a stern silence in places of worship.

The Japanese temples are living places of worship, not foreign tourist traps, and so finding someone who speaks English or other Western languages may be more difficult than you would expect.

Flights from the U.S. to Asia often make a stop overnight at Tokyo's Narita airport, and if the visitor is blessed with even a few spare hours, local temples can be visited. One of these is the temple to Kwannon (similar to Kuan Yin, though here in male form), which can be reached by taxi from downtown. Be prepared for quite a bite on the taxi fare—they're expensive ($70–90) and you will need to ask the driver to wait. This temple also offers a small museum of primitive Japanese sculpture, and is one of the oldest wooden temples in existence.

The peace and beauty of Japanese temples stays with the visitor for a long time. For the Western Wiccan or Neo-Pagan, it is especially memorable to be in a place where the belief in gods and goddesses, nature spirits and sea spirits, is alive and well and considered to be nothing out of the ordinary.

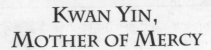

KWAN YIN,
MOTHER OF MERCY

BY ESTELLE DANIELS

Kwan Yin is one of the most widespread and variously depicted deities in India and China. She is also known as Guan Yin, Avalokita, and Avalokiteshvara. She is a Bodhisattva, which means she achieved enlightenment, yet chooses to stay in this plane of existence until all living beings have attained enlightenment also. Originally a Hindu deity, she also became a Buddhist Bodhisattva and was brought to China through Tibet during the Tang dynasty.

Kwan Yin is usually shown as a woman sitting or standing on a lotus. She has a serene expression, and is called the Mother of Mercy. She is the personification of compassion and love. She protects all women and children, and especially pregnant women and women in childbirth. She is compassionate, the reliever of suffering, the remover of obstacles, and the comforter.

As Avalokiteshvara, this deity is able to assume whatever form is necessary to alleviate suffering. Avalokiteshvara was originally male, but Kwan Yin is usually female, though male versions of Kwan Yin also exist. The attributes of goodness, reliever of suffering, and helper of mankind, as well as being a Bodhisattva, are universal to all her various forms.

She is the cosmic mother and guardian. She is a goddess of fertility, and those who pray to her have found themselves able to conceive where they were barren before. She is the goddess of health and healing, and many miraculous cures are attributed to her intervention. She can bestow physical prowess in addition to health. She is a guardian of education and knowledge and can bestow learning and wisdom to those who follow her ways. She is also the goddess of last resort. When all hope is gone Kwan Yin can answer the most desperate prayers.

She is called the Melodious Voice, and is associated with music and song. All things pleasant and harmonious are beloved by her and can be bestowed by her. As Avalokiteshvara, she created the chant "Om Mane Padme Om," the jewel of creation in the lotus.

Kwan Yin is depicted in many forms, and her images are readily available. She can look Indian, Mongol, or contemporary, she can be depicted as Chinese, as a young maiden, or as a more sedate matron. She is usually shown with some sort of flower, preferably the lotus.

I like Kwan Yin because she is a goddess who has no enemies, and being part of a greater pantheon is content as one of many deities I revere. She is not my main deity, but in times of pain or hurt she is there, the comforter—the universal mother-figure who will bind up my hurts, and rock me to sleep singing soothing lullabies. She helps remind me when compassion is called for.

Sometimes it seems that Kwan Yin is a bit, well, boring. She has no great lore or stories. She has no tales of her friends and enemies. There are no real myths of her interaction with mortals, no miracles, no rescues, no last-minute interventions and much-needed help.

Myths and stories are not all that makes a goddess, however. She is real and revered in a wide area of the world. She is a vital and living goddess. Her worship has been more or less continuous since she came on the scene. She is a goddess well acquainted with the modern world and she understands the pressures and obligations of modern-day living. She is an ideal deity for children because she is kind, gentle, and compassionate, yet protecting. She is a good role model for children, more so than some of the more raucous deities like Aries or Thor. As a guardian of learning, she can help a child understand the gifts of schooling and knowledge.

When you have asked the other deities for help, invoked them and asked for action, after all is said and done and you are lying in bed, feeling a bit hurt and alone, Kwan Yin will come and comfort you. She will soothe you and make things all better. That's just one of her roles, and she is a good friend to have. Blessed Be.

How to Consecrate a Statue

By Ann Moura (Aoumiel)

Deity images, normal features on a Witch's altar, are not consecrated in the manner of magical tools. Statues, usually hollow with and opening at the base, may be enlivened to draw the potent power of the Divine within them in a consecration ritual that has links to the ancient customs still practiced in India.

Prepare your altar as for a Full Moon Esbat ritual and cast your circle. For your statue, you will be combining in your cauldron one herb from the goddess, god, or dual deity listing, along with one herb from the matching elemental list. This echoes the pentagram with a deity spirit and four relating elementals.

Goddess Herbs

Marjoram, moonwort, elder flower. Her earth: cypress, honeysuckle, jasmine. Her air: anise seed, comfrey, elder wood, eyebright, hazel, lavender, mugwort. Her fire: angelica, celandine, coriander, heliotrope, hyssop, nettle, primrose, rowan. Her water: camomile, camphor, catnip, geranium, hawthorn, hyacinth, ivy, rose, willow.

God Herbs

Woodruff, yarrow, bergamot. His earth: cedar, fern, High John the Conqueror, horehound, pine. His air: acacia, benzoin, mistletoe, nutmeg, thyme, wormwood. His fire: alder, basil, betony, cinnamon, clove, holly, oak, peppercorn, thistle. His water: ash, burdock, hops, orris root, yarrow.

DUAL DEITY HERBS

Mullein, dianthus, heather. Their earth: cinquefoil, mandrake, patchouli, sage, slippery elm. Their air: eucalyptus, lemon verbena, mugwort, peppermint, sandalwood, spearmint. Their fire: bay, juniper, marigold, rosemary, rue, saffron, St. John's wort, vervain. Their water: apple, elecampane, heather, meadowsweet, poppy, star anise.

Place the cauldron on your pentacle. Hold each herb over the cauldron before dropping it in and say:

I call upon thee (herb) to lend unto me thy power for the consecration and enlivening of this image of (deity name).

Stir all with your athame:

Through the power of the Goddess and the God are these herbs blessed to enliven this image of (deity name).

Place the herbs in a small pouch. If your pouch has drawstrings, wrap the ends around the stuffed bag, otherwise fold the pouch shut. Set the cauldron aside. Pass the herbal pouch through the elements:

By earth you have form (sprinkle with salt).
By air you have breath (pass through incense smoke).
By fire you have energy (pass through candle flame).
By water you have the fluids of life (sprinkle with water).

Place the pouch on the pentacle. With your athame in your power hand, raise your open arms overhead to gather in energy:

I call upon the power of the Lady and the Lord to bless and empower these herbs with their divine essence.

Bring your hands together to hold the knife. Bring the athame down to touch the pouch with the tip and see the energy flow through the blade into the pouch. Set down the athame. Place your hands with palms down above the pouch:

By Spirit are you charged and enlivened.

Now the image is given spiritual birth through the materials of the sacred cow. This image is found in Hathor, the most ancient goddess of Egypt, portrayed in some statues as the sacred cow with the solar disk resting between Her horns.

With the essences of the sacred cow, who gives of herself in many ways for the lives of others, is this image now blessed.

Rub the statue all over with soft butter.

With butter are you anointed.

Rub it all over with a soft cheese like a brie, cottage cheese, or use yogurt or sour cream.

With cheese are you fed.

Wash the statue with about a cup of milk.

With milk are you given the substance of life.

Rinse the statue off with spring water or running water.

With water are you cleansed and purified.

Dry the statue and anoint it with consecration oil.

In the names of the Goddess and the God, I consecrate this statue. Let this image of (name) draw (His/Her) divine power into my home and into my Craft. Let this image remind me that (name) is always close to me, as I am always close to (name).

Pick up the herb bundle and tuck it securely inside the statue. If you are concerned that the bundle may fall out, you can close off the bottom of the statue with a piece of felt cut to fit and glued along the edges. Usually the curves of the figure are sufficient to hold the pouch in place.

Set the image on the pentacle and cover it completely with a black cloth. Pick up your athame or wand—athame for images of the God and Dual Deity, and the wand for images of the Goddess—to call the Divine into the statue. Hold the athame or wand upright with your arms raised and open before the covered statue and say:

I call upon thee elemental earth, elemental air, elemental fire, and elemental water to bring thy energy and thy power that this image of (deity name) be made ready for enlivening.

Bring your hands together to hold the tool and slowly point it toward the statue as you say:

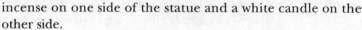

Come Great Lady (Great Lord) and inhabit this image I have prepared for you. Let your presence in my life and in my home be a comfort and joy to me.

Touch the statue with the tip of the tool and feel the power of the Divine entering into the image. Leave the statue on the pentacle for grounding and set the athame on the altar.

Carefully unveil the statue and set aside the cloth. Verbally welcome the deity by name and place an offering before it such as a cornbread muffin, fruit, or flowers, or you may want use a dish with food and a small cup with milk or some other beverage. Light an incense such as frankincense on one side of the statue and a white candle on the other side.

Welcome to my home and my heart, Great Lady/Lord (name). I am blessed by thy presence, and my blessings I give unto thee. Let the light of thy love be with me always.

After an hour, place the statue where you plan to keep it. Offerings, incense, and candles will change in accordance with your needs, the season, the Sabbat and so forth because the statue is now a focal point for your practice. Do not feel odd about talking to the image or meditating on it, for this is an ancient practice that strengthens the ties between yourself and the Divine.

For statues that have no hollow space for an herb bundle, touch the herb pouch to the statue. Lightly anoint the image with a consecration oil, then set the statue on the pentacle and cover it with a black cloth with the herb bundle under the cloth as well, either under the statue, or behind it or somehow draped against it. Follow the rest of the procedure as above, keeping the herb bundle close to the statue, perhaps in a small covered jar behind the image.

ENHEDUANNA

BY deTRACI REGULA

Ancient Sumer rose, thrived, and then fell to the superior armies of the Akkadians, led by Sargon the First. The Sumerians became a subjugated people, but they soon found an unlikely ally in the daughter of Sargon himself: Enheduanna. Enheduanna sought her own spiritual fulfillment in an ancient goddess of the Sumerians, Inanna. Almost five thousand years ago, Enheduanna learned the language of the Sumerians and began writing her praise-poems to Inanna. Sargon, perhaps seeing a political advantage in his religiously-gifted daughter, installed her as the official high priestess of Ur.

But Enheduanna had challenges to face. A falling-out with her brother led to her being cast out from the temple where she was High Priestess of Ur, and her despair still echoes in her poems. Inanna did not turn her face from her adopted daughter, and with another change in the political winds, she was reinstated and her poems reflect her joy. The *Nin-me-sarra,* commonly translated as *The Exaltation of Inanna,* is her best-known work, though there are dozens of others and still more that may be by her hand. The quality that strikes modern readers is that Enheduanna writes personally of things that happened to her within her work for Inanna. She is not an anonymous scribe, but a royal princess and priestess completely caught up in her devotion to Inanna.

Enheduanna, also sometimes transliterated Enkeduanna, is unique in another way: She is not only the first named priestess of history, she is also the first known author. Most early praise hymns and songs were anonymous, but perhaps because of Enheduanna's high rank, her creations were identified as clearly her own.

When you write a rite, express joy in a poem, or go through troubled spiritual times, think of Enheduanna, a priestess-ancestress for us all.

USING COLORS FOR MAGICAL CHARGING

BY RAVEN GRIMASSI

The effect of color on human emotions is a well-known phenomenon. Color has a vibration. In a certain respect it is a visual energy, but each color has its own individual vibratory essence, and therefore each is unique in its influence. Just as color can be used to enhance the atmosphere of a room or an object, it can also be used to enhance magical energy. There are many different methods of accomplishing this task. Colored bottles can be used to store things such as incense or oils. Light can be passed through a colored filter, such as stained glass, and focused on an amulet of talisman. In this article, we shall explore this method of using color for magical charges.

Centuries ago, occultists devised a table of correspondences indicating the metaphysical properties of various colors. A color code was created so that an individual could refer to it when needed for ritual or magical work. The belief in the magical power of the color red, for example, dates back to ancient Roman times, where it symbolized the sacred liquid of life and the heat of the sacred flame. Blue was the color of the sky, the Great Spirit, associating it with divine blessings. Silver, as a lunar color, held power over spirits of the astral world. The following is a basic list of colors you can use for magical charges involving oils, potions, or incense:

AMBER: grounding, calming, condensing, and preserving.

BLACK: hidden forces, binding, and guarding secrets.

BLUE: blessing, well-being, and peace.

GOLD: material success and gain.

GREEN: healing, nurturing, growth, and fertility.

GREY: neutrality and contentment.

PINK: friendships and relationships.

PURPLE: magical energy.

RED: passion, vitality, and success in matters of love.

SILVER: spirits or spiritual forces at work.

YELLOW: mental activity and communication.

A TECHNIQUE FOR MAGICAL CHARGING

You will first need to decide on the material you want to use. Stained glass is an excellent choice, but you can also use translucent-colored paper or plastic. The light spectrum is more important than the filter itself, although crystalline properties do further enhance the vibratory energy of the light. Colored glass bottles can easily be found in antique stores, and most department stores carry them during the holiday seasons.

Both the Sun and the Moon are used as sources of light when charging by color. Sunlight is employed first, followed by moonlight, and never the reverse unless you wish to remove or negate the magical charge. Sunlight passing through colored glass will impart the vibratory essence of the color. Moonlight will impart the etheric or metaphysical properties. You can think of sunlight as the body and moonlight as the spirit.

When preparing to charge by color, consider the phase of the Moon and the season of the year. Both cycles exert an influence upon the light spectrum. The waxing Moon is best for works of gain, growth, or outcome. The waning Moon is best for works of decline, dissipation, binding, and introspection. The same is true of the waxing and waning seasons of the year.

Using a color charge can also capture and condense the energy of the Full Moon, equinox, or solstice. This can then be passed into an oil, potion, or incense specifically formulated as is appropriate to the season or event. To accomplish this, first consult a calendar for the specific day and hour. You may wish to check on the planetary influences as well. Remember that you will perform this both during the day and at night, so check both times. To obtain the precise nature of the charge desired may require performing the charge on two different calendar days.

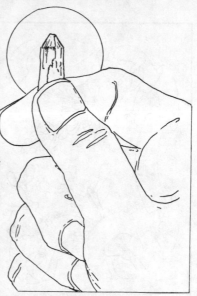

When the time is right in accord with the desired nature of the charge, select the appropriate-colored filter or bottle. Place the bottle containing the material you wish to charge in the sunlight at noon for one hour. If using a colored filter, prop it so that the sunlight sheds colored light through the filter on the material. After the time has passed, remove the filter/bottle and material from the sunlight. When the phase of the Moon is right for your needs, repeat the same technique at either 9:00 PM or midnight. During the charging process you can recite an invocation or the words of a spell to further enhance the charge. This is extremely useful as it helps to "inform" the material with the condensed energy of your thoughts and desires.

Additional energy can be added when using a colored bottle by adding a crystal. At noon, pinch the crystal between your thumb and index finger of the left hand. Trace a wide sweeping arch from your right shoulder, over your head, and down to your left shoulder. At the peak of the sweep, just above your head, quickly close all of your fingers around the crystal as though you were snatching the Sun out of the sky, pressing it into the crystal. Then simply drop the crystal into the bottle containing the oil, potion, or incense. There it will act as a battery of power, maintaining and vitalizing the magical charge.

The same technique can be used for capturing the magical influence of the Moon when it occupies a specific astrological sign, or is Full on the night of a Solstice or Equinox. Since this only occurs once during an eight-year cycle it is considered particularly magical. Keep a selection of charged bottles and label them according to their magical nature. Recharge them each Full Moon by setting them out beneath the moonlight for an hour. Do not set them out beneath the Sun, as the light of day will dispel the astral energy.

Druids in America

By Roslyn Reid

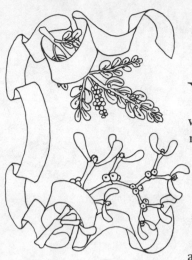

You may have seen them at conventions, perhaps even wearing long white robes. You might have stumbled upon one or two of their websites. There could even be a few in your place of business, working incognito in the next cubicle. They are modern-day Druids, followers of the religion of the ancient Celts. So who are these Druid dudes, anyway? Many people think they died out in old days, but they are very much a part of today's society. Keeping in mind that today's Druids are quite different from yesterday's, we shall explore this question.

The original Druids were identified in the writings of Julius Caesar as one of two social levels of the ancient Celts, the people who were the ancestors of all modern Europeans. This particular level of their society concerned itself with religion and laws, and is sometimes referred to as a "priesthood." (The other level was identified in Caesar's writings as "knights." The common peasants in those days were barely noticed.) From the lumping together of these two disciplines, religion and law, one can start to get a feeling for just how important religion must have been to these ancient people.

Now, some people consider ancient writings on the Druids to be highly suspect because they were written by the conquerors of the Celts. However, as one respected authority on the Celts points out, Diviciacus, who was a learned king of the ancient Celts, was also a close personal friend of Julius Caesar. Therefore, when Caesar wrote about the structure of Celtic society, he was almost certainly getting his information right from the horse's mouth.

The history of the ancient Celts dates back to the migration of the Indo-European-speaking people approximately 4,000 years ago. At that time, nomadic tribes who occupied the area around the Caspian Sea in southern Russia began to migrate southeast into the Indus Valley (now India) and west into Asia Minor (now Turkey), the Balkans, and across eastern Europe. Around the tenth century B.C., a people recognizable as Celts began to emerge from Bohemia, in western Czechoslovakia.

In the eighth to the sixth centuries B.C., these people started to migrate down into Italy and Spain, further westward into France and Belgium, and eventually into the British Isles. It was in the fifth century B.C. that these people were first referred to as "Celts" (actually *Keltoi* in Greek) by the Greek historian Herodotus. Legend has it that Hu Gadarn, or "Hu the Mighty," whose name survives today as one of the ancient Celtic hero-gods, led a party of settlers from Asia Minor to the British Isles and established a religious practice among the Celts that we now refer to as Druidism.

Several meanings are attributed to the word "Druid," including "a servant of truth," "all knowing, or wise man," "an oak" (from the Gaelic *duir*), or "equal in honor." Robert Graves considers the word to be derived from the Welsh *derwydd,* "oak-seer," due to the association of oak groves with Druids.

By the fourth century B.C., the Romans viewed the Druids as an established institution. Posidonius, the philosopher-historian, traveled throughout Gaul during the time of the Druids and wrote about them in his *Histories* at the end of the second century B.C. Unfortunately, these writings were lost, but portions were later referred to by the historian Strabo (63 B.C.–A.D. 21). By the year 37, Gaul and much of Britain were under Roman control, and the Romans strictly prohibited Druidic practices due to the possibility of insurrection. Thus began the decline of Druidry; although some people maintain that the ancient Druidic beliefs and practices have survived to this day in various forms.

Despite many scholarly and classical writings on the ancient Celts, very little is known about them and the activities of the Druids. The best accounts of the Druids, which were written by their actual contemporaries, are Caesar's *Conquest of Gaul* and Pliny the Elder's *Natural History.* Archaeological evidence and early writings don't reveal much beyond their existence—and some people dispute even that!

MISCONCEPTIONS ABOUT THE DRUIDS

There are a few popular misconceptions about the ancient Druids, one being that they never wrote anything down. Although they had a long history of oral tradition, they did indeed use written language (Greek and some Latin). However, this was used only for everyday mundane items such as receipts and letters. The Druids considered it improper to use writing in their important studies and relied on the memorization of a great deal of verse.

Another controversial legend about the ancient Druids is that of human sacrifice. While this has never been confirmed—or denied—by archaeological evidence, it would not be unusual for conquerors (the Romans) to portray a conquered culture (the Celts) as a bloodthirsty gang of savage barbarians. Indeed, some of the classical Roman writers described a few of the procedures the Celts supposedly used for these sacrifices: burning, stabbing, and impaling. It's also possible the association of Druids with human sacrifice may have arisen because the Celts worshipped the human head as the seat of all wisdom and felt quite comfortable with several of their enemies' severed heads mounted on pikes around their villages. A sight like this would understandably unnerve any foreigner. In any case, it's entirely likely the ancient Celts actually did practice human sacrifice— quite a few cultures indulged in it at that time. The point is moot, though, because there are many things ancient Pagans did that we don't do today.

In the latter part of the eighteenth century, Druidic cults and societies appeared all over Western Europe. One of the first was the Ancient Order of Druids, which was founded by an Englishman, Henry Hurle. Later this group became more of a benefit society, similar to the Elks Club. Some members who were more interested in the esoteric side of Druidism split off to form other Orders.

PRESENT-DAY DRUIDS

Now you know more about the ancient Druids than you may have cared to. So let's fast forward to a Minnesota college campus in 1963, when Carleton College has just instituted a rule that all students attend a certain number of religious services as a requirement of enrollment. Some students, aghast at what they perceived as an encroachment on their religious freedom, decided to organize a group called the Reformed Druids of North America (RDNA). Because the college's rule permitted the requirement to be fulfilled in a religion of one's own choosing, the students chose Druidry. They reasoned that if religious credit were granted to them (even though the group was bogus at the time, having been created only as a protest), then the college's religious requirement could be exposed as totally ineffective. On the other hand, if credit were denied to them, the college could be charged with bigotry.

This sounded cleverly effective, and it was. Carleton College repealed the religious requirement the following year. However, although elated with its victory, the RDNA did not fold its robes and go away. The students realized that Druidry had developed a meaning in their lives, and after graduation, they went on to continue the RDNA and even start other Druidic groups.

Today there are three major national Druidic organizations: the RDNA, now called the NRDNA, or "New" Reformed Druids of North America; the ADF, or Ar nDraiocht Fein (sometimes called the "American Druid Foundation" by the Gaelic-impaired); and the Henge of Keltria. Many smaller groups also exist.

Although Druids tend to be among the most organized of Pagans, there is no real conformity to standards outside of a few basics. Such strictness would be un-Druidlike. One good example is that some leaders of national Druidic organizations are called ArchDruids, but others are called Presidents. At certain times, the same person might even use both titles at once!

Whatever the differences, one standard seems to have been agreed on. The smaller groups of Druids that comprise the national organizations are called "groves." Grove leaders might have titles such as "senior Druid," or they may have no title at all. Each organization handles the details differently.

WHAT DO DRUIDS DO?

Probably the most-asked question these days by non-Druids is "What do Druids do?" Although this question is also asked about every other Pagan sect, I always find it to be absolutely hilarious. Can you imagine asking, "What do Christians do?" and getting an intelligible answer? Now that we've put it into perspective, here is no more than an attempt to answer that question.

Druids do ritual. Most groves make up their own litany and may share it with the other groves. These days, however, the Druids write it down! The national organization might give suggestions or have written material to help out with this task, but the officers of these groups are more concerned with promoting community, setting standards for advancement, and representing the organization to the outside world than with dealing with these details.

As in most Pagan groups, rites and rituals are preferably held outdoors, typically in a grove of trees (oaks, if we can find them) or around a stone circle. Druids celebrate the four major Sabbaths: Samhain–Harvest (Halloween), Imbolc/Oimelc–the feast of lights (February 2), Beltane–the fertility festival (May Day), and Lughnasadh–the feast of bread or first fruits (August 1). There are also four lesser Sabbaths related to the changing of the seasons: the Spring and Autumn Equinoxes, and the Summer and Winter Solstices.

Some groves hold sermons during a ritual, much like an ordinary mainstream church would. Other groves use color magic. Some groves have a Norse focus, others are Celtic. Generally, Druidic rituals are fun times, with feasting, dancing, and singing, where feelings of love for the gods and goddesses are expressed and an appreciation for nature's abundance is celebrated.

STONEHENGE

Conceivably the second most-asked question about Druids is characterized by a friend of mine who said, "So what is it with you guys and Stonehenge, anyway?" While Stonehenge is a magnet for modern-day Druids (along with other Pagans), there is little, if any, evidence that the ancient Druids used it for anything, or what they may have used it for. It is now commonly agreed that Stonehenge was built in four stages. The first period was about 3100–2300 B.C., also known as the Neolithic Age. At this time, Stonehenge consisted of nothing more than a circular ditch with an internal bank and a northeast entrance. Along the inside of the ditch were a ring of fifty-six pits, now known as the Aubrey holes (after John Aubrey, who discovered them in the seventeenth century). These pits were later used to bury cremated remains. On the outside of the entrance was the monolith we now call the Heelstone, along with a timber gate.

The second period, ranging from approximately 2100–2000 B.C., was the work of the people now known as the Beaker Culture. These ambitious folks built an approach road (now called the Avenue), brought bluestone from the Preseli Mountains in southwestern Wales, and set up the double concentric circle of huge stones known as the Menhirs. Both this circle and the Avenue were oriented toward the Summer Solistice, although the double circle was never completed and was later dismantled.

During the third period, around 2000–1550 B.C., the existing circle of sarcen stones was erected, as well as the horseshoe-shaped structure in its center, and Stonehenge assumed its present configuration. The sarcen stones were imported from a quarry in what is now Marlboro Downs, twenty miles away. In the fourth period, about 1100 B.C., the Avenue was extended to the River Avon, a little over a mile away. That's

99

the story of Stonehenge. No mention of Druids is made in the archaeological writings.

OTHER ASPECTS OF DRUIDRY

Sometimes I'm asked whether Druids hex or put curses on people. Certainly the ancient Druids had no compunction about doing such things—in fact, it was part of their job to do this to the enemy during battles. Modern-day Druids, however, tend to avoid such activities because of their belief that whatever you work upon the universe will eventually return to you—"what goes around comes around."

On the other hand, probably one of the best-known aspects of the ancient Druids is their association with mistletoe. Why did they prize the mistletoe so highly as to call it "all-heal?"

Well, first of all, they didn't prize all mistletoe highly—only mistletoe that grew on oak trees. Why? Because although mistletoe grows on deciduous trees, it prefers trees with soft bark such as the apple and ash. Rarely does the mistletoe grow on an oak tree.

However, it wasn't just this scarcity that made mistletoe a prized plant. It was what the scarcity represented. In *The Golden Bough* (titled after an ancient Greek name for the mistletoe), Sir James Frazer postulates an interesting theory based on a popular name for mistletoe in Germany during his time: "thunder-besom." The mistletoe was so designated in the folklore of that area because it was thought to be a product of a tree's being struck by lightning. "If there is any truth in this conjecture," Frazer goes on to say, "the real reason why the Druids worshipped a mistletoe-bearing oak above all other trees of the forest was a belief that every such oak had not only been struck by lightning but bore among its branches a visible emanation of the celestial fire; so that in cutting the mistletoe with mystic rites they were securing for themselves all the magical properties of a thunderbolt." If we consider how magic is supposed to work, this sounds like a fairly reasonable speculation.

WHERE CAN WE FIND DRUIDS TODAY?

Druids generally do not wander around town in flowing robes any more, carrying a long staff and bearing a raven on each shoulder (if indeed they ever did). Due to the scholarly nature of

Druidry, and what Margot Adler calls "its thirst for structure and study," the Druids of today do tend to be less "in the broom closet" than many other types of Pagans.

Every year the ADF holds a national gathering called Wellspring, usually at a location in Ohio, with guest speakers, workshops, and group rituals. Many groves gather together for festivals and other occasions on a regular basis. There are even cybergroves who get together daily online.

Unlike their spiritual ancestors, today's Druids are doing their best to adapt to modern challenges. This flexibility will enable Druidry to change with the times and once again be a living part of the national scene. You never can tell, you might even know a Druid...there could be one working right in the next cubicle.

GROUPS

Although keeping current with the ever-changing face of Druidry is like trying to push water, I have endeavored to collect here the most recent contact information for these Druid organizations. It is suggested that you enclose a SASE when writing for information.

AR NDRAIOCHT FEIN

(Sometimes listed as American Druid Foundation)

ADDRESS: PO Box 15259, Ann Arbor, MI 48106-5259.

HOT LINE: 1-800-DRUIDRY.

WEBSITE: http://www.adf.org.

HENGE OF KELTRIA

ADDRESS: P.O. Box 48369, Minneapolis, MN 55448.

WEBSITES: Henge of Keltria, http://www.magusbooks.com/keltria; *Keltria Journal,* http://www.keltria.org/journal.

In addition to these major organizations, there are many smaller Druid groups, as well as what are called "seed" groups of the Order of Bards, Ovates and Druids, a British group that is gaining in popularity in the U.S. It's likely there is a Druidic group near you, or there will soon be one.

Mixing Magical Systems

By Silver RavenWolf

Most magical people are enterprising souls with an insatiable desire to increase their knowledge in the occult sciences. With that desire comes curiosity. Once we learn a system and move on to something else, we discover that within each system are similarities and differences. We also discover that one system may have enhanced an area where a different system is weak. Is it possible to take the strengths of various systems and cobble them together to create something that is unique for our personal use?

Although purists will tell us that we should not tinker with the mechanism of a working magical system, we must remember that all systems used today are a result of human massage from that system's inception. Then again, removing part of a system because we do not understand how it works or why the component is there in the first place is not a good idea either. When a modifed system is passed to another person it will more than likely become weaker, rather than stronger, than its original blueprint.

Change is growth, but tradition is stability. What do we do?

Perhaps there are really two questions here rather than one. First, can we mix systems? The answer would be yes, though I would agree, cautiously. Should we change the original systems and pass them on? Only if we can (1) Indicate we made a change, and why, and (2) Continue to provide the original version. Through my personal studies I have discovered that there is less damage from mixing magical practices than if we were to mix deity energies. For example, if an individual followed Celtic Craft for deity influences but has learned that he can mix his tarot techniques with the technique of divining with the runes or with sortilege (shell divination) he will probably have excellent success (as long as he keeps in mind the original correspondences of the tools). However, if we change the lesser banishing ritual by removing Christian/Judaic correspondences and replace

102

those same correspondences with Celtic deities, then you are changing the spiritual focus and you alter the energy of the original technique. If you went one step further and replaced the Celtic deity associations with a compendium of pantheons, then you have stepped even further from the original energy pattern This is fine if the new technique works for you and you have researched the complete history of the technique, but what about the students that you teach? If you fail to give them the original system that gave you the point of reference for your experimentation and eventual changes, then you are doing a disservice to the new students.

The same thing happens with a traditional study, such as Alexandrian or Gardnerian. In a decade of composing and teaching from my own materials I've seen exactly how things get changed, and many times not for a good reason. For example, in the Black Forest Clan (we are not a tradition because technically the person who starts a tradition has to be dead for the teachings to become a tradition, and I'm not dead yet) we have a specific number of lessons, a specific set of quarter calls, a specific circle casting, and initiation rituals and elevation rituals that are not to be changed for any reason. Why? To keep the group mind linked through repetition and to prepare the student systematically for more challenging lessons. Several years ago one of my trainers decided that she didn't like the lessons as they were provided. Without my knowledge she tore apart the first two lessons in my training program and gave the students only the portions that she felt were relevant. Consequently, the students did not receive the exercises needed to prepare them for the more advanced lessons. Several students quit out of confusion before reaching the advanced lessons, while many students got stuck further on in their training and had to repeat the original lessons because they didn't have the necessary information or exercises to successfully complete the more difficult material. For some, it took an extra year of training to reach the same elevations that their peers in other training groups had completed in a shorter amount of time. Had I been dead, and not able to oversee the training groups as I currently do, one section of Black Forest students would have lost the original integrity of the training and would not have had the same information as a student in the other eleven training groups across the country. I realize that this is a minor example, but it does show you what can (and has) happened to magical systems and traditions over the years. As a result of this situation in our own group, trainers were required to meet a more rigorous criteria than previously given, and no one was given permission to train unless they had worked through the Black Forest materials from lesson one through the advanced lessons. Switched Witches (those that moved from a different tradition into mine) were no longer given authority to train until they completed the original training program themselves, regardless of what tradition they came from.

Cut 'n' paste activity has occurred in several Alexandrian and Gardnerian groups, especially when the High Priest or High Priestess did not finish his or her training with the original group, took the Book of Shadows and ran (so to speak), eventually producing students who may carry the lineage, but not the training. It is harder for that student to backtrack and find the adequate training than if he or she had been able to receive the training and lineage at the same time, or simply trained as a solitary. I was, and still am, such a student, and I can tell you that the road was often frustrating and difficult. Power without knowledge is just as confusing as knowledge without power. Remarrying these two elements of training is possible, but the amount of crud you will wade through to get there is phenomenal.

Should we experiment? Should we mix systems? Should we change aspects and techniques to enhance our personal practice? Absolutely, but we should always honor that which has gone before our changes, and make a concerted effort to offer our students every opportunity to enjoy the original knowledge that we, ourselves, investigated. It is the only fair way to treat the new generation of Witches.

WHAT'S BUGGING YOU?

BY MARGUERITE ELSBETH

I nsects fascinate me, so I am chagrined to read books on shamanism that point out the inherent dangers of having a bug for one's totem animal. What's the deal? Here are some reasons why shamans relegate insects to the Underworld, that mystical place of initiation and magic, where devouring demons and other dark pesties reside.

SHAMANS SAY, "BUG OFF"

The insect world is filled with chaos and destruction. Ant against ant, spider against fly, and hornet against spider, Bugland is a microcosmic continuum of the macrocosm in which we live. Violent crime, war, spousal abuse, and not-so-sudden death are commonplace as they go about their day dismembering, killing, and consuming each other in the name of food, territory, and sensual pleasure. Therefore, insect consciousness is thought to be inimical to human consciousness, and having insect totems may only serve to emphasize our lowest instinctual tendencies.

Besides, bugs are venomous little vampires where humans are concerned. Just ask any nature-loving, wood-roving, tree-hugging, Goddess-worshiping Pagan and they'll tell you: these bugs bite, suck blood, and/or inject poison, leaving itchy welts, oozy infections, life-threatening allergens, or virulent diseases without so much as a thank you very much. Some even stick around like unwanted house pests until you force them or their stingers loose from the burrow of your skin via bleach, nail polish remover, tweezers, or a lit match. Preventing this assault means that you must spray yourself from head to toe with toxic chemicals, smell like lemongrass oil, or go around brandishing a citronella candle.

Does all of the above incline you to bug off? I have been known to declare war on bugs too, especially the ones that like to hum in my ear at three in the morning before eating me for dinner. But there is another way to co-habitate, and even be on friendly, magical terms, with these hard-shelled, soft-bellied, multi-legged critters.

I SAY "BUG OUT"

Humans are in the minority when it comes to insects, a factor leaving us with few choices in beating the odds of surviving their onslaughts. We could buy into their militant mentality (meaning a fight to the death), run screaming upon contact, or Zen out with passive resistance. However, insects are teachers too, just like the more cuddly variety of feathered and four-legged tutelary animals, and there is much we can learn from them.

WELCOME HOUSE PESTS

Throughout the year ants invade my kitchen, raiding cereal boxes, sugar bowls, and anything else they can crawl into. Being adverse to killing anything, I've tried talking to them, requesting that they leave. No dice. Natural and chemical deterrents seem to do nothing but lend encouragement, so I've resorted to letting them be. What are they trying to tell me?

Ants were once used in soothsaying, being totems of Ceres, a Roman goddess associated with divination. Moroccan shamans feed ants to their lethargic patients. South American and Guiana natives use large black ants in their purification rituals. Their bite packs a wallop, chasing away evil spirits. My own observations indicate that ants are tenacious, obsessive, clean, orderly, never idle, and always moving. Considering I'm a diviner prone to indolence with a need to purify my home atmosphere often, having ants in my pantry makes sense.

Spiders seem drawn to me also. Wolf spiders and harmless browns are allowed to decorate the corners of my home, while black widows and violins are nimbly captured and sent packing. A few have even set up shop in the kitchen, my allies in helping to keep the ant population down.

Spiders are both feared and worshipped by tribal peoples. Teton natives kill the bad ones, sending their spirits to Grandfather Thunder; other Amerindians revere Spider Grandmother, a world creatrix. Lunar creatures, spiders alternate between weaving and destroying. Their spiral webs symbolize timeless space in the spirit world.

SPIRITS IN THE SLY

As a child I collected bees in makeshift hives to watch them make honey (which, of course, they couldn't do without a queen). Little did I know that in Mayan cosmology four giant bees hold up the sky, one in each of the four directions, or that in Greek mythology bees represent the soul, and their honey a symbol of wisdom and rebirth through initiation. However, as Venus/Aphrodite, the Greco-Roman love goddess, had a following of bees, it was for this romantic reason that I came to think of them as my familiars also. But, synchronicity happens...

Some nineteen years ago I traveled to Uxmal-Kabah, a Mayan ruin in Yucatán, Mexico. More amazing than the pyramids were the hoards of white butterflies that hovered in thick clouds over the area. Strange that they decided to make me their landing site, until a local guide said they were the souls of the Mayan dead striving for light and rebirth in the spirit world. I had recently embarked on a spiritual pathway, and my trip to Yucatán represented purification, transcendence, and a fresh start in life.

JOURNEY WORK

More recently, my husband, a country-western musician, decided to quit the band in which he was playing. We thought this was the right decision, but still, uncertainty lingered. Upon arriving home from the road we knew not to worry. We found two baby grasshoppers living in what was left of my fennel plant (a protective guardian spirit in its own right, they had eaten it down to a nub). I sensed this was a good omen, appearances notwithstanding.

Grasshoppers are destructive when it comes to crops and foliage. The Sumatran Bataks have a ceremony to get rid of them, called "making the curse fly away." Albanian women catch and drown a few grasshoppers, thinking to magically kill them all in the process. However, unwed girls of Madagascar use grasshoppers in a charm to protect their unborn children from premature death. Grasshoppers are great at destroying plants, but they are incredible jumpers, too. Therefore, Madagascar natives sacrifice them so the grasshopper-souls may leap forward to the spirit world in place of their prospective children. Similarly, I felt the baby grasshoppers to be the spirit messengers telling my husband and me that our leap toward building a new future was the correct decision.

Shaman Hunt Sites

By Bernyce Barlow

In my book *Sacred Sites of the West,* I discussed the buffalo hunt of the Plains Indian Nations, the Summer Circle. Now, I would like to explore the hunt ritual sites of the Northern Paiute, whose territory stretched from Central California through Northern Nevada and into parts of Oregon and Washington. The Northern bands of Pauite were nomadic, following the migrational patterns of the deer, antelope, and mountain sheep. Of course water was a big deal too, but the herds knew where the watering holes, rivers, and streams were, so therefore did the nomadic communities that followed them.

The hunt itself was orchestrated by the hunt shaman, resulting in days of preparation and rituals that date back at least 5,000 years. We know this due to the dating of the petroglyphs found at hunt sites like Wellington, Nevada or Lake County, Oregon. Today, the sites provide us with a wealth of information through ruins and remnants scattered on the high desert floor like pieces of a puzzle waiting to be put together.

I had the opportunity to put one of these puzzles together over a period of a few months at an unexcavated location in Northern Nevada. This chapter is as personal as it is professional because the spirit of place brought about many changes in my life that would not have happened if I had not stumbled onto this sacred site. In the chapter of my book titled "Grimes Point," I joke about the energy that is found at these types of sites. All joking aside, this kind of energy is powerful and maintained by Mother Earth and the on-site spirit of place.

I have always been intrigued with the physics found at shaman hunt sites. They are often located near a fault line, giving the site a natural charge. When you combine this energy with the imprint of ritual and intent, it really packs a wallop! As a matter of fact, the energy is somewhat addicting, and I used to find myself wandering around the site for no other reason than to receive a charge, even when the ground was covered with snow! I knew I was in trouble when I found myself spending more time on site than with my family or working.

The layout of the site was typical. A small knoll had been chosen to build a number of shaman circles that were specific in their use. The hunt shamans used only basalt and tufa rocks to record the hunts. Basalt was especially favored due to its ability to confine and retain high levels of magnetic energy. The altars and sacred pit and groove rocks were made of basalt, as were the sitting stones and rocks used as tool benches. Only the hunt shamans were allowed to pit or paint the rocks. To ignore this tabu could bring bad luck, even death, to those who did not honor this tradition.

The altars and pit and groove stones were painted by the shaman, therefore some of the circles on the knoll were set aside as paint areas, containing bowl-shaped rocks where the paints could be mixed and applied. Identification of these paint pot circles was easy due to leftover paint stains and small deposits of paint not yet washed away by the weathering forces of the basin and range topography. Earth dyes, such as the mineral ochre, were crushed with a catalyst of animal fat, blood, or water and used as paint. Sometimes the hunt was recorded through petroglyphs that would be painted after they were pecked into the basalt boulders. At other times the symbology was only painted onto the rocks. The second tier of circles contained some rock cores from the sacred mountain, Mt. Grant, where red ochre is abundant. The colors red, black, yellow, and white were especially favored by the shaman, who would collect the dyes at sacred earth wells and holy mountains. Again, only the hunt shaman could collect the minerals to paint the rocks.

The pit and groove rocks were considered shaman's tools and a part of his altar. The rocks were usually basalt, with pits carved into them connected with grooves. The pits would be painted accordingly. During each hunt, pits would be carved into the stones. Some pit and groove rocks have as many as forty or fifty pits carved into them, red being the color of choice for this type of altar rock. Pit and groove rocks date back five thousand years and are considered one of the earliest styles of hunt petroglyphs of the Great Basin, Central California, and Oregon. Their meaning has been lost, but it is assumed that the pits represented the number of hunts the shaman had participated in at any given site. The pit and groove altar stones

were placed in the main circles where much of the shaman's hunt magic was conjured up, or near hunt blinds that concealed the hunters. One rock may have been pitted by many different shamans, but always for the same purpose: a successful hunt.

Often, pictures of animals were pecked or painted onto the surrounding boulders. It was the hunt shaman's business to capture the soul of an animal and keep it until the animal came to retrieve it. When the animal came for its soul, it was believed others in the herd would follow, maintaining successful numbers for ambush. Some mountain sheep have been depicted without legs or a torso. This represented the shaman's influence over the animal, making it disappear, then reappear after the soul had been snatched. These types of journeys were usually induced through the use of mind-altering drugs and recorded on the rocks found within the shaman's circles. Sometimes the sacred journeys were recorded in nearby caves. At the site I researched, there were fading outlines of deer and antelope whose spirits had been captured by hunt shamans, both inside the main circles and near the existing hunt blind ruins.

The circles were tiered around a large hub circle connected to six smaller circles, each having a workbench rock, a paint pot rock, a sitting stone, an altar stone, and a stone with a flat surface on one side that had been placed upright—about nine to fifteen inches in height, near the center of the circle. The next tier consisted of fire circles with burned rocks that were used in the processing of paints, dyes, herbs and tools. The next tier contained fewer but larger circles that were covered with points and chippings from chert and jasper. Scraping tools, awls, and puncture tools were in abundance on this tier, as were cores of rock matrix used to make arrowheads. There was no evidence of chipping or tool making on the first two tiers of the knoll where the shaman's area was.

The circle's sitting stones were lightning rocks that had been chosen and carried to the site. People with illness came to these sitting rocks to be cured. The shaman used them to enhance visions and states of spirituality. The rocks were usually flat and worn smooth on top, discolored brownish by a lightning hit, and large enough to comfortably sit on with a few inches to spare. The top two

tiers of circles contained sitting rocks. One was especially powerful and was instrumental in healing some of my friends with back problems. Healing was an important part of the hunt. It was believed a person could sabotage a hunt if he carried an illness or was spiritually unclean, so purification ceremonies and healing rituals were incorporated into the shaman's magic.

Understanding the dynamics of the hunt shaman helps us to discern the artifacts and ruins left on site. The site I researched was typical of a shaman's circle center with a few exceptions. There were no obsidian points or chippings found anywhere on the grounds around the site, just jasper and chert. However, a few miles away, in the community living area, lots of obsidian points and arrowheads lay strewn on the ground. Most hunt sites in the Sweetwater Range and along the Eastern Sierra Nevada contain obsidian chips and points, but not this one. This led me to the conclusion obsidian was tabu at this location for some unknown reason.

Another difference I saw was that the hunt blinds were at some distance from the ceremonial knoll. This may be due to the fact the site was flat and large with plenty of room for hunters, animals, and shamans. Sometimes the blinds are within a few yards of the circle encampments, but this is usually where there is a narrow pass that the game must migrate through, or at watering holes.

What was not typical was the energy I felt whenever I visited the site. It was smooth and even, promoting creativity and a hertz rate that fell into the Shumann Resonance. The site was not combative or warrior-like—it was healing. Folks felt relaxed at the site, and those who usually bicker didn't. Time seemed to slow down there, and one could get lost just surveying the ground. The lightning rocks both grounded as well as sent us soaring. The anomaly energy registered higher than the norm, but I feel it was the combined energies of the site that gave it such a distinctive spirit of place. Obviously, the shamans knew what they were doing when they chose this spot as their ceremonial center. I am grateful that they did. It gave me the opportunity to research another powerful healing site that was set up for hunt and healing magic.

The Legend of Feathered Serpent

By Kenneth Johnson

We've all seen the planet Venus as it moves gracefully through its cycle. First, it rises in the morning, just before the Sun, and we call it the Morning Star. Then, for a time, Venus vanishes from sight, too close to the Sun to be seen by us mortals here on Earth. Finally, Venus reappears, but now it is the Evening Star, shining in the night sky.

Throughout the Western world, we think of Venus as the goddess of love and beauty, and our myths about her planet reflect that belief. But different peoples, in different parts of the world, see things in a very different way. Among the Aztecs of ancient Mexico, for example, the cycle of the planet Venus is embodied in one of the most important myths of their civilization—the legend of Feathered Serpent.

In the Aztec language, his name was Quetzalcoatl, and it is said that he was originally a king of the Toltecs, an empire that flourished in central Mexico between 600 and 1000 A.D. If he was a king, he was also a god, the product of a magical birth. Feathered Serpent brought culture and enlightenment to his people. He taught them to turn away from human sacrifice, and that the true "sacrifice" to the gods was incense, flowers, and poetic songs. He lived the pure life of a sage.

But then one day his enemy, the god Smoking Mirror, arrived disguised as a sorcerer. He held up his

magic mirror, in which
we always see our dark
side reflected. His poise
shattered by the sad, broken, aging image of his
own darker nature, Feath-
ered Serpent began to fall
from grace, just as Venus
the Morning Star begins to "fall" toward its union with the Sun. Feathered Serpent began to drink heavily, and to indulge too much in the
magic mushroom, as well as in the company of women. Finally, he
committed incest with his sister, and lost his "magic" altogether.

Sadly, Feathered Serpent set aside his kingdom and built for
himself a coffin. His loyal followers carried the coffin that contained
their lord all the way to the shores of the Gulf of Mexico. It took
them eight days, which is just as long as the planet Venus remains
"dark" during its union with the Sun. Then Feathered Serpent rose
up again and built for himself a funeral pyre. He set himself aflame,
and his heart rose up into the heavens. There he remained, now embodied in the Evening Star.

Feathered Serpent was one of the most important figures in the
religious history of ancient Mexico and Central America. Some said
that even though his heart had traveled to the stars, he himself had
actually sailed away across the sea in a boat made of serpents. It was
prophesied that he would return someday. Unfortunately, some
Aztecs mistook the conqueror Cortez for the returning Quetzalcoatl,
though he came to destroy rather than restore their civilization. But
some of the Mayan prophecies insist that Feathered Serpent is due to
return during the last twenty-year cycle of the Mayan Calendar.
When will this cycle occur? It runs from 1993 to 2012. If the Mayan
prophets were right, the return of Feathered Serpent is not far off.

HISTORY AND DANCES OF THE MAYPOLE

BY BREID FOXSONG

Some of the most popular activities of Beltane were centered around the maypole. The symbolic phallus (some were more graphic than others) was planted in the earth to fertilize her.

Historically, maypoles vary in height. These poles were placed permanently in the town square and were often left up for ten to fifteen years. Villages would vie with each other to see who could find and erect the tallest maypole. Obviously, a pole of this height was not plaited with ribbons, although it was the center of a variety of ring dances. Generally it was brightly painted and decorated with wreaths, garlands, and fresh flowers each year.

In 1644, the English Puritan Long Parliament banned these "devilish instruments," and ordered all existing maypoles to be taken down and burned. Despite the reintroduction of the maypole, the Puritan Reformation had its effect on Beltane festivities, and many of the Pagan elements were lost. Those of us who want to make our own maypoles are happily unencumbered by the weight of tradition and can change the design and the meanings to suit our modern purposes.

When choosing a maypole, take into consideration what you will do with it after the ceremony. Will it end up in your garage, or remain in the circle area for the rest of the summer? Will you have to transport it to your ritual site and home again?

For the purposes of this article, let us assume that you are not able to plant a twenty-foot pole and leave it. Let us also assume that you have fairly limited resources, both financial and otherwise. You can certainly elaborate on this basic pole.

MAKING A MAYPOLE

The easiest way to make a maypole is to purchase it. Check out any lumber yard (or "seconds" lumberyard if you have them in your area) for dowels or banister rails. For making an eight to nine foot maypole, a one-inch dowel is perfectly adequate. You will probably not find dowels longer than twelve feet, but an eight or nine foot maypole should be big enough for any group of less than twenty.

If you are going to go over twelve feet, you will have to go to a much thicker pole. At that point, start looking for old telephone poles. A more techno-Pagan approach is to use PVC pipe. You will have to start with two-inch pipe due to the higher flexibility, but it will last forever and is easily extended to be whatever size you need.

MAKING THE BASE

Once you have acquired the pole, you will need to fix it to a stand. The stability of the stand is important. Unless you have a good one, you will have to be careful not to pull too hard on the ribbons when you dance. The easiest type of stand is a Christmas tree stand, if you own one. If you don't own one, check at local thrift stores for them. Most of the stands have holes in the feet to allow you to anchor them with stakes outdoors. If you don't own or can't find a tree stand, making a stand is simple.

You will need two two-foot lengths of one-by-four inch boards, and two pieces of one-by-four that are only a couple inches long. You will also need a floor flange (you'll find them in the plumbing department, cost is about three dollars) that will fit the end of the dowel. Nail the two foot boards together in a cross. Use the smaller pieces on the ends of the upper board to make the stand level.

Screw the floor flange to the center of the crossed boards (screws are much more stable than nails). You will need five screws; four to screw the flange into the wood and one that will screw up through the wood and into the center of the pole for greater stability. Two more small blocks may be needed to secure the flange on the lower board, depending on the width of the flange.

Sand bags can be placed in the boards to weight them down if needed. If you are outside, you can drill holes in the ends of the one-by-fours and stake them down.

SUSPENDING THE RIBBONS

Total cost on the maypole should average about twelve dollars plus ribbons. An additional piece that adds to the symbolism is an acorn-shaped banister top. This can be purchased at a lumber yard and

screwed or nailed to the top of the pole after attaching the ribbons to give it that proper phallic "look."

Many people make a suspended ring to hold the ribbons away from the pole at the top. For this, use an old embroidery hoop covered with bright cloth. You can also attach flowers, narrow ribbons, bows, or other decorations to make this more attractive. Attach wire or thin cord on four sides so that it balances nicely, and firmly affix it to the top of the pole before attaching the ribbons.

The next step is to choose your "ribbons." There are several options. All of them have their virtues and vices. Crepe paper is inexpensive but tears easily and the color runs if it gets wet. Ribbons are more expensive but don't tear. Cloth is fairly cheap, but bulky. It also tends to fray on the edges, making it hard to unwrap. The ribbons should be longer than the pole by about two or three feet. This allows for the extra length needed for braiding the ribbons. To attach the ribbons, simply nail them to the top of the pole.

Since most people use a maypole in a group context, you will have to decide how many ribbons you want. The easiest solution is to have one ribbon for each member who wants to dance around it. The pole will plait easier if there is an even number of ribbons, but that may mean that one person takes two, which can be awkward.

The "proper" colors of the maypole vary, depending on who you ask. The dance described below uses only two colors, but that is primarily so that you can tell who is supposed to do what when.

THE MAYPOLE DANCE

The maypole dance is usually a couples dance; it apparently originated as a form of courting. Most versions have a formal procession to the maypole in two lines with partners coming forward to get ribbons together. It certainly avoids confusion to have people getting their ribbons one at a time, and keeps the ribbons from getting tangled. Since rare is the coven that is perfectly balanced, count off by ones and twos. "Ones" get the white ribbons, "twos," the red (or whatever combination of colors you are using).

Once you have gotten your ribbon, move back out and form a circle around the pole. White ribbon holders face widdershins (counter-clockwise), and red ribbon holders face deosil (clockwise).

Music helps keep everyone together. Any standard Morris tune or waltz will work. The primary point of the music is to keep everyone moving at about the same speed.

When the music starts, or someone says "Go," begin weaving. Whites should start by going to the outside of the person facing them, then to the inside of the next person, then to the outside, then the inside, etc. Reds begin by going to the inside, then the outside, then the inside, then the outside, etc. This is called the "grand right and left." Contin-

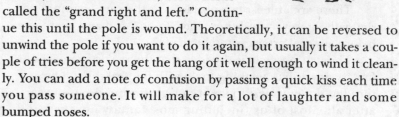

ue this until the pole is wound. Theoretically, it can be reversed to unwind the pole if you want to do it again, but usually it takes a couple of tries before you get the hang of it well enough to wind it cleanly. You can add a note of confusion by passing a quick kiss each time you pass someone. It will make for a lot of laughter and some bumped noses.

A more formal version of the maypole dance might go something like this: Each person curtsies or bows to his or her partner, then curtsies or bows to the pole (god/dess image). Repeat. Then all face deosil and walk around the pole once, stop, face widdershins and repeat. All face deosil and hop, glide, step once around the pole, then face widdershins and repeat. All white ribbons take two steps toward the pole and form an inside circle. Red ribbons form an outside circle. Inside circle faces deosil, outside faces widdershins. All move in hop, glide, step once around the pole. Inside and outside circles curtsy or bow to each other, face opposite direction, and return in the same way. All curtsy or bow to partners, then to the pole. Begin grand right and left. Whites go to the outside of the person facing them, then to the inside of the next person, then to the outside, then the inside, etc. Reds go to the inside, then the outside, then the inside, then the outside, etc., until done. When the pole is plaited, curtsy or bow to your partner, drop the ribbons, join hands, and leave area in procession.

Whichever you decide to do, enjoy the dance. Beltane should be a day of joy. With a lighthearted attitude, the maypole can be a lot of fun, even if you end up with a tangled mess. It is truly a dance of life!

So You Want to Be a Real Magician

By John Michael Greer

If you're reading *Llewellyn's Magical Almanac*, you're almost certainly interested in magic, and if you're interested in magic, it's likely that you want to learn how to do it yourself. You may even be thinking about taking up magic in a serious way. If so, you've turned to the right page. The path that leads to magical mastery is long and sometimes difficult, but it can be followed by anyone willing to dedicate the time, effort, and energy involved.

There are at least two obstacles at the very beginning of the path, however, and these have to be faced and overcome before any real progress can be made.

The first obstacle is the idea that the magic in movies or fantasy novels has anything to do with the real thing. Our culture has done its best to ignore magic for hundreds of years, after all. Most of us (including most fantasy novelists and movie producers) grew up around technology, not magic, and thus most of our ideas about magic are actually based on technology. We expect magic to do flashy things—levitate heavy objects, shoot lightning bolts from fingertips, and so on—because flashy things are something technology is good at.

Applied to magic, though, this is completely wrongheaded. Magic is not technology. It does different things in different ways. It works through subtle natural connections between the two realms of human experience we call "mind" and "matter"—connections our modern sciences have long forgotten, and are only just beginning to rediscover. Its powers are natural powers, woven into the fabric of existence, and it uses them in ways that follow the natural flow of events. As a result, when magic works, its results come about naturally, as if by coincidence. (This is one of the main reasons why our culture has been able to ignore magic for so long; successful magic can always be dismissed by the skeptical as "coincidence.")

The first thing to do if you intend to get serious about magic, then, is to set aside the ideas you've picked up from fiction, movies, and the media. This isn't always easy; after all, these images are often what draw people to the occult arts in the first place. Still, no amount of magical training is going to give you the power to fly like a comic-book superhero, make things explode with a wave of your hand, and so on. The real powers of magic are different, as you'll find if you read any good book on the subject. The sooner you become clear about this, the less likely you are to end up disappointed.

So much for the first obstacle. The second is the idea that knowledge about magic is all you need. Again, this is a common notion in the media images we've just discussed. At the same time, there's also some truth behind it, because knowledge is an absolute necessity if you want to become a competent magician. The problem is that you can learn vast amounts about magic and still have no clue how to put that knowledge into practice. It's even possible to know exactly how a magical operation should be done, and still be unable to do it.

After all, the same thing is true elsewhere. For example, someone might read hundreds of books about music, picking up a vast amount of knowledge on the subject, and still have no idea how it's applied in practice. He might even read detailed descriptions of how to play the piano, and still be unable to sit down and pick out *Chopsticks*—much less something by Mozart or Elton John.

Knowledge, in other words, is not enough. Neither is talent. Neither, it has to be said, is the kind of fashion statement that involves dressing in black, wearing pounds of mystical jewelry, and leaving occult books on your coffee table for visitors to see. If you intend to become a real magician, you're going to have to do something more.

What is enough, then? Ask yourself the same question about almost anything else, and the answer is obvious.

Let's imagine that you meet someone who says he's a musician. He tells you that he's read dozens of books on playing the piano; piano-playing has been a tradition in his family for generations; he has a really good piano at home, and always dresses like Beethoven. When you ask him how much time he puts into practice every day, though, you get a blank look. It turns out that once a month, he and a few friends get together and play one tune out of a book—and this is the only time he ever touches piano keys. Odds are you would go away shaking your head, convinced that this would-be "musician" didn't have a clue. Surprisingly, though, many people think that the same things will make them competent magicians.

The moral to this little story is that you become a magician the same way you become a musician, a martial artist, or anything else—by practicing. The best way to begin learning magic, in fact, is to choose a basic practice to do every day without fail. What you choose for your practice will depend on the tradition that most appeals to you. Many Wiccans find that casting a circle and calling the quarters makes a good daily practice; Hermetic magicians have the Lesser Ritual of the Pentagram and the Middle Pillar exercise; other traditions have their own possibilities. The important thing is that you choose something, and then do it each and every day.

Sticking to a daily practice isn't easy. What magicians call the lower self—the ramshackle structure of the ordinary personality—will almost always try to weasel out of a process that's guaranteed to reshape it. You'll come up with any number of reasons to set aside your practice "just this once." Ignore them, and keep at it. As days add up to weeks, months, and years of regular practice, you'll find your magical abilities growing accordingly.

There are several other things you can do to help lay the foundations for your magical development. It's useful to keep a record of your work, a magical diary in which you write down details of all your practices and workings. It's useful to set aside time regularly for magical reading and study—after all, you're going to have to learn a good deal. Nothing, though, is more important than regular practice. If you want to become a real magician, and not just a "wannabee," there is no other way.

2000
ALMANAC SECTION

Calendar

Time Changes

Full Moon Listings

Sabbat Listings

Lunar Phase Listings

Moon Sign Listings

World Holiday Listings

Color Correspondences

Incense Correspondences

ALMANAC LISTINGS

I n these listings you will find the date, day, lunar phase, Moon sign, color and incense for the day, and festivals from around the world.

THE DATE

The date is used in numerological calculations that govern magical rites.

THE DAY

Each day is ruled by a planet that possesses specific magical influences:

MONDAY (MOON): Peace, sleep, healing, compassion, friends, psychic awareness, purification, and fertility.

TUESDAY (MARS): Passion, sex, courage, aggression, and protection.

WEDNESDAY (MERCURY): The conscious mind, study, travel, divination, and wisdom.

THURSDAY (JUPITER): Expansion, money, prosperity, and generosity.

FRIDAY (VENUS): Love, friendship, reconciliation, and beauty.

SATURDAY (SATURN): Longevity, exorcism, endings, homes, and houses.

SUNDAY (SUN): Healing, spirituality, success, strength, and protection.

THE LUNAR PHASE

The lunar phase is important in determining the best times for magic.

THE WAXING MOON (from the New Moon to the Full) is the ideal time for magic to draw things toward you.

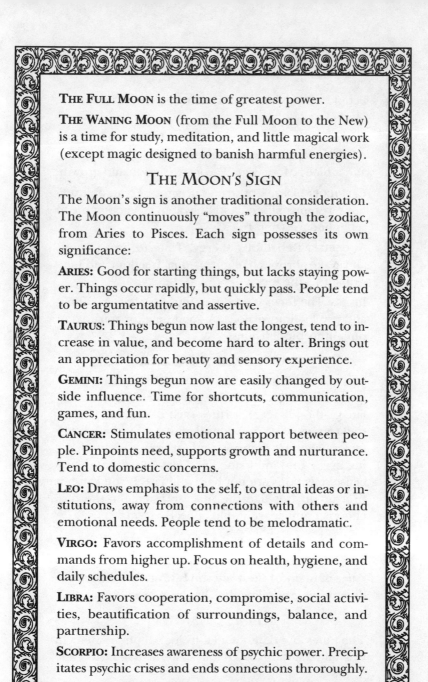

THE FULL MOON is the time of greatest power.

THE WANING MOON (from the Full Moon to the New) is a time for study, meditation, and little magical work (except magic designed to banish harmful energies).

THE MOON'S SIGN

The Moon's sign is another traditional consideration. The Moon continuously "moves" through the zodiac, from Aries to Pisces. Each sign possesses its own significance:

ARIES: Good for starting things, but lacks staying power. Things occur rapidly, but quickly pass. People tend to be argumentatitve and assertive.

TAURUS: Things begun now last the longest, tend to increase in value, and become hard to alter. Brings out an appreciation for beauty and sensory experience.

GEMINI: Things begun now are easily changed by outside influence. Time for shortcuts, communication, games, and fun.

CANCER: Stimulates emotional rapport between people. Pinpoints need, supports growth and nurturance. Tend to domestic concerns.

LEO: Draws emphasis to the self, to central ideas or institutions, away from connections with others and emotional needs. People tend to be melodramatic.

VIRGO: Favors accomplishment of details and commands from higher up. Focus on health, hygiene, and daily schedules.

LIBRA: Favors cooperation, compromise, social activities, beautification of surroundings, balance, and partnership.

SCORPIO: Increases awareness of psychic power. Precipitates psychic crises and ends connections throroughly.

People tend to brood and become secretive under this Moon sign.

SAGITTARIUS: Encourages flights of imagination and confidence. This is an adventurous, philosophical, and athletic Moon sign. Favors expansion and growth.

CAPRICORN: Develops strong structure. Focus on traditions, responsibilities, and obligations. A good time to set boundaries and rules.

AQUARIUS: Rebellious energy. Time to break habits and make abrupt change. Personal freedom and individuality is the focus.

PISCES: The focus is on dreaming, nostalgia, intuition, and psychic impressions. A good time for spiritual or philanthropic activities.

COLOR AND INCENSE

The color and incense for the day are based on information from *Personal Alchemy* by Amber Wolfe, and relate to the planet that rules each day. This information can be taken into consideration along with other factors when planning works of magic or when blending magic into mundane life. Please note that the incense selections are not hard and fast. If you can not find or do not like the incense listed for the day, choose a similar scent that appeals to you.

FESTIVALS AND HOLIDAYS

Festivals are listed throughout the year. **The exact dates of many of these ancient festivals are difficult to determine; prevailing data has been used.**

TIME CHANGES

The times and dates of all astrological phenomena in this almanac are based on **Eastern Standard Time**

(EST). If you live outside of EST, you will need to make the following changes:

PACIFIC STANDARD TIME: subtract three hours.

MOUNTAIN STANDARD TIME: subtract two hours.

CENTRAL STANDARD TIME: subtract one hour.

ALASKA/HAWAII: subtract five hours.

DAYLIGHT SAVING TIME: add an hour. Daylight saving time runs from April 2 to October 29, 2000.

2000 SABBATS AND FULL MOONS

January 20	Full Moon 11:40 PM
February 2	Imbolc
February 19	Full Moon 11:27 AM
March 19	Full Moon 11:44 PM
March 20	Ostara (Spring Equinox)
April 18	Full Moon 12:41 PM
May 1	Beltane
May 18	Full Moon 2:34 AM
June 16	Full Moon 5:27 PM
June 20	Litha (Summer Solstice)
July 16	Full Moon 8:55 AM
August 1	Lammas
August 15	Full Moon 12:13 AM
September 13	Full Moon 2:37 PM
September 22	Mabon (Fall Equinox)
October 13	Full Moon 3:53 AM
October 31	Samhain
November 11	Full Moon 4:15 PM
December 11	Full Moon 4:03 AM
December 21	Yule (Winter Solstice)

CAPRICORN ♑

1 SATURDAY
New Year's Day • Kwanzaa ends
Waning Moon
Moon Phase: Fourth Quarter
Color: Indigo
Moon Sign: Scorpio
Incense: Jasmine

2 SUNDAY
Disting Moon • Birthday of Inanna
Waning Moon
Moon Phase: Fourth Quarter
Color: Gold
Moon Sign: Scorpio
Moon enters Sagittarius 4:32 pm
Incense: Myrrh

3 MONDAY
Pueblo Deer Dances (Native American)
Waning Moon
Moon Phase: Fourth Quarter
Color: Silver
Moon Sign: Sagittarius
Incense: Clove

4 TUESDAY
Martyrs of Independence (Zaire)
Waning Moon
Moon Phase: Fourth Quarter
Color: Red
Moon Sign: Sagittarius
Incense: Sage

5 WEDNESDAY
George Washington Carver Day
Waning Moon
Moon Phase: Fourth Quarter
Color: Yellow
Moon Sign: Sagittarius
Moon enters Capricorn 5:24 am
Incense: Sandalwood

☽ THURSDAY
Ramadan ends
Waning Moon
Moon Phase: New Moon 1:14 pm
Color: Turquoise
Moon Sign: Capricorn
Incense: Poplar

7 FRIDAY
Feast of Sekhmet (Egypt)
Waxing Moon
Moon Phase: First Quarter
Color: Blue
Moon Sign: Capricorn
Moon enters Aquarius 5:53 pm
Incense: Geranium

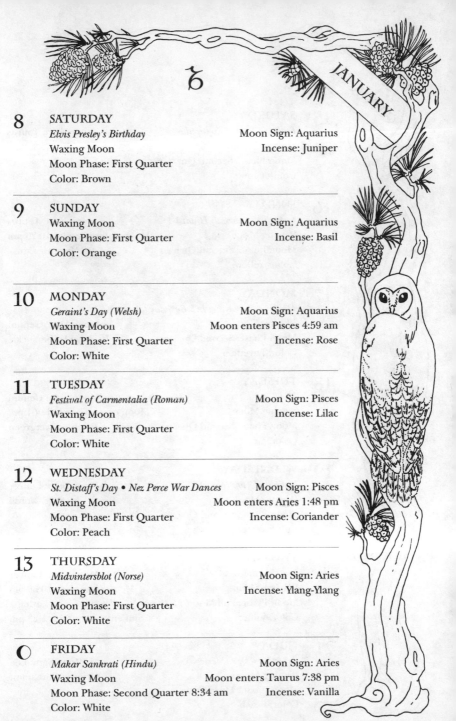

8   **SATURDAY**
Elvis Presley's Birthday
Waxing Moon
Moon Phase: First Quarter
Color: Brown

Moon Sign: Aquarius
Incense: Juniper

---

9   **SUNDAY**
Waxing Moon
Moon Phase: First Quarter
Color: Orange

Moon Sign: Aquarius
Incense: Basil

---

10   **MONDAY**
Geraint's Day (Welsh)
Waxing Moon
Moon Phase: First Quarter
Color: White

Moon Sign: Aquarius
Moon enters Pisces 4:59 am
Incense: Rose

---

11   **TUESDAY**
Festival of Carmentalia (Roman)
Waxing Moon
Moon Phase: First Quarter
Color: White

Moon Sign: Pisces
Incense: Lilac

---

12   **WEDNESDAY**
St. Distaff's Day • Nez Perce War Dances
Waxing Moon
Moon Phase: First Quarter
Color: Peach

Moon Sign: Pisces
Moon enters Aries 1:48 pm
Incense: Coriander

---

13   **THURSDAY**
Midvintersblot (Norse)
Waxing Moon
Moon Phase: First Quarter
Color: White

Moon Sign: Aries
Incense: Ylang-Ylang

◗   **FRIDAY**
Makar Sankrati (Hindu)
Waxing Moon
Moon Phase: Second Quarter 8:34 am
Color: White

Moon Sign: Aries
Moon enters Taurus 7:38 pm
Incense: Vanilla

CAPRICORN ♑

15 SATURDAY
Feast of Christ of Esquipulas
Waxing Moon
Moon Phase: Second Quarter
Color: Gray

Moon Sign: Taurus
Incense: Pine

16 SUNDAY
Festival of Ganesha (Hindu)
Waxing Moon
Moon Phase: Second Quarter
Color: Yellow

Moon Sign: Taurus
Moon enters Gemini 10:25 pm
Incense: Musk

17 MONDAY
Martin Luther King, Jr.'s Birthday (observed)
Waxing Moon
Moon Phase: Second Quarter
Color: Lavender

Moon Sign: Gemini
Incense: Honeysuckle

18 TUESDAY
Surya
Waxing Moon
Moon Phase: Second Quarter
Color: Gray

Moon Sign: Gemini
Moon enters Cancer 11:01 pm
Incense: Evergreen

19 WEDNESDAY
Festival of Thor (Norse)
Waxing Moon
Moon Phase: Second Quarter
Color: White

Moon Sign: Cancer
Incense: Neroli

☺ THURSDAY
Lunar Eclipse
Waxing Moon
Moon Phase: Full Moon 11:40 pm
Color: Violet

Moon Sign: Cancer
Moon enters Leo 10:58 pm
Incense: Gardenia
Sun enters Aquarius 1:23 pm

21 FRIDAY
Santa Ines' Day (Mexican)
Waning Moon
Moon Phase: Third Quarter
Color: Peach

Moon Sign: Leo
Incense: Cinnamon

22 SATURDAY
St. Vincent's Day
Waning Moon
Moon Phase: Third Quarter
Color: Brown

Moon Sign: Leo
Incense: Patchouli

23 SUNDAY
New Year of the Trees (Jewish)
Waning Moon
Moon Phase: Third Quarter
Color: Peach

Moon Sign: Leo
Moon enters Virgo 12:07 am
Incense: Nutmeg

24 MONDAY
Blessing of the Happy Woman's Candle (Hungarian)
Waning Moon
Moon Phase: Third Quarter
Color: Gray

Moon Sign: Virgo
Incense: Cedar

25 TUESDAY
Burns' Night (Scottish)
Waning Moon
Moon Phase: Third Quarter
Color: Red

Moon Sign: Virgo
Moon enters Libra 4:09 am
Incense: Ginger

26 WEDNESDAY
Festival of Ekeko (Bolivian)
Waning Moon
Moon Phase: Third Quarter
Color: Brown

Moon Sign: Libra
Incense: Pine

27 THURSDAY
Sementivae Feria (Roman)
Waning Moon
Moon Phase: Third Quarter
Color: Green

Moon Sign: Libra
Moon enters Scorpio 12:01 pm
Incense: Parsley

◖ FRIDAY
Upelly-Aa (Scottish)
Waning Moon
Moon Phase: Fourth Quarter 2:57 am
Color: Rose

Moon Sign: Scorpio
Incense: Dill

29 SATURDAY
Martyr's Day (Nepalese)
Waning Moon
Moon Phase: Fourth Quarter
Color: Indigo

Moon Sign: Scorpio
Moon enters Sagittarius 11:17 pm
Incense: Jasmine

30 SUNDAY
Three Hierarchs Day (Eastern Orthodox)
Waning Moon
Moon Phase: Fourth Quarter
Color: Orange

Moon Sign: Sagittarius
Incense: Clove

31 MONDAY
Hecate's Feast (Greek)
Waning Moon
Moon Phase: Fourth Quarter
Color: White

Moon Sign: Sagittarius
Incense: Chrysanthemum

FULL MOONS

January	Cold Moon, Moon after Yule
February	Snow Moon, Wolf Moon, Hunger Moon
March	Quickening Moon, Storm Moon, Sap Moon
April	Wind Moon, Grass Moon
May	Flower Moon, Planting Moon
June	Strong Sun Moon
July	Blessing Moon, Honey Moon
August	Corn Moon, Thunder Moon
September	Harvest Moon, Grain Moon, Fruit Moon
October	Blood Moon, Hunter's Moon
November	Mourning Moon, Frosty Moon
December	Moon Before Yule, Long Nights Moon

The second Full Moon of any month is called a Blue Moon.

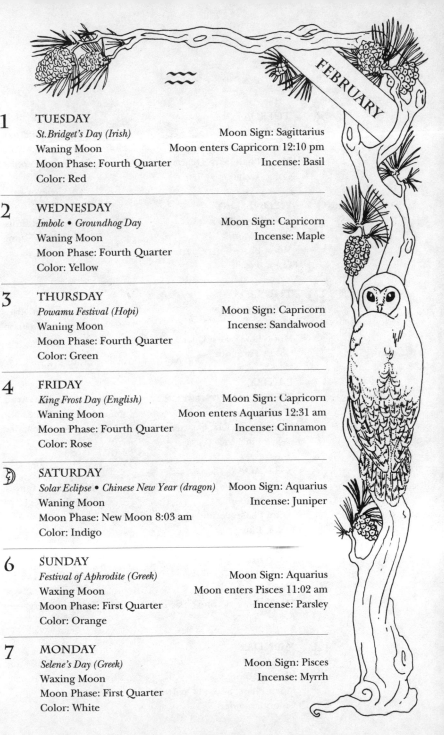

1 TUESDAY
St.Bridget's Day (Irish)
Waning Moon
Moon Phase: Fourth Quarter
Color: Red

Moon Sign: Sagittarius
Moon enters Capricorn 12:10 pm
Incense: Basil

2 WEDNESDAY
Imbolc • Groundhog Day
Waning Moon
Moon Phase: Fourth Quarter
Color: Yellow

Moon Sign: Capricorn
Incense: Maple

3 THURSDAY
Powamu Festival (Hopi)
Waning Moon
Moon Phase: Fourth Quarter
Color: Green

Moon Sign: Capricorn
Incense: Sandalwood

4 FRIDAY
King Frost Day (English)
Waning Moon
Moon Phase: Fourth Quarter
Color: Rose

Moon Sign: Capricorn
Moon enters Aquarius 12:31 am
Incense: Cinnamon

5 SATURDAY
Solar Eclipse • Chinese New Year (dragon)
Waning Moon
Moon Phase: New Moon 8:03 am
Color: Indigo

Moon Sign: Aquarius
Incense: Juniper

6 SUNDAY
Festival of Aphrodite (Greek)
Waxing Moon
Moon Phase: First Quarter
Color: Orange

Moon Sign: Aquarius
Moon enters Pisces 11:02 am
Incense: Parsley

7 MONDAY
Selene's Day (Greek)
Waxing Moon
Moon Phase: First Quarter
Color: White

Moon Sign: Pisces
Incense: Myrrh

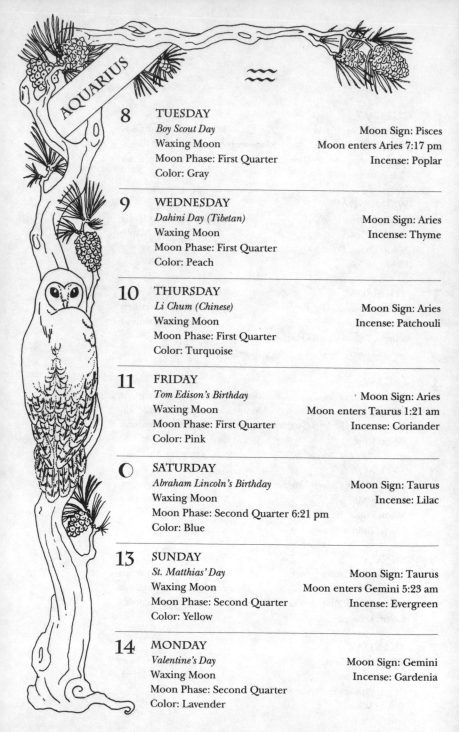

AQUARIUS ≈

8 TUESDAY
Boy Scout Day
Waxing Moon
Moon Phase: First Quarter
Color: Gray

Moon Sign: Pisces
Moon enters Aries 7:17 pm
Incense: Poplar

9 WEDNESDAY
Dahini Day (Tibetan)
Waxing Moon
Moon Phase: First Quarter
Color: Peach

Moon Sign: Aries
Incense: Thyme

10 THURSDAY
Li Chum (Chinese)
Waxing Moon
Moon Phase: First Quarter
Color: Turquoise

Moon Sign: Aries
Incense: Patchouli

11 FRIDAY
Tom Edison's Birthday
Waxing Moon
Moon Phase: First Quarter
Color: Pink

Moon Sign: Aries
Moon enters Taurus 1:21 am
Incense: Coriander

☽ SATURDAY
Abraham Lincoln's Birthday
Waxing Moon
Moon Phase: Second Quarter 6:21 pm
Color: Blue

Moon Sign: Taurus
Incense: Lilac

13 SUNDAY
St. Matthias' Day
Waxing Moon
Moon Phase: Second Quarter
Color: Yellow

Moon Sign: Taurus
Moon enters Gemini 5:23 am
Incense: Evergreen

14 MONDAY
Valentine's Day
Waxing Moon
Moon Phase: Second Quarter
Color: Lavender

Moon Sign: Gemini
Incense: Gardenia

15 TUESDAY
Lupercalia
Waxing Moon
Moon Phase: Second Quarter
Color: White

Moon Sign: Gemini
Moon enters Cancer 7:45 am
Incense: Almond

16 WEDNESDAY
Waxing Moon
Moon Phase: Second Quarter
Color: Brown

Moon Sign: Cancer
Incense: Pine

17 THURSDAY
Waxing Moon
Moon Phase: Second Quarter
Color: White

Moon Sign: Cancer
Moon enters Leo 9:11 am
Incense: Geranium

18 FRIDAY
Spenta Armaiti (Zoroastrian)
Waxing Moon
Moon Phase: Second Quarter
Color: Peach

Moon Sign: Leo
Incense: Clove

SATURDAY
Mahashivatri (The Great Night of Shiva)
Waxing Moon
Moon Phase: Full Moon 11:27 am
Color: Gray

Moon Sign: Leo
Moon enters Virgo 10:53 am
Incense: Eucalyptus
Sun enters Pisces 3:33 am

20 SUNDAY
Day of Tacita (Roman)
Waning Moon
Moon Phase: Third Quarter
Color: Peach

Moon Sign: Virgo
Incense: Ginger

21 MONDAY
President's Day (observed)
Waning Moon
Moon Phase: Third Quarter
Color: Gray

Moon Sign: Virgo
Moon enters Libra 2:21 pm
Incense: Maple

133

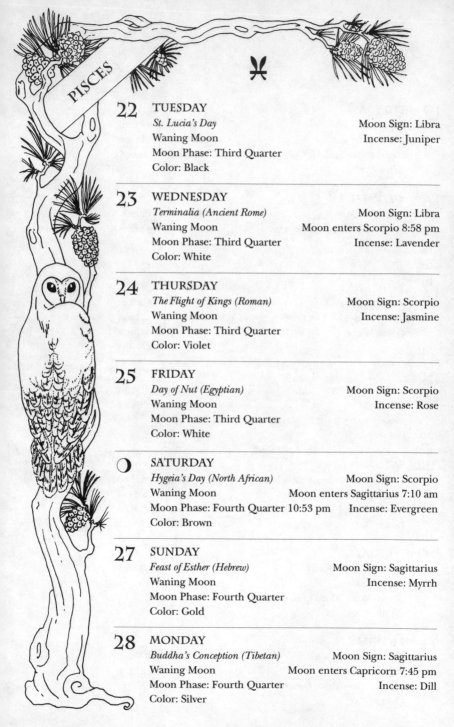

PISCES

22 **TUESDAY**
St. Lucia's Day
Waning Moon
Moon Phase: Third Quarter
Color: Black

Moon Sign: Libra
Incense: Juniper

23 **WEDNESDAY**
Terminalia (Ancient Rome)
Waning Moon
Moon Phase: Third Quarter
Color: White

Moon Sign: Libra
Moon enters Scorpio 8:58 pm
Incense: Lavender

24 **THURSDAY**
The Flight of Kings (Roman)
Waning Moon
Moon Phase: Third Quarter
Color: Violet

Moon Sign: Scorpio
Incense: Jasmine

25 **FRIDAY**
Day of Nut (Egyptian)
Waning Moon
Moon Phase: Third Quarter
Color: White

Moon Sign: Scorpio
Incense: Rose

◐ **SATURDAY**
Hygeia's Day (North African)
Waning Moon
Moon Phase: Fourth Quarter 10:53 pm
Color: Brown

Moon Sign: Scorpio
Moon enters Sagittarius 7:10 am
Incense: Evergreen

27 **SUNDAY**
Feast of Esther (Hebrew)
Waning Moon
Moon Phase: Fourth Quarter
Color: Gold

Moon Sign: Sagittarius
Incense: Myrrh

28 **MONDAY**
Buddha's Conception (Tibetan)
Waning Moon
Moon Phase: Fourth Quarter
Color: Silver

Moon Sign: Sagittarius
Moon enters Capricorn 7:45 pm
Incense: Dill

134

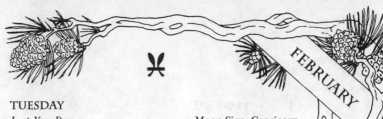

29 TUESDAY

Leap Year Day
Waning Moon
Moon Phase: Fourth Quarter
Color: Red

Moon Sign: Capricorn
Incense: Ginger

HUMOR

In our increasingly solemn times, many of us are tempted to forget one of the most important facets of human existence: laughter. Humor is an ancient magical tool used for protection, to dispell negative energies, and to erase stress.

If you're depressed, angry, tense, worried, ill, or otherwise afflicted, create situations in which you'll laugh. Watch comedies. Tell jokes. Remember comical occasions from the past. Read funny books. Ensure that laughter is part of your everyday experience.

Laughter is a powerful force that releases large amounts of energy from the body that can be channelled to blast away unwanted energies that may be directed to the laughter.

Those who believe they're the victims of a curse are frequently told to laugh at the situation, not out of disbelief, but out of the firm and solid conviction that no negative energy can possibly affect she or he who doesn't desire it.

Too often, we allow ourselves to wallow in misery. Follow the light and lighten up!

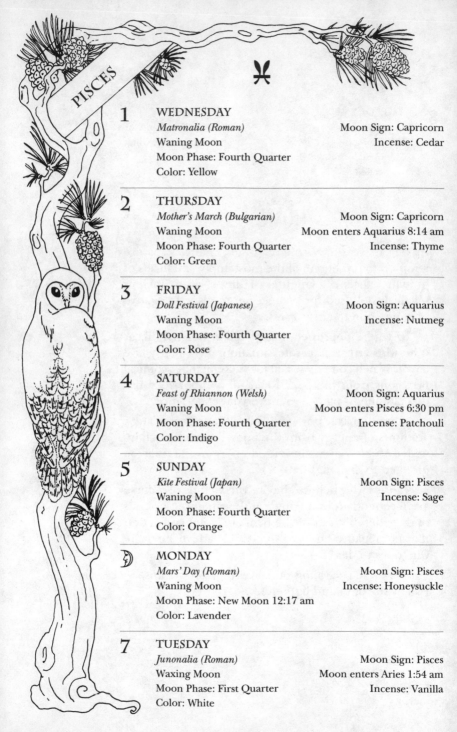

PISCES

♓

1 WEDNESDAY
Matronalia (Roman)
Waning Moon
Moon Phase: Fourth Quarter
Color: Yellow

Moon Sign: Capricorn
Incense: Cedar

2 THURSDAY
Mother's March (Bulgarian)
Waning Moon
Moon Phase: Fourth Quarter
Color: Green

Moon Sign: Capricorn
Moon enters Aquarius 8:14 am
Incense: Thyme

3 FRIDAY
Doll Festival (Japanese)
Waning Moon
Moon Phase: Fourth Quarter
Color: Rose

Moon Sign: Aquarius
Incense: Nutmeg

4 SATURDAY
Feast of Rhiannon (Welsh)
Waning Moon
Moon Phase: Fourth Quarter
Color: Indigo

Moon Sign: Aquarius
Moon enters Pisces 6:30 pm
Incense: Patchouli

5 SUNDAY
Kite Festival (Japan)
Waning Moon
Moon Phase: Fourth Quarter
Color: Orange

Moon Sign: Pisces
Incense: Sage

6 MONDAY
Mars' Day (Roman)
Waning Moon
Moon Phase: New Moon 12:17 am
Color: Lavender

Moon Sign: Pisces
Incense: Honeysuckle

7 TUESDAY
Junonalia (Roman)
Waxing Moon
Moon Phase: First Quarter
Color: White

Moon Sign: Pisces
Moon enters Aries 1:54 am
Incense: Vanilla

8 **WEDNESDAY**
Ash Wednesday (Christian)   Moon Sign: Aries
Waxing Moon   Incense: Sandalwood
Moon Phase: First Quarter
Color: Peach

9 **THURSDAY**
Feast of the Forty Martyrs (Greek)   Moon Sign: Aries
Waxing Moon   Moon enters Taurus 7:01 am
Moon Phase: First Quarter   Incense: Poplar
Color: Turquoise

10 **FRIDAY**
Siamese New Year   Moon Sign: Taurus
Waxing Moon   Incense: Coriander
Moon Phase: First Quarter
Color: Pink

11 **SATURDAY**
Hercules' Day (Greek)   Moon Sign: Taurus
Waxing Moon   Moon enters Gemini 10:46 am
Moon Phase: First Quarter   Incense: Peony
Color: Blue

12 **SUNDAY**
Feast of Marduk (Mesopotamian)   Moon Sign: Gemini
Waxing Moon   Incense: Maple
Moon Phase: First Quarter
Color: Yellow

☾ **MONDAY**
Purification Feast (Balinese)   Moon Sign: Gemini
Waxing Moon   Moon enters Cancer 1:51 pm
Moon Phase: Second Quarter 1:59 am   Incense: Violet
Color: White

14 **TUESDAY**
Veturius Mamurius (Roman)   Moon Sign: Cancer
Waxing Moon   Incense: Musk
Moon Phase: Second Quarter
Color: Gray

♓

15 WEDNESDAY
Offerings to Ra, Asar, Horus (Egyptian) — Moon Sign: Cancer
Waxing Moon — Moon enters Leo 4:43 pm
Moon Phase: Second Quarter — Incense: Eucalyptus
Color: Brown

16 THURSDAY
Festival of Dionysus — Moon Sign: Leo
Waxing Moon — Incense: Rose
Moon Phase: Second Quarter
Color: White

17 FRIDAY
St. Patrick's Day — Moon Sign: Leo
Waxing Moon — Moon enters Virgo 7:48 pm
Moon Phase: Second Quarter — Incense: Cinnamon
Color: Peach

18 SATURDAY
Sheelah's Day (Icelandic) — Moon Sign: Virgo
Waxing Moon — Incense: Pine
Moon Phase: Second Quarter
Color: Gray

☺ **SUNDAY**
Quintania (Greek) — Moon Sign: Virgo
Waxing Moon — Moon enters Libra 11:57 pm
Moon Phase: Full Moon 11:44 pm — Incense: Rosemary
Color: Peach

20 MONDAY
Ostara • Spring Equinox — Moon Sign: Libra
Waning Moon — Sun enters Aries 2:35 am
Moon Phase: Third Quarter — Incense: Juniper
Color: Gray

21 TUESDAY
Purim (Jewish) — Moon Sign: Libra
Waning Moon — Incense: Evergreen
Moon Phase: Third Quarter
Color: Black

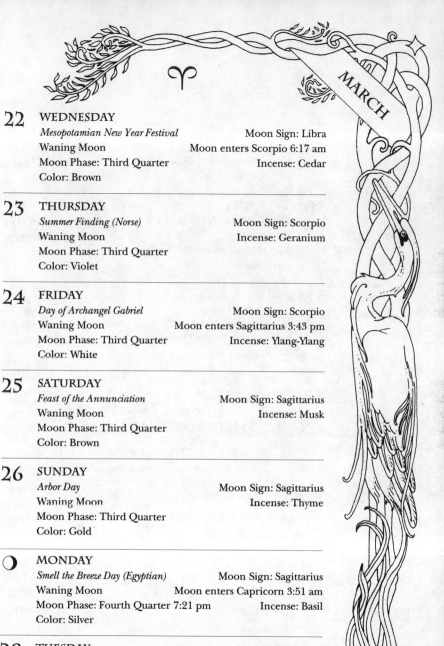

22 WEDNESDAY
Mesopotamian New Year Festival   Moon Sign: Libra
Waning Moon   Moon enters Scorpio 6:17 am
Moon Phase: Third Quarter   Incense: Cedar
Color: Brown

---

23 THURSDAY
Summer Finding (Norse)   Moon Sign: Scorpio
Waning Moon   Incense: Geranium
Moon Phase: Third Quarter
Color: Violet

---

24 FRIDAY
Day of Archangel Gabriel   Moon Sign: Scorpio
Waning Moon   Moon enters Sagittarius 3:43 pm
Moon Phase: Third Quarter   Incense: Ylang-Ylang
Color: White

---

25 SATURDAY
Feast of the Annunciation   Moon Sign: Sagittarius
Waning Moon   Incense: Musk
Moon Phase: Third Quarter
Color: Brown

---

26 SUNDAY
Arbor Day   Moon Sign: Sagittarius
Waning Moon   Incense: Thyme
Moon Phase: Third Quarter
Color: Gold

◖ MONDAY
Smell the Breeze Day (Egyptian)   Moon Sign: Sagittarius
Waning Moon   Moon enters Capricorn 3:51 am
Moon Phase: Fourth Quarter 7:21 pm   Incense: Basil
Color: Silver

---

28 TUESDAY
Wapynshaws of Scotland   Moon Sign: Capricorn
Waning Moon   Incense: Sage
Moon Phase: Fourth Quarter
Color: Red

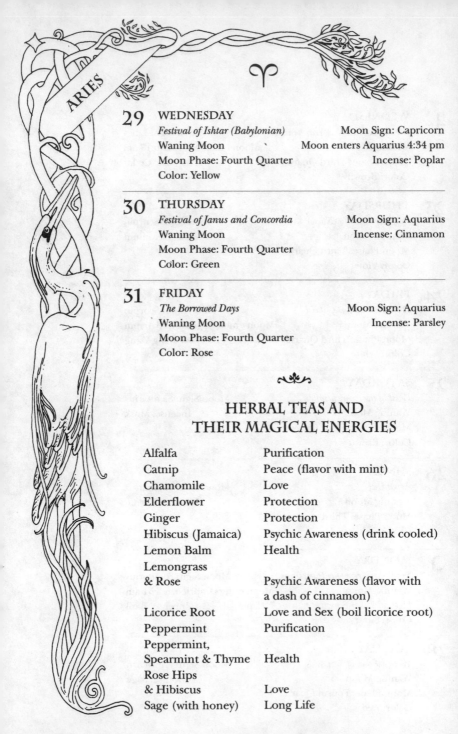

♈

29 WEDNESDAY
Festival of Ishtar (Babylonian)   Moon Sign: Capricorn
Waning Moon   Moon enters Aquarius 4:34 pm
Moon Phase: Fourth Quarter   Incense: Poplar
Color: Yellow

30 THURSDAY
Festival of Janus and Concordia   Moon Sign: Aquarius
Waning Moon   Incense: Cinnamon
Moon Phase: Fourth Quarter
Color: Green

31 FRIDAY
The Borrowed Days   Moon Sign: Aquarius
Waning Moon   Incense: Parsley
Moon Phase: Fourth Quarter
Color: Rose

HERBAL TEAS AND THEIR MAGICAL ENERGIES

Alfalfa	Purification
Catnip	Peace (flavor with mint)
Chamomile	Love
Elderflower	Protection
Ginger	Protection
Hibiscus (Jamaica)	Psychic Awareness (drink cooled)
Lemon Balm	Health
Lemongrass & Rose	Psychic Awareness (flavor with a dash of cinnamon)
Licorice Root	Love and Sex (boil licorice root)
Peppermint	Purification
Peppermint, Spearmint & Thyme	Health
Rose Hips & Hibiscus	Love
Sage (with honey)	Long Life

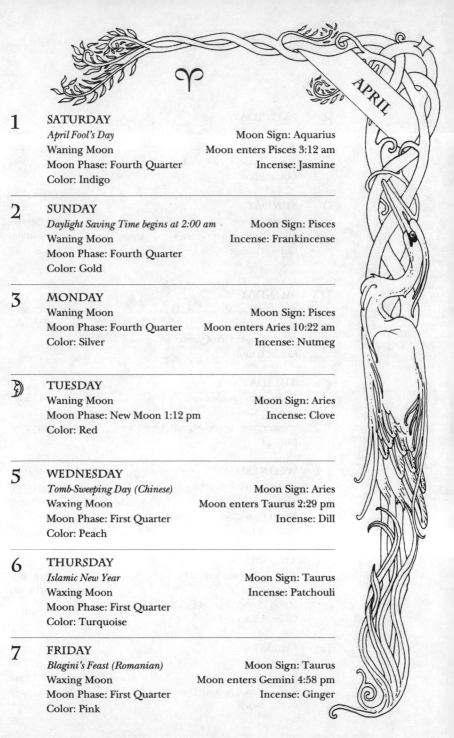

1 SATURDAY
April Fool's Day   Moon Sign: Aquarius
Waning Moon   Moon enters Pisces 3:12 am
Moon Phase: Fourth Quarter   Incense: Jasmine
Color: Indigo

2 SUNDAY
Daylight Saving Time begins at 2:00 am   Moon Sign: Pisces
Waning Moon   Incense: Frankincense
Moon Phase: Fourth Quarter
Color: Gold

3 MONDAY
Waning Moon   Moon Sign: Pisces
Moon Phase: Fourth Quarter   Moon enters Aries 10:22 am
Color: Silver   Incense: Nutmeg

4 TUESDAY
Waning Moon   Moon Sign: Aries
Moon Phase: New Moon 1:12 pm   Incense: Clove
Color: Red

5 WEDNESDAY
Tomb-Sweeping Day (Chinese)   Moon Sign: Aries
Waxing Moon   Moon enters Taurus 2:29 pm
Moon Phase: First Quarter   Incense: Dill
Color: Peach

6 THURSDAY
Islamic New Year   Moon Sign: Taurus
Waxing Moon   Incense: Patchouli
Moon Phase: First Quarter
Color: Turquoise

7 FRIDAY
Blagini's Feast (Romanian)   Moon Sign: Taurus
Waxing Moon   Moon enters Gemini 4:58 pm
Moon Phase: First Quarter   Incense: Ginger
Color: Pink

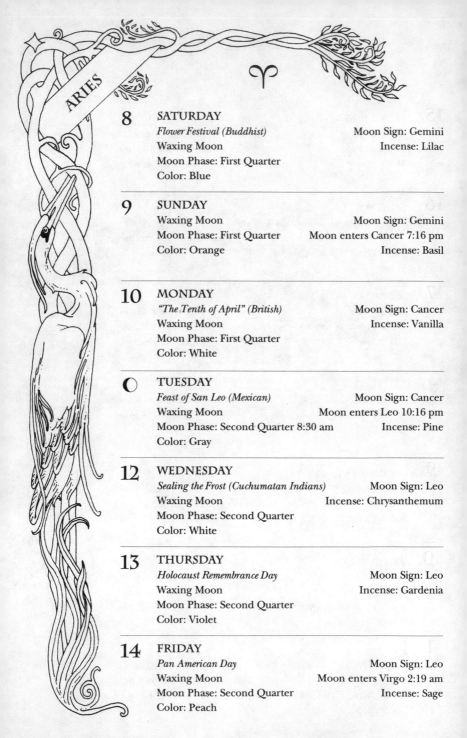

♈

8 **SATURDAY**
Flower Festival (Buddhist)   Moon Sign: Gemini
Waxing Moon   Incense: Lilac
Moon Phase: First Quarter
Color: Blue

9 **SUNDAY**
Waxing Moon   Moon Sign: Gemini
Moon Phase: First Quarter   Moon enters Cancer 7:16 pm
Color: Orange   Incense: Basil

10 **MONDAY**
"The Tenth of April" (British)   Moon Sign: Cancer
Waxing Moon   Incense: Vanilla
Moon Phase: First Quarter
Color: White

☾ **TUESDAY**
Feast of San Leo (Mexican)   Moon Sign: Cancer
Waxing Moon   Moon enters Leo 10:16 pm
Moon Phase: Second Quarter 8:30 am   Incense: Pine
Color: Gray

12 **WEDNESDAY**
Sealing the Frost (Cuchumatan Indians)   Moon Sign: Leo
Waxing Moon   Incense: Chrysanthemum
Moon Phase: Second Quarter
Color: White

13 **THURSDAY**
Holocaust Remembrance Day   Moon Sign: Leo
Waxing Moon   Incense: Gardenia
Moon Phase: Second Quarter
Color: Violet

14 **FRIDAY**
Pan American Day   Moon Sign: Leo
Waxing Moon   Moon enters Virgo 2:19 am
Moon Phase: Second Quarter   Incense: Sage
Color: Peach

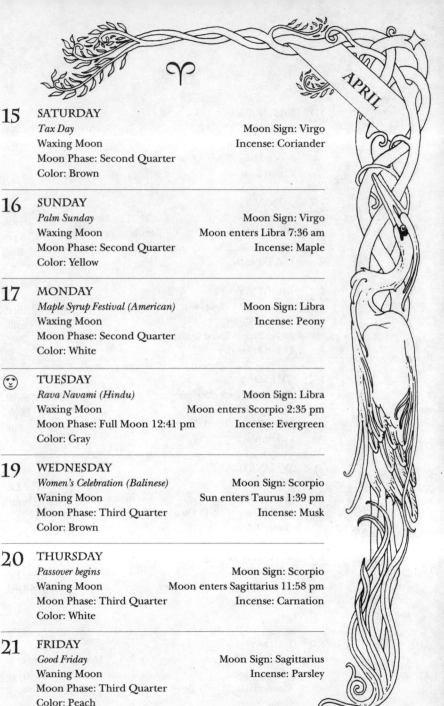

15 SATURDAY
Tax Day   Moon Sign: Virgo
Waxing Moon   Incense: Coriander
Moon Phase: Second Quarter
Color: Brown

16 SUNDAY
Palm Sunday   Moon Sign: Virgo
Waxing Moon   Moon enters Libra 7:36 am
Moon Phase: Second Quarter   Incense: Maple
Color: Yellow

17 MONDAY
Maple Syrup Festival (American)   Moon Sign: Libra
Waxing Moon   Incense: Peony
Moon Phase: Second Quarter
Color: White

18 TUESDAY
Rava Navami (Hindu)   Moon Sign: Libra
Waxing Moon   Moon enters Scorpio 2:35 pm
Moon Phase: Full Moon 12:41 pm   Incense: Evergreen
Color: Gray

19 WEDNESDAY
Women's Celebration (Balinese)   Moon Sign: Scorpio
Waning Moon   Sun enters Taurus 1:39 pm
Moon Phase: Third Quarter   Incense: Musk
Color: Brown

20 THURSDAY
Passover begins   Moon Sign: Scorpio
Waning Moon   Moon enters Sagittarius 11:58 pm
Moon Phase: Third Quarter   Incense: Carnation
Color: White

21 FRIDAY
Good Friday   Moon Sign: Sagittarius
Waning Moon   Incense: Parsley
Moon Phase: Third Quarter
Color: Peach

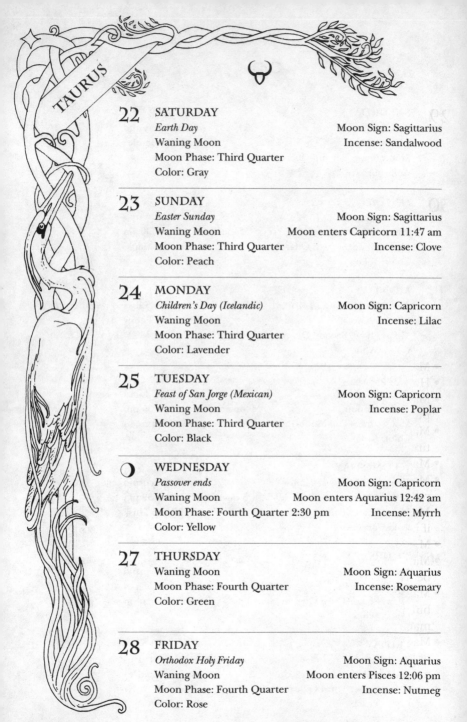

22 SATURDAY
Earth Day   Moon Sign: Sagittarius
Waning Moon   Incense: Sandalwood
Moon Phase: Third Quarter
Color: Gray

23 SUNDAY
Easter Sunday   Moon Sign: Sagittarius
Waning Moon   Moon enters Capricorn 11:47 am
Moon Phase: Third Quarter   Incense: Clove
Color: Peach

24 MONDAY
Children's Day (Icelandic)   Moon Sign: Capricorn
Waning Moon   Incense: Lilac
Moon Phase: Third Quarter
Color: Lavender

25 TUESDAY
Feast of San Jorge (Mexican)   Moon Sign: Capricorn
Waning Moon   Incense: Poplar
Moon Phase: Third Quarter
Color: Black

○ WEDNESDAY
Passover ends   Moon Sign: Capricorn
Waning Moon   Moon enters Aquarius 12:42 am
Moon Phase: Fourth Quarter 2:30 pm   Incense: Myrrh
Color: Yellow

27 THURSDAY
Waning Moon   Moon Sign: Aquarius
Moon Phase: Fourth Quarter   Incense: Rosemary
Color: Green

28 FRIDAY
Orthodox Holy Friday   Moon Sign: Aquarius
Waning Moon   Moon enters Pisces 12:06 pm
Moon Phase: Fourth Quarter   Incense: Nutmeg
Color: Rose

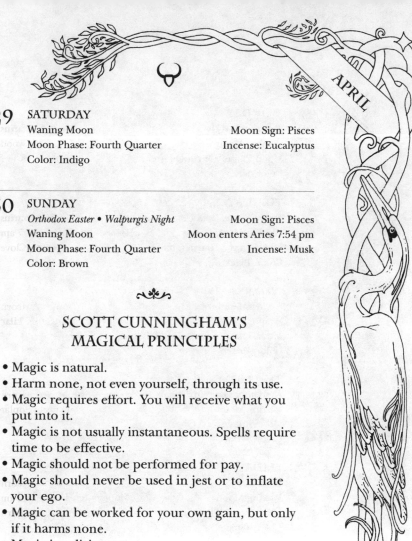

29 SATURDAY

Waning Moon
Moon Phase: Fourth Quarter
Color: Indigo

Moon Sign: Pisces
Incense: Eucalyptus

30 SUNDAY

Orthodox Easter • Walpurgis Night
Waning Moon
Moon Phase: Fourth Quarter
Color: Brown

Moon Sign: Pisces
Moon enters Aries 7:54 pm
Incense: Musk

SCOTT CUNNINGHAM'S MAGICAL PRINCIPLES

- Magic is natural.
- Harm none, not even yourself, through its use.
- Magic requires effort. You will receive what you put into it.
- Magic is not usually instantaneous. Spells require time to be effective.
- Magic should not be performed for pay.
- Magic should never be used in jest or to inflate your ego.
- Magic can be worked for your own gain, but only if it harms none.
- Magic is a divine act.
- Magic can be used for defense but should never be used for attack.
- Magic is knowledge — not only of its way and laws, but also of its effectiveness. Do not believe that magic works — know it!
- Magic is love. All magic should be performed out of love. The moment anger or hatred tinges your magic you have crossed the border into a dangerous world, one that will ultimately consume you.

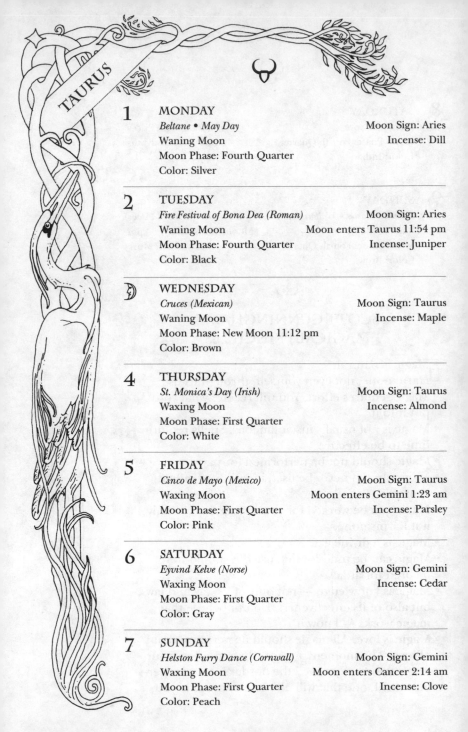

1 MONDAY
Beltane • May Day
Waning Moon
Moon Phase: Fourth Quarter
Color: Silver

Moon Sign: Aries
Incense: Dill

2 TUESDAY
Fire Festival of Bona Dea (Roman)
Waning Moon
Moon Phase: Fourth Quarter
Color: Black

Moon Sign: Aries
Moon enters Taurus 11:54 pm
Incense: Juniper

☽ WEDNESDAY
Cruces (Mexican)
Waning Moon
Moon Phase: New Moon 11:12 pm
Color: Brown

Moon Sign: Taurus
Incense: Maple

4 THURSDAY
St. Monica's Day (Irish)
Waxing Moon
Moon Phase: First Quarter
Color: White

Moon Sign: Taurus
Incense: Almond

5 FRIDAY
Cinco de Mayo (Mexico)
Waxing Moon
Moon Phase: First Quarter
Color: Pink

Moon Sign: Taurus
Moon enters Gemini 1:23 am
Incense: Parsley

6 SATURDAY
Eyvind Kelve (Norse)
Waxing Moon
Moon Phase: First Quarter
Color: Gray

Moon Sign: Gemini
Incense: Cedar

7 SUNDAY
Helston Furry Dance (Cornwall)
Waxing Moon
Moon Phase: First Quarter
Color: Peach

Moon Sign: Gemini
Moon enters Cancer 2:14 am
Incense: Clove

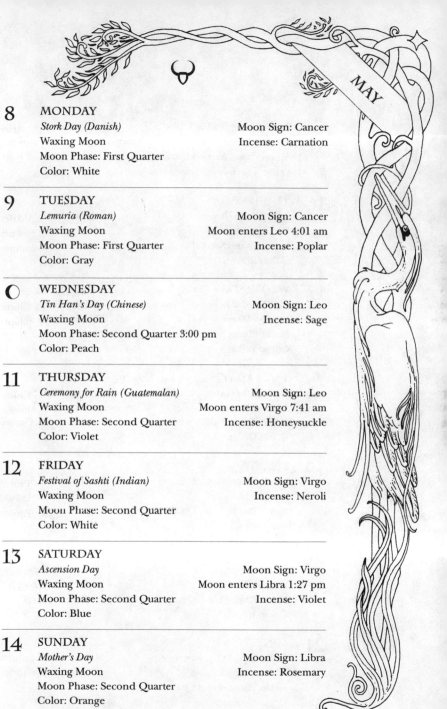

8 MONDAY
Stork Day (Danish)
Waxing Moon
Moon Phase: First Quarter
Color: White

Moon Sign: Cancer
Incense: Carnation

9 TUESDAY
Lemuria (Roman)
Waxing Moon
Moon Phase: First Quarter
Color: Gray

Moon Sign: Cancer
Moon enters Leo 4:01 am
Incense: Poplar

WEDNESDAY
Tin Han's Day (Chinese)
Waxing Moon
Moon Phase: Second Quarter 3:00 pm
Color: Peach

Moon Sign: Leo
Incense: Sage

11 THURSDAY
Ceremony for Rain (Guatemalan)
Waxing Moon
Moon Phase: Second Quarter
Color: Violet

Moon Sign: Leo
Moon enters Virgo 7:41 am
Incense: Honeysuckle

12 FRIDAY
Festival of Sashti (Indian)
Waxing Moon
Moon Phase: Second Quarter
Color: White

Moon Sign: Virgo
Incense: Neroli

13 SATURDAY
Ascension Day
Waxing Moon
Moon Phase: Second Quarter
Color: Blue

Moon Sign: Virgo
Moon enters Libra 1:27 pm
Incense: Violet

14 SUNDAY
Mother's Day
Waxing Moon
Moon Phase: Second Quarter
Color: Orange

Moon Sign: Libra
Incense: Rosemary

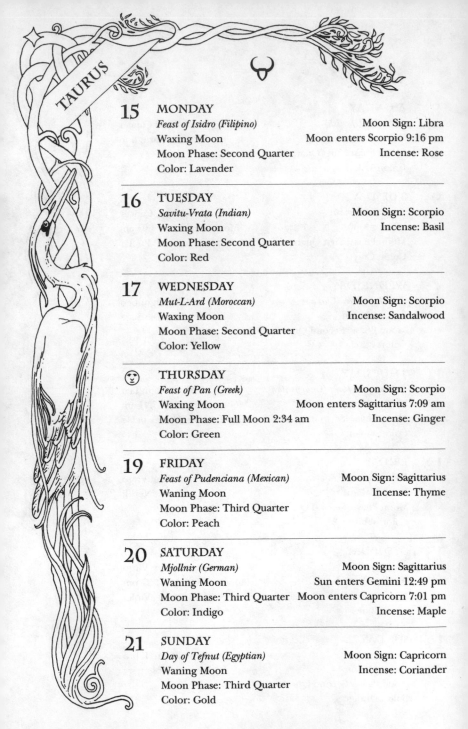

TAURUS

15 MONDAY
Feast of Isidro (Filipino)
Waxing Moon
Moon Phase: Second Quarter
Color: Lavender

Moon Sign: Libra
Moon enters Scorpio 9:16 pm
Incense: Rose

16 TUESDAY
Savitu-Vrata (Indian)
Waxing Moon
Moon Phase: Second Quarter
Color: Red

Moon Sign: Scorpio
Incense: Basil

17 WEDNESDAY
Mut-L-Ard (Moroccan)
Waxing Moon
Moon Phase: Second Quarter
Color: Yellow

Moon Sign: Scorpio
Incense: Sandalwood

THURSDAY
Feast of Pan (Greek)
Waxing Moon
Moon Phase: Full Moon 2:34 am
Color: Green

Moon Sign: Scorpio
Moon enters Sagittarius 7:09 am
Incense: Ginger

19 FRIDAY
Feast of Pudenciana (Mexican)
Waning Moon
Moon Phase: Third Quarter
Color: Peach

Moon Sign: Sagittarius
Incense: Thyme

20 SATURDAY
Mjollnir (German)
Waning Moon
Moon Phase: Third Quarter
Color: Indigo

Moon Sign: Sagittarius
Sun enters Gemini 12:49 pm
Moon enters Capricorn 7:01 pm
Incense: Maple

21 SUNDAY
Day of Tefnut (Egyptian)
Waning Moon
Moon Phase: Third Quarter
Color: Gold

Moon Sign: Capricorn
Incense: Coriander

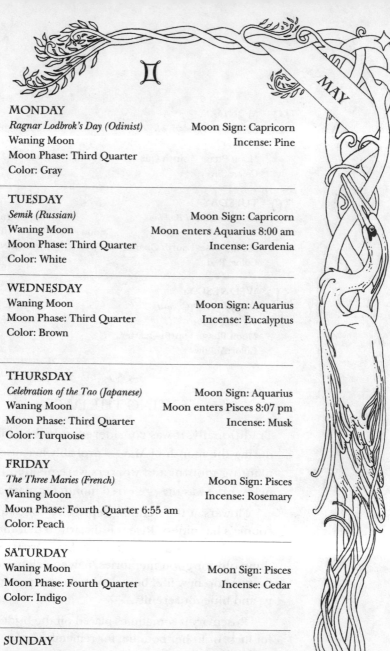

22 MONDAY
Ragnar Lodbrok's Day (Odinist)
Waning Moon
Moon Phase: Third Quarter
Color: Gray

Moon Sign: Capricorn
Incense: Pine

23 TUESDAY
Semik (Russian)
Waning Moon
Moon Phase: Third Quarter
Color: White

Moon Sign: Capricorn
Moon enters Aquarius 8:00 am
Incense: Gardenia

24 WEDNESDAY
Waning Moon
Moon Phase: Third Quarter
Color: Brown

Moon Sign: Aquarius
Incense: Eucalyptus

25 THURSDAY
Celebration of the Tao (Japanese)
Waning Moon
Moon Phase: Third Quarter
Color: Turquoise

Moon Sign: Aquarius
Moon enters Pisces 8:07 pm
Incense: Musk

○ FRIDAY
The Three Maries (French)
Waning Moon
Moon Phase: Fourth Quarter 6:55 am
Color: Peach

Moon Sign: Pisces
Incense: Rosemary

27 SATURDAY
Waning Moon
Moon Phase: Fourth Quarter
Color: Indigo

Moon Sign: Pisces
Incense: Cedar

28 SUNDAY
Holy Well (British)
Waning Moon
Moon Phase: Fourth Quarter
Color: Peach

Moon Sign: Pisces
Moon enters Aries 5:08 am
Incense: Basil

♊

29 MONDAY
Memorial Day (observed)
Waning Moon
Moon Phase: Fourth Quarter
Color: Silver

Moon Sign: Aries
Incense: Ginger

30 TUESDAY
Enlightenment of Buddha
Waning Moon
Moon Phase: Fourth Quarter
Color: Red

Moon Sign: Aries
Moon enters Taurus 10:02 am
Incense: Nutmeg

31 WEDNESDAY
Day of Oggum (Cuban)
Waning Moon
Moon Phase: Fourth Quarter
Color: Yellow

Moon Sign: Taurus
Incense: Clove

❧

SETTING THE DATE

Traditionally, it was considered unlucky to marry during the month of May — probably because it's a planting month, and workers were needed in the fields. June was the preferred month for marriage.

Flowers at the wedding represent wishes for the couple's happiness. Rice was thrown so that the couple would never go hungry. The bride wears something old for good memories, new to celebrate new friends and new life, borrowed to encourage frugality, and blue for serenity.

Rosemary is sometimes placed on the bride's bed for luck, or in her bouquet for remembrance.

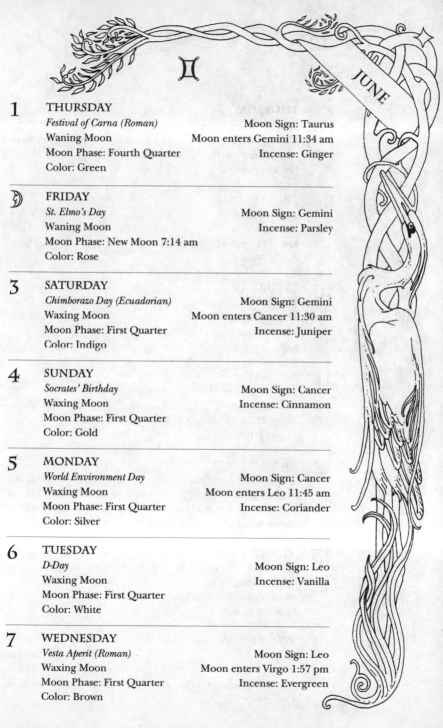

♊

1 THURSDAY
Festival of Carna (Roman)
Waning Moon
Moon Phase: Fourth Quarter
Color: Green

Moon Sign: Taurus
Moon enters Gemini 11:34 am
Incense: Ginger

☽ **2 FRIDAY**
St. Elmo's Day
Waning Moon
Moon Phase: New Moon 7:14 am
Color: Rose

Moon Sign: Gemini
Incense: Parsley

3 SATURDAY
Chimborazo Day (Ecuadorian)
Waxing Moon
Moon Phase: First Quarter
Color: Indigo

Moon Sign: Gemini
Moon enters Cancer 11:30 am
Incense: Juniper

4 SUNDAY
Socrates' Birthday
Waxing Moon
Moon Phase: First Quarter
Color: Gold

Moon Sign: Cancer
Incense: Cinnamon

5 MONDAY
World Environment Day
Waxing Moon
Moon Phase: First Quarter
Color: Silver

Moon Sign: Cancer
Moon enters Leo 11:45 am
Incense: Coriander

6 TUESDAY
D-Day
Waxing Moon
Moon Phase: First Quarter
Color: White

Moon Sign: Leo
Incense: Vanilla

7 WEDNESDAY
Vesta Aperit (Roman)
Waxing Moon
Moon Phase: First Quarter
Color: Brown

Moon Sign: Leo
Moon enters Virgo 1:57 pm
Incense: Evergreen

GEMINI

♊

☽ THURSDAY
Lindisfarne Day (Odinist) Moon Sign: Virgo
Waxing Moon Incense: Patchouli
Moon Phase: Second Quarter 10:29 pm
Color: Turquoise

9 FRIDAY
Shavuot Moon Sign: Virgo
Waxing Moon Moon enters Libra 6:58 pm
Moon Phase: Second Quarter Incense: Sage
Color: Pink

10 SATURDAY
Day of Anahita (Persian) Moon Sign: Libra
Waxing Moon Incense: Lilac
Moon Phase: Second Quarter
Color: Blue

11 SUNDAY
King Kamehameha I Day (Hawaiian) Moon Sign: Libra
Waxing Moon Incense: Maple
Moon Phase: Second Quarter
Color: Yellow

12 MONDAY
Riding the Marches (Scottish) Moon Sign: Libra
Waxing Moon Moon enters Scorpio 2:55 am
Moon Phase: Second Quarter Incense: Lavender
Color: White

13 TUESDAY
Tibetan All Souls' Day Moon Sign: Scorpio
Waxing Moon Incense: Pine
Moon Phase: Second Quarter
Color: Gray

14 WEDNESDAY
Flag Day Moon Sign: Scorpio
Waxing Moon Moon enters Sagittarius 1:18 pm
Moon Phase: Second Quarter Incense: Basil
Color: Peach

JUNE

♊

15 THURSDAY
St. Vitus' Day   Moon Sign: Sagittarius
Waxing Moon   Incense: Rose
Moon Phase: Second Quarter
Color: White

☻ FRIDAY
Night of the Drop (Egyptian)   Moon Sign: Sagittarius
Waxing Moon   Incense: Rosemary
Moon Phase: Full Moon 5:27 pm
Color: Peach

17 SATURDAY
Ludi Piscatari (Roman)   Moon Sign: Sagittarius
Waning Moon   Moon enters Capricorn 1:26 am
Moon Phase: Third Quarter   Incense: Eucalyptus
Color: Gray

18 SUNDAY
Father's Day   Moon Sign: Capricorn
Waning Moon   Incense: Nutmeg
Moon Phase: Third Quarter
Color: Orange

19 MONDAY
Waa-Laa begins (Native American)   Moon Sign: Capricorn
Waning Moon   Moon enters Aquarius 2:26 pm
Moon Phase: Third Quarter   Incense: Myrrh
Color: Gray

20 TUESDAY
Litha • Summer Solstice   Moon Sign: Aquarius
Waning Moon   Sun enters Cancer 8:48 pm
Moon Phase: Third Quarter   Incense: Poplar
Color: Black

21 WEDNESDAY
Feast of the King's Daughter (Egyptian)   Moon Sign: Aquarius
Waning Moon   Incense: Honeysuckle
Moon Phase: Third Quarter
Color: White

CANCER ♋

22 **THURSDAY**
Feast of San Aloisio (Mexican)   Moon Sign: Aquarius
Waning Moon   Moon enters Pisces 2:52 am
Moon Phase: Third Quarter   Incense: Jasmine
Color: Violet

---

23 **FRIDAY**
St. John's Eve   Moon Sign: Pisces
Waning Moon   Incense: Ylang-Ylang
Moon Phase: Third Quarter
Color: White

○ **SATURDAY**
Aztec Feast of the Sun   Moon Sign: Pisces
Waning Moon   Moon enters Aries 12:55 pm
Moon Phase: Fourth Quarter 8:00 pm   Incense: Pine
Color: Brown

---

25 **SUNDAY**
Well-Dressing Festival (British)   Moon Sign: Aries
Waning Moon   Incense: Parsley
Moon Phase: Fourth Quarter
Color: Peach

---

26 **MONDAY**
Green Corn Festival (Iroquois)   Moon Sign: Aries
Waning Moon   Moon enters Taurus 7:19 pm
Moon Phase: Fourth Quarter   Incense: Clove
Color: Silver

---

27 **TUESDAY**
Day of Seven Sleepers (Muslim)   Moon Sign: Taurus
Waning Moon   Incense: Ginger
Moon Phase: Fourth Quarter
Color: Red

---

28 **WEDNESDAY**
Festival of the Tarasque (French)   Moon Sign: Taurus
Waning Moon   Moon enters Gemini 9:59 pm
Moon Phase: Fourth Quarter   Incense: Dill
Color: Yellow

29 THURSDAY

Feast of Ogun (Santerian)
Waning Moon
Moon Phase: Fourth Quarter
Color: Green

Moon Sign: Gemini
Incense: Sage

30 FRIDAY

The Burning of the Three Firs (French)
Waning Moon
Moon Phase: Fourth Quarter
Color: Rose

Moon Sign: Gemini
Moon enters Cancer 10:09 pm
Incense: Sandalwood

∽✤∾

HIGH TIDES

The Norse, a seafaring race, were especially attuned to the time of day when the tide came in, and they attributed great significance to its arrival.

- Morning tides represented awakenings, fertility, and life.
- Day tides brought gentility, growth, and finances.
- A tide during midday represented sustenance, willpower, and perseverance.
- A tide before dusk offered change, perceptiveness, and parenting.
- An evening tide represented joy, spirituality, pregnancy, and children.
- A night tide meant creativity, deeper knowledge, and enlightenment.
- A tide at midnight meant recuperation.

CANCER ♋

☽ **SATURDAY**
Solar Eclipse • Canada Day　　　　Moon Sign: Cancer
Waning Moon　　　　　　　　　　　Incense: Juniper
Moon Phase: New Moon 2:20 pm
Color: Gray

2 **SUNDAY**
Feast of Expectant Mothers (European)　　Moon Sign: Cancer
Waxing Moon　　　　　　　Moon enters Leo 9:38 pm
Moon Phase: First Quarter　　　　Incense: Coriander
Color: Gold

3 **MONDAY**
Sothis (Egyptian)　　　　　　　Moon Sign: Leo
Waxing Moon　　　　　　　　　Incense: Clove
Moon Phase: First Quarter
Color: Silver

4 **TUESDAY**
Independence Day　　　　　　　Moon Sign: Leo
Waxing Moon　　　　　Moon enters Virgo 10:19 pm
Moon Phase: First Quarter　　　　Incense: Ginger
Color: Red

5 **WEDNESDAY**
Old Midsummer's Day　　　　　Moon Sign: Virgo
Waxing Moon　　　　　　　　Incense: Rosemary
Moon Phase: First Quarter
Color: Peach

6 **THURSDAY**
Feast of Julian the Blessed　　　Moon Sign: Virgo
Waxing Moon　　　　　　　　　Incense: Musk
Moon Phase: First Quarter
Color: Turquoise

7 **FRIDAY**
Tanabata (Japanese)　　　　　　Moon Sign: Virgo
Waxing Moon　　　　　Moon enters Libra 1:47 am
Moon Phase: First Quarter　　　　Incense: Thyme
Color: Pink

SATURDAY ☽
St. Sunniva's Day
Waxing Moon
Moon Phase: Second Quarter 7:53 am
Color: Blue

Moon Sign: Libra
Incense: Lilac

---

9 SUNDAY
Martyrdom of the Bab (Baha'i)
Waxing Moon
Moon Phase: Second Quarter
Color: Orange

Moon Sign: Libra
Moon enters Scorpio 8:48 am
Incense: Coriander

---

10 MONDAY
Lady Godiva Day (English)
Waxing Moon
Moon Phase: Second Quarter
Color: White

Moon Sign: Scorpio
Incense: Neroli

---

11 TUESDAY
Naadam Festival (Mongolian)
Waxing Moon
Moon Phase: Second Quarter
Color: Black

Moon Sign: Scorpio
Moon enters Sagittarius 7:06 pm
Incense: Evergreen

---

12 WEDNESDAY
Lobster Carnival (Nova Scotian)
Waxing Moon
Moon Phase: Second Quarter
Color: White

Moon Sign: Sagittarius
Incense: Almond

---

13 THURSDAY
Reed Dance Day (African)
Waxing Moon
Moon Phase: Second Quarter
Color: Violet

Moon Sign: Sagittarius
Incense: Carnation

---

14 FRIDAY
Bastille Day (French)
Waxing Moon
Moon Phase: Second Quarter
Color: Peach

Moon Sign: Sagittarius
Moon enters Capricorn 7:27 am
Incense: Dill

CANCER ♋

15 SATURDAY
Day of Rauni (Finnish) Moon Sign: Capricorn
Waxing Moon Incense: Cedar
Moon Phase: Second Quarter
Color: Gray

☺ SUNDAY
Lunar Eclipse • Rosa Mundi (Palestinian) Moon Sign: Capricorn
Waxing Moon Moon enters Aquarius 8:27 pm
Moon Phase: Full Moon 8:55 am Incense: Basil
Color: Yellow

17 MONDAY
Festival of Ama-terasu-O-Mi-Kami (Japanese)
Waning Moon Moon Sign: Aquarius
Moon Phase: Third Quarter Incense: Peony
Color: Lavender

18 TUESDAY
Birthday of Nephthys (Egyptian) Moon Sign: Aquarius
Waning Moon Incense: Juniper
Moon Phase: Third Quarter
Color: Gray

19 WEDNESDAY
Wedding of Adonis and Aphrodite (Greek) Moon Sign: Aquarius
Waning Moon Moon enters Pisces 8:44 am
Moon Phase: Third Quarter Incense: Frankincense
Color: Brown

20 THURSDAY
Binding of Wreaths (Lithuanian) Moon Sign: Pisces
Waning Moon Incense: Geranium
Moon Phase: Third Quarter
Color: White

21 FRIDAY
Damo's Day (Greek) Moon Sign: Pisces
Waning Moon Moon enters Aries 7:09 pm
Moon Phase: Third Quarter Incense: Parsley
Color: Rose

22 SATURDAY
St. Mary Magdalene's Birthday
Waning Moon
Moon Phase: Third Quarter
Color: Brown

Moon Sign: Aries
Sun enters Leo 7:43 am
Incense: Patchouli

23 SUNDAY
Neptunalia
Waning Moon
Moon Phase: Third Quarter
Color: Peach

Moon Sign: Aries
Incense: Sage

○ MONDAY
Fete of St. Eloi (French)
Waning Moon
Moon Phase: Fourth Quarter 6:02 am
Color: Gray

Moon Sign: Aries
Moon enters Taurus 2:44 am
Incense: Musk

25 TUESDAY
Feast of Salacia (Roman)
Waning Moon
Moon Phase: Fourth Quarter
Color: White

Moon Sign: Taurus
Incense: Lavender

26 WEDNESDAY
Sleipnir (Odinist)
Waning Moon
Moon Phase: Fourth Quarter
Color: Yellow

Moon Sign: Taurus
Moon enters Gemini 7:01 am
Incense: Pine

27 THURSDAY
Hatshepsut's Day (Egyptian)
Waning Moon
Moon Phase: Fourth Quarter
Color: Green

Moon Sign: Gemini
Incense: Rosemary

28 FRIDAY
Pythias' Day (Greek)
Waning Moon
Moon Phase: Fourth Quarter
Color: White

Moon Sign: Gemini
Moon enters Cancer 8:30 am
Incense: Rose

LEO ♌

29 SATURDAY
Feast of Santa Maria (Mexican)
Waning Moon
Moon Phase: Fourth Quarter
Color: Indigo

Moon Sign: Cancer
Incense: Maple

☽ **SUNDAY**
Solar Eclipse
Waning Moon
Moon Phase: New Moon 9:25 pm
Color: Gold

Moon Sign: Cancer
Moon enters Leo 8:23 am
Incense: Cinnamon

31 MONDAY
Day of Loki and Sigyn (Odinist)
Waxing Moon
Moon Phase: First Quarter
Color: Silver

Moon Sign: Leo
Incense: Dill

MONTH BIRTHSTONE FLOWERS

Month	Birthstone	Flowers
January	*Garnet*	*Carnations, Snowdrops*
February	*Amethyst*	*Violets, Primroses*
March	*Bloodstone*	*Daffodils, Jonquils*
April	*Diamond*	*Daisies, Sweet Peas*
May	*Emerald*	*Lilies of the Valley, Hawthorn*
June	*Pearl*	*Roses, Honeysuckle*
July	*Ruby*	*Water Lilies, Larkspur*
August	*Peridot*	*Gladiolus, Poppies*
September	*Sapphire*	*Morning Glories, Asters*
October	*Opal*	*Calendula, Cosmos*
November	*Topaz*	*Chrysanthemums, Dahlias*
December	*Turquoise*	*Narcissus, Holly*

ᒕ

1 TUESDAY
Lammas　　　　　　　　　　　　Moon Sign: Leo
Waxing Moon　　　　　　　Moon enters Virgo 8:27 am
Moon Phase: First Quarter　　　　Incense: Coriander
Color: Red

2 WEDNESDAY
Feast of Our Lady of Angels (Central American)　Moon Sign: Virgo
Waxing Moon　　　　　　　　　　Incense: Basil
Moon Phase: First Quarter
Color: Yellow

3 THURSDAY
Asheville Mountain Festival (American)　　Moon Sign: Virgo
Waxing Moon　　　　　　Moon enters Libra 10:31 am
Moon Phase: First Quarter　　　　Incense: Evergreen
Color: Turquoise

4 FRIDAY
Feast of the Blessed Virgin Mary　　　Moon Sign: Libra
Waxing Moon　　　　　　　　　　Incense: Nutmeg
Moon Phase: First Quarter
Color: Peach

5 SATURDAY
St. Oswald's Day　　　　　　　Moon Sign: Libra
Waxing Moon　　　　　　Moon enters Scorpio 4:04 pm
Moon Phase: First Quarter　　　　Incense: Violet
Color: Blue

☾ **SUNDAY**
Tan Hill Festival (Celtic)　　　　Moon Sign: Scorpio
Waxing Moon　　　　　　　　　　Incense: Poplar
Moon Phase: Second Quarter 8:02 pm
Color: Yellow

7 MONDAY
Breaking of the Nile (Egyptian)　　Moon Sign: Scorpio
Waxing Moon　　　　　　　　　　Incense: Lilac
Moon Phase: Second Quarter
Color: Lavender

LEO

8 TUESDAY
Tij Day (Nepalese)
Waxing Moon
Moon Phase: Second Quarter
Color: White

Moon Sign: Scorpio
Moon enters Sagittarius 1:30 am
Incense: Gardenia

9 WEDNESDAY
Milky Way Festival (Chinese)
Waxing Moon
Moon Phase: Second Quarter
Color: Peach

Moon Sign: Sagittarius
Incense: Thyme

10 THURSDAY
St. Lawrence's Day
Waxing Moon
Moon Phase: Second Quarter
Color: White

Moon Sign: Sagittarius
Moon enters Capricorn 1:44 pm
Incense: Chrysanthemum

11 FRIDAY
Puck Fair (Irish)
Waxing Moon
Moon Phase: Second Quarter
Color: Rose

Moon Sign: Capricorn
Incense: Clove

12 SATURDAY
Lights of Isis (Egyptian)
Waxing Moon
Moon Phase: Second Quarter
Color: Gray

Moon Sign: Capricorn
Incense: Juniper

13 SUNDAY
Hecate's Day (Greek)
Waxing Moon
Moon Phase: Second Quarter
Color: Orange

Moon Sign: Capricorn
Moon enters Aquarius 2:43 am
Incense: Parsley

14 MONDAY
Fieschi's Cake Day (Italian)
Waxing Moon
Moon Phase: Second Quarter
Color: White

Moon Sign: Aquarius
Incense: Jasmine

TUESDAY
Assumption Day
Waxing Moon
Moon Phase: Full Moon 12:13 am
Color: Gray

Moon Sign: Aquarius
Moon enters Pisces 2:41 pm
Incense: Cedar

---

16 WEDNESDAY
Festival of Minstrels (European)
Waning Moon
Moon Phase: Third Quarter
Color: White

Moon Sign: Pisces
Incense: Rose

---

17 THURSDAY
Amenartus (Egyptian)
Waning Moon
Moon Phase: Third Quarter
Color: Violet

Moon Sign: Pisces
Incense: Vanilla

---

18 FRIDAY
Blessing of the Grapes (Armenian)
Waning Moon
Moon Phase: Third Quarter
Color: Pink

Moon Sign: Pisces
Moon enters Aries 12:44 am
Incense: Ginger

---

19 SATURDAY
Rustic Vinalia (Roman)
Waning Moon
Moon Phase: Third Quarter
Color: Brown

Moon Sign: Aries
Incense: Poplar

---

20 SUNDAY
Day of Inanna (Mesopotamian)
Waning Moon
Moon Phase: Third Quarter
Color: Gold

Moon Sign: Aries
Moon enters Taurus 8:31 am
Incense: Nutmeg

---

21 MONDAY
Odin's Ordeal
Waning Moon
Moon Phase: Third Quarter
Color: Silver

Moon Sign: Taurus
Incense: Myrrh

TUESDAY ☽
Aedesia's Day (Greek)
Waning Moon
Moon Phase: Fourth Quarter 1:51 pm
Color: Red

Moon Sign: Taurus
Moon enters Gemini 1:55 pm
Incense: Basil
Sun enters Virgo 2:48 pm

---

23 WEDNESDAY
Moira's Day (Greek)
Waning Moon
Moon Phase: Fourth Quarter
Color: Yellow

Moon Sign: Gemini
Incense: Maple

---

24 THURSDAY
St. Bartholomew's Day
Waning Moon
Moon Phase: Fourth Quarter
Color: Green

Moon Sign: Gemini
Moon enters Cancer 4:59 pm
Incense: Dill

---

25 FRIDAY
Paryushana Parva (Hindu)
Waning Moon
Moon Phase: Fourth Quarter
Color: Peach

Moon Sign: Cancer
Incense: Thyme

---

26 SATURDAY
Ilmatar's Day (Finnish)
Waning Moon
Moon Phase: Fourth Quarter
Color: Blue

Moon Sign: Cancer
Moon enters Leo 6:17 pm
Incense: Lavender

---

27 SUNDAY
Worship of Mother Goddess Devaki (East Indian)
Waning Moon
Moon Phase: Fourth Quarter
Color: Peach

Moon Sign: Leo
Incense: Sage

---

28 MONDAY
Nativity of Nephthys (Egyptian)
Waning Moon
Moon Phase: Fourth Quarter
Color: Gray

Moon Sign: Leo
Moon enters Virgo 6:55 pm
Incense: Eucalyptus

TUESDAY
Hathor's Day (Egyptian)
Waning Moon
Moon Phase: New Moon 5:19 am
Color: White

Moon Sign: Virgo
Incense: Honeysuckle

30 WEDNESDAY
St. Rose of Lima Day (Peruvian)
Waxing Moon
Moon Phase: First Quarter
Color: Peach

Moon Sign: Virgo
Moon enters Libra 8:33 pm
Incense: Rosemary

31 THURSDAY
Unto These Hills Pageant (Cherokee)
Waxing Moon
Moon Phase: First Quarter
Color: Turquoise

Moon Sign: Libra
Incense: Evergreen

THE FOURTEEN CONSTELLATIONS OF THE ZODIAC

Believe it or not, the Sun actually crosses through fourteen constellations — not twelve — in its annual trek past the stars.

Starting on the first day of spring, the Sun passes Pisces and Cetus, goes back through Pisces, and then crosses through Aries, Taurus, Gemini, Cancer, Leo, Virgo, Libra, Scorpius, Ophiuchus, Sagittarius, Capricornus, and Aquarius.

These fourteen constellations were designated by scientists in the eighteenth century and do not take any astrology into account at all; so, twelve astrological signs of the zodiac is correct for astrologers and fourteen constellations of the zodiac is correct for astronomers.

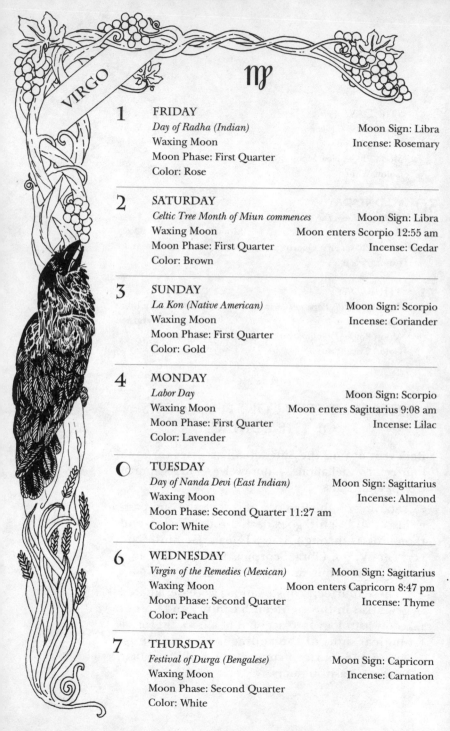

VIRGO ♍

1
FRIDAY
Day of Radha (Indian)
Waxing Moon
Moon Phase: First Quarter
Color: Rose

Moon Sign: Libra
Incense: Rosemary

2
SATURDAY
Celtic Tree Month of Miun commences
Waxing Moon
Moon Phase: First Quarter
Color: Brown

Moon Sign: Libra
Moon enters Scorpio 12:55 am
Incense: Cedar

3
SUNDAY
La Kon (Native American)
Waxing Moon
Moon Phase: First Quarter
Color: Gold

Moon Sign: Scorpio
Incense: Coriander

4
MONDAY
Labor Day
Waxing Moon
Moon Phase: First Quarter
Color: Lavender

Moon Sign: Scorpio
Moon enters Sagittarius 9:08 am
Incense: Lilac

☽ TUESDAY
Day of Nanda Devi (East Indian)
Waxing Moon
Moon Phase: Second Quarter 11:27 am
Color: White

Moon Sign: Sagittarius
Incense: Almond

6
WEDNESDAY
Virgin of the Remedies (Mexican)
Waxing Moon
Moon Phase: Second Quarter
Color: Peach

Moon Sign: Sagittarius
Moon enters Capricorn 8:47 pm
Incense: Thyme

7
THURSDAY
Festival of Durga (Bengalese)
Waxing Moon
Moon Phase: Second Quarter
Color: White

Moon Sign: Capricorn
Incense: Carnation

♍

8 FRIDAY
Pinnhut Festival (Native American)
Waxing Moon
Moon Phase: Second Quarter
Color: Pink
Moon Sign: Capricorn
Incense: Nutmeg

9 SATURDAY
Horned Dance at Abbots Bromley (English)
Waxing Moon
Moon Phase: Second Quarter
Color: Blue
Moon Sign: Capricorn
Moon enters Aquarius 9:44 am
Incense: Peony

10 SUNDAY
Festival of the Poets (Japanese)
Waxing Moon
Moon Phase: Second Quarter
Color: Orange
Moon Sign: Aquarius
Incense: Sage

11 MONDAY
Egyptian Day of Queens
Waxing Moon
Moon Phase: Second Quarter
Color: Gray
Moon Sign: Aquarius
Moon enters Pisces 9:34 pm
Incense: Poplar

12 TUESDAY
Astraea's Day (Greek)
Waxing Moon
Moon Phase: Second Quarter
Color: Red
Moon Sign: Pisces
Incense: Rosemary

☺ WEDNESDAY
Lectisternia (Roman)
Waxing Moon
Moon Phase: Full Moon 2:37 pm
Color: White
Moon Sign: Pisces
Incense: Geranium

14 THURSDAY
Feast of Lights (Egyptian)
Waning Moon
Moon Phase: Third Quarter
Color: Green
Moon Sign: Pisces
Moon enters Aries 7:00 am
Incense: Sandalwood

15 FRIDAY
Birthday of the Moon (Chinese) Moon Sign: Aries
Waning Moon Incense: Violet
Moon Phase: Third Quarter
Color: White

16 SATURDAY
St. Ninian's Day Moon Sign: Aries
Waning Moon Moon enters Taurus 2:05 pm
Moon Phase: Third Quarter Incense: Maple
Color: Gray

17 SUNDAY
Hildegard of Bingen's Day (German) Moon Sign: Taurus
Waning Moon Incense: Patchouli
Moon Phase: Third Quarter
Color: Yellow

18 MONDAY
Dividing the Cheese Festival (Swiss) Moon Sign: Taurus
Waning Moon Moon enters Gemini 7:22 pm
Moon Phase: Third Quarter Incense: Poplar
Color: Gray

19 TUESDAY
"The Scouring of the White Horse" (British) Moon Sign: Gemini
Waning Moon Incense: Neroli
Moon Phase: Third Quarter
Color: White

☽ WEDNESDAY
Birth of Quetzalcoatl (Aztec) Moon Sign: Gemini
Waning Moon Moon enters Cancer 11:16 pm
Moon Phase: Fourth Quarter 8:28 pm Incense: Evergreen
Color: Brown

21 THURSDAY
Raud the Strong's Martyrdom (Norwegian) Moon Sign: Cancer
Waning Moon Incense: Pine
Moon Phase: Fourth Quarter
Color: Turquoise

22 FRIDAY
Mabon • Fall Equinox   Moon Sign: Cancer
Waning Moon   Sun enters Libra 12:28 pm
Moon Phase: Fourth Quarter   Incense: Coriander
Color: Peach

23 SATURDAY
Waning Moon   Moon Sign: Cancer
Moon Phase: Fourth Quarter   Moon enters Leo 2:00 am
Color: Indigo   Incense: Jasmine

24 SUNDAY
Feast of Obatala (Santeria)   Moon Sign: Leo
Waning Moon   Incense: Parsley
Moon Phase: Fourth Quarter
Color: Peach

25 MONDAY
Salute to the Sun (Chinese)   Moon Sign: Leo
Waning Moon   Moon enters Virgo 4:02 am
Moon Phase: Fourth Quarter   Incense: Ginger
Color: Silver

26 TUESDAY
Feast of Santa Justina (Mexican)   Moon Sign: Virgo
Waning Moon   Incense: Eucalyptus
Moon Phase: Fourth Quarter
Color: Black

☽ WEDNESDAY
Day of Willows (Mesopotamian)   Moon Sign: Virgo
Waning Moon   Moon enters Libra 6:22 am
Moon Phase: New Moon 2:53 pm   Incense: Juniper
Color: Yellow

28 THURSDAY
Confucius' Birthday   Moon Sign: Libra
Waxing Moon   Incense: Honeysuckle
Moon Phase: First Quarter
Color: Violet

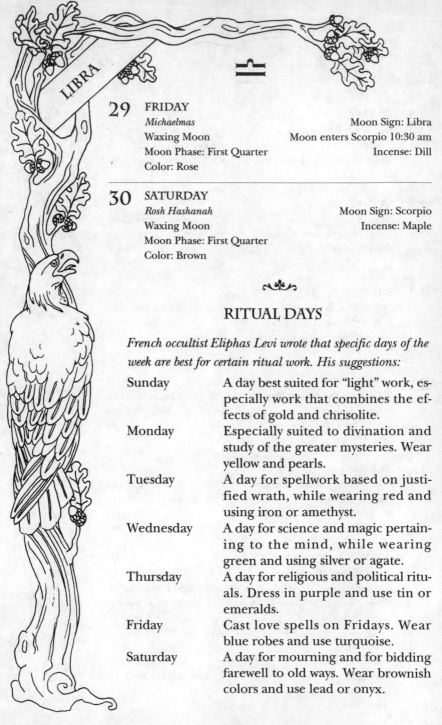

LIBRA

29 FRIDAY
Michaelmas
Waxing Moon
Moon Phase: First Quarter
Color: Rose

Moon Sign: Libra
Moon enters Scorpio 10:30 am
Incense: Dill

30 SATURDAY
Rosh Hashanah
Waxing Moon
Moon Phase: First Quarter
Color: Brown

Moon Sign: Scorpio
Incense: Maple

RITUAL DAYS

French occultist Eliphas Levi wrote that specific days of the week are best for certain ritual work. His suggestions:

Sunday	A day best suited for "light" work, especially work that combines the effects of gold and chrisolite.
Monday	Especially suited to divination and study of the greater mysteries. Wear yellow and pearls.
Tuesday	A day for spellwork based on justified wrath, while wearing red and using iron or amethyst.
Wednesday	A day for science and magic pertaining to the mind, while wearing green and using silver or agate.
Thursday	A day for religious and political rituals. Dress in purple and use tin or emeralds.
Friday	Cast love spells on Fridays. Wear blue robes and use turquoise.
Saturday	A day for mourning and for bidding farewell to old ways. Wear brownish colors and use lead or onyx.

≏ **OCTOBER**

1 SUNDAY
Waxing Moon
Moon Phase: First Quarter
Color: Peach
Moon Sign: Scorpio
Moon enters Sagittarius 5:50 pm
Incense: Basil

2 MONDAY
Waxing Moon
Moon Phase: First Quarter
Color: Gray
Moon Sign: Sagittarius
Incense: Cedar

3 TUESDAY
Moroccan New Year's Day
Waxing Moon
Moon Phase: First Quarter
Color: Red
Moon Sign: Sagittarius
Incense: Cinnamon

4 WEDNESDAY
Elk Festival (Native American)
Waxing Moon
Moon Phase: First Quarter
Color: Yellow
Moon Sign: Sagittarius
Moon enters Capricorn 4:42 am
Incense: Myrrh

☽ THURSDAY
Romanian Wine Festival
Waxing Moon
Moon Phase: Second Quarter 5:59 am
Color: Turquoise
Moon Sign: Capricorn
Incense: Patchouli

6 FRIDAY
Water Festival
Waxing Moon
Moon Phase: Second Quarter
Color: White
Moon Sign: Capricorn
Moon enters Aquarius 5:33 pm
Incense: Rose

7 SATURDAY
Pallas Athena's Day (Roman)
Waxing Moon
Moon Phase: Second Quarter
Color: Gray
Moon Sign: Aquarius
Incense: Pine

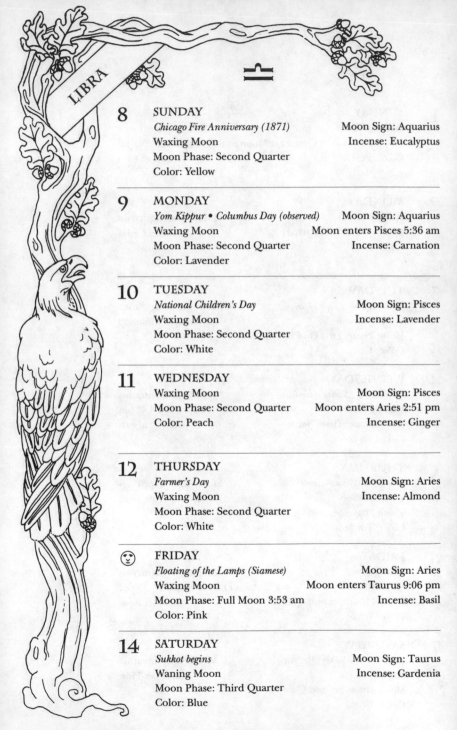

LIBRA ♎

8 SUNDAY
Chicago Fire Anniversary (1871)
Waxing Moon
Moon Phase: Second Quarter
Color: Yellow

Moon Sign: Aquarius
Incense: Eucalyptus

9 MONDAY
Yom Kippur • Columbus Day (observed)
Waxing Moon
Moon Phase: Second Quarter
Color: Lavender

Moon Sign: Aquarius
Moon enters Pisces 5:36 am
Incense: Carnation

10 TUESDAY
National Children's Day
Waxing Moon
Moon Phase: Second Quarter
Color: White

Moon Sign: Pisces
Incense: Lavender

11 WEDNESDAY
Waxing Moon
Moon Phase: Second Quarter
Color: Peach

Moon Sign: Pisces
Moon enters Aries 2:51 pm
Incense: Ginger

12 THURSDAY
Farmer's Day
Waxing Moon
Moon Phase: Second Quarter
Color: White

Moon Sign: Aries
Incense: Almond

FRIDAY
Floating of the Lamps (Siamese)
Waxing Moon
Moon Phase: Full Moon 3:53 am
Color: Pink

Moon Sign: Aries
Moon enters Taurus 9:06 pm
Incense: Basil

14 SATURDAY
Sukkot begins
Waning Moon
Moon Phase: Third Quarter
Color: Blue

Moon Sign: Taurus
Incense: Gardenia

15 SUNDAY
Ides of October (Roman)   Moon Sign: Taurus
Waning Moon   Incense: Parsley
Moon Phase: Third Quarter
Color: Orange

16 MONDAY
Festival of Pandrosus (Greek)   Moon Sign: Taurus
Waning Moon   Moon enters Gemini 1:19 am
Moon Phase: Third Quarter   Incense: Violet
Color: White

17 TUESDAY
St. Audrey's Day   Moon Sign: Gemini
Waning Moon   Incense: Pine
Moon Phase: Third Quarter
Color: Gray

18 WEDNESDAY
Alaska Day   Moon Sign: Gemini
Waning Moon   Moon enters Cancer 4:37 am
Moon Phase: Third Quarter   Incense: Cedar
Color: Brown

19 THURSDAY
Waning Moon   Moon Sign: Cancer
Moon Phase: Third Quarter   Incense: Chrysanthemum
Color: Violet

( ) FRIDAY
Sukkot ends   Moon Sign: Cancer
Waning Moon   Moon enters Leo 7:42 am
Moon Phase: Fourth Quarter 2:59 am   Incense: Thyme
Color: Rose

21 SATURDAY
Festival of Ishhara (Mesopotamian)   Moon Sign: Leo
Waning Moon   Incense: Poplar
Moon Phase: Fourth Quarter
Color: Indigo

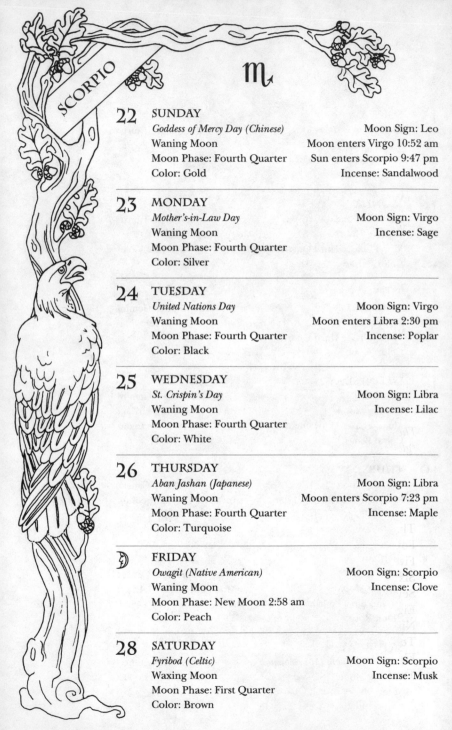

♏

22 SUNDAY
Goddess of Mercy Day (Chinese)   Moon Sign: Leo
Waning Moon   Moon enters Virgo 10:52 am
Moon Phase: Fourth Quarter   Sun enters Scorpio 9:47 pm
Color: Gold   Incense: Sandalwood

23 MONDAY
Mother's-in-Law Day   Moon Sign: Virgo
Waning Moon   Incense: Sage
Moon Phase: Fourth Quarter
Color: Silver

24 TUESDAY
United Nations Day   Moon Sign: Virgo
Waning Moon   Moon enters Libra 2:30 pm
Moon Phase: Fourth Quarter   Incense: Poplar
Color: Black

25 WEDNESDAY
St. Crispin's Day   Moon Sign: Libra
Waning Moon   Incense: Lilac
Moon Phase: Fourth Quarter
Color: White

26 THURSDAY
Aban Jashan (Japanese)   Moon Sign: Libra
Waning Moon   Moon enters Scorpio 7:23 pm
Moon Phase: Fourth Quarter   Incense: Maple
Color: Turquoise

☽ FRIDAY
Owagit (Native American)   Moon Sign: Scorpio
Waning Moon   Incense: Clove
Moon Phase: New Moon 2:58 am
Color: Peach

28 SATURDAY
Fyribod (Celtic)   Moon Sign: Scorpio
Waxing Moon   Incense: Musk
Moon Phase: First Quarter
Color: Brown

♏

OCTOBER

29 SUNDAY
Daylight Saving Time ends at 2:00 am   Moon Sign: Scorpio
Waxing Moon   Moon enters Sagittarius 2:40 am
Moon Phase: First Quarter   Incense: Thyme
Color: Peach

30 MONDAY
Los Angelitos (Mexican)   Moon Sign: Sagittarius
Waxing Moon   Incense: Eucalyptus
Moon Phase: First Quarter
Color: Gray

31 TUESDAY
Halloween • Samhain   Moon Sign: Sagittarius
Waxing Moon   Moon enters Capricorn 1:01 pm
Moon Phase: First Quarter   Incense: Rosemary
Color: Red

༒

BUTTONHOLING THE FUTURE

*The first person you meet on Halloween can give you a
glimpse of the year to come. Just count the number of
buttons they're wearing.*

One   Luck
Two   Happiness
Three   A new vehicle
Four   Another form of transportation
Five   New clothes
Six   Accessories
Seven   A new dog
Eight   A new cat
Nine   An unexpected letter
Ten   Pleasure
Eleven   Extreme joy
Twelve   A treasure soon to be discovered

175

1 WEDNESDAY
All Saints' Day
Waxing Moon
Moon Phase: First Quarter
Color: Brown

Moon Sign: Capricorn
Incense: Evergreen

---

2 THURSDAY
Animas (Mexican)
Waxing Moon
Moon Phase: First Quarter
Color: Turquoise

Moon Sign: Capricorn
Incense: Patchouli

---

3 FRIDAY
Festival for the New Year (Gaelic)
Waxing Moon
Moon Phase: First Quarter
Color: Peach

Moon Sign: Capricorn
Moon enters Aquarius 1:41 am
Incense: Basil

◐ **SATURDAY**
Will Rogers' Birthday
Waxing Moon
Moon Phase: Second Quarter 2:27 am
Color: Brown

Moon Sign: Aquarius
Incense: Nutmeg

---

5 SUNDAY
Guy Fawkes' Day
Waxing Moon
Moon Phase: Second Quarter
Color: Peach

Moon Sign: Aquarius
Moon enters Pisces 2:13 pm
Incense: Coriander

---

6 MONDAY
Birthday of Tiamat (Babylonian)
Waxing Moon
Moon Phase: Second Quarter
Color: Lavender

Moon Sign: Pisces
Incense: Vanilla

---

7 TUESDAY
General Election Day
Waxing Moon
Moon Phase: Second Quarter
Color: Red

Moon Sign: Pisces
Incense: Dill

♏︎

8 WEDNESDAY
Festival of Kami of the Hearth (Japanese)   Moon Sign: Pisces
Waxing Moon   Moon enters Aries 12:02 am
Moon Phase: Second Quarter   Incense: Lilac
Color: White

9 THURSDAY
Feast of the Four Crowned Martyrs   Moon Sign: Aries
Waxing Moon   Incense: Gardenia
Moon Phase: Second Quarter
Color: Violet

10 FRIDAY
Festival of the Goddess of Reason (French)   Moon Sign: Aries
Waxing Moon   Moon enters Taurus 6:12 am
Moon Phase: Second Quarter   Incense: Almond
Color: White

SATURDAY
Veterans' Day   Moon Sign: Taurus
Waxing Moon   Incense: Jasmine
Moon Phase: Full Moon 4:15 pm
Color: Blue

12 SUNDAY
Birthday of Baha'u'llah (Baha'i)   Moon Sign: Taurus
Waning Moon   Moon enters Gemini 9:27 am
Moon Phase: Third Quarter   Incense: Clove
Color: Gold

13 MONDAY
Festival of Jupiter (Roman)   Moon Sign: Gemini
Waning Moon   Incense: Neroli
Moon Phase: Third Quarter
Color: White

14 TUESDAY
Moccas' Day (Celtic)   Moon Sign: Gemini
Waning Moon   Moon enters Cancer 11:21 am
Moon Phase: Third Quarter   Incense: Cedar
Color: Black

15 WEDNESDAY
Seven-Five-Three Festival (Japanese)
Waning Moon
Moon Phase: Third Quarter
Color: Peach

Moon Sign: Cancer
Incense: Coriander

---

16 THURSDAY
Night of Hecate (Greek)
Waning Moon
Moon Phase: Third Quarter
Color: Green

Moon Sign: Cancer
Moon enters Leo 1:19 pm
Incense: Ginger

---

17 FRIDAY
Festival of the Pearly Bouquet (Hungarian)
Waning Moon
Moon Phase: Third Quarter
Color: Pink

Moon Sign: Leo
Incense: Cinnamon

SATURDAY
Day of Ardvi Sura (Persian)
Waning Moon
Moon Phase: Fourth Quarter 10:24 am
Color: Gray

Moon Sign: Leo
Moon enters Virgo 4:15 pm
Incense: Pine

---

19 SUNDAY
Feast of Santa Isabel (Mexican)
Waning Moon
Moon Phase: Fourth Quarter
Color: Orange

Moon Sign: Virgo
Incense: Parsley

---

20 MONDAY
St. Edmund's Day
Waning Moon
Moon Phase: Fourth Quarter
Color: Silver

Moon Sign: Virgo
Moon enters Libra 8:35 pm
Incense: Thyme

---

21 TUESDAY
Feast of Hathor (Egyptian)
Waning Moon
Moon Phase: Fourth Quarter
Color: Gray

Moon Sign: Libra
Sun enters Sagittarius 7:19 pm
Incense: Maple

22 WEDNESDAY
Ydalir (Norse)   Moon Sign: Libra
Waning Moon   Incense: Evergreen
Moon Phase: Fourth Quarter
Color: Yellow

23 THURSDAY
Thanksgiving Day   Moon Sign: Libra
Waning Moon   Moon enters Scorpio 2:33 am
Moon Phase: Fourth Quarter   Incense: Ylang-Ylang
Color: White

24 FRIDAY
Stir-Up Sunday (British)   Moon Sign: Scorpio
Waning Moon   Incense: Rosemary
Moon Phase: Fourth Quarter
Color: Rose

SATURDAY
St. Catherine's Day (French)   Moon Sign: Scorpio
Waning Moon   Moon enters Sagittarius 10:33 am
Moon Phase: New Moon 6:11 pm   Incense: Cedar
Color: Indigo

26 SUNDAY
Festival of Lights (Tibetan)   Moon Sign: Sagittarius
Waxing Moon   Incense: Musk
Moon Phase: First Quarter
Color: Yellow

27 MONDAY
Waxing Moon   Moon Sign: Sagittarius
Moon Phase: First Quarter   Moon enters Capricorn 8:57 pm
Color: Lavender   Incense: Geranium

28 TUESDAY
Ramadan begins   Moon Sign: Capricorn
Waxing Moon   Incense: Violet
Moon Phase: First Quarter
Color: White

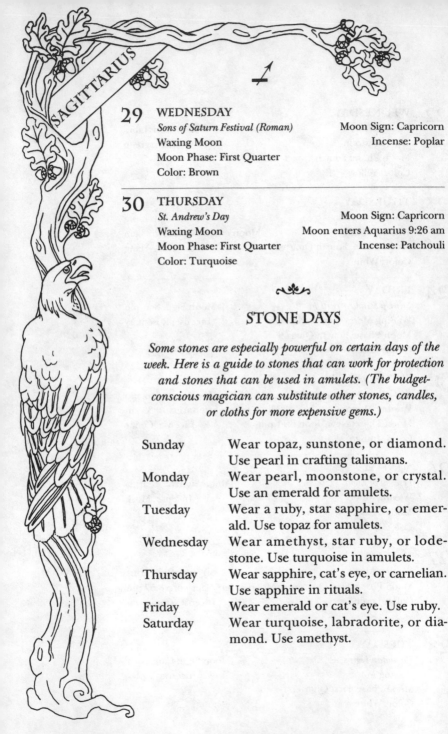

29 WEDNESDAY
Sons of Saturn Festival (Roman)
Waxing Moon
Moon Phase: First Quarter
Color: Brown

Moon Sign: Capricorn
Incense: Poplar

30 THURSDAY
St. Andrew's Day
Waxing Moon
Moon Phase: First Quarter
Color: Turquoise

Moon Sign: Capricorn
Moon enters Aquarius 9:26 am
Incense: Patchouli

STONE DAYS

Some stones are especially powerful on certain days of the week. Here is a guide to stones that can work for protection and stones that can be used in amulets. (The budget-conscious magician can substitute other stones, candles, or cloths for more expensive gems.)

Sunday	Wear topaz, sunstone, or diamond. Use pearl in crafting talismans.
Monday	Wear pearl, moonstone, or crystal. Use an emerald for amulets.
Tuesday	Wear a ruby, star sapphire, or emerald. Use topaz for amulets.
Wednesday	Wear amethyst, star ruby, or lodestone. Use turquoise in amulets.
Thursday	Wear sapphire, cat's eye, or carnelian. Use sapphire in rituals.
Friday	Wear emerald or cat's eye. Use ruby.
Saturday	Wear turquoise, labradorite, or diamond. Use amethyst.

1 FRIDAY
Festival of Poseidon (Greek)
Waxing Moon
Moon Phase: First Quarter
Color: Rose

Moon Sign: Aquarius
Incense: Nutmeg

2 SATURDAY
Feast of Shiva (Hindu)
Waxing Moon
Moon Phase: First Quarter
Color: Indigo

Moon Sign: Aquarius
Moon enters Pisces 10:23 pm
Incense: Maple

☾ **SUNDAY**
Waxing Moon
Moon Phase: Second Quarter 10:55 pm
Color: Peach

Moon Sign: Pisces
Incense: Clove

4 MONDAY
St. Barbara's Day
Waxing Moon
Moon Phase: Second Quarter
Color: Silver

Moon Sign: Pisces
Incense: Cinnamon

5 TUESDAY
Eve of St. Nicholas' Day
Waxing Moon
Moon Phase: Second Quarter
Color: Gray

Moon Sign: Pisces
Moon enters Aries 9:17 am
Incense: Poplar

6 WEDNESDAY
St. Nicholas' Day
Waxing Moon
Moon Phase: Second Quarter
Color: Brown

Moon Sign: Aries
Incense: Cedar

7 THURSDAY
Burning the Devil (Guatemalan)
Waxing Moon
Moon Phase: Second Quarter
Color: Turquoise

Moon Sign: Aries
Moon enters Taurus 4:26 pm
Incense: Myrrh

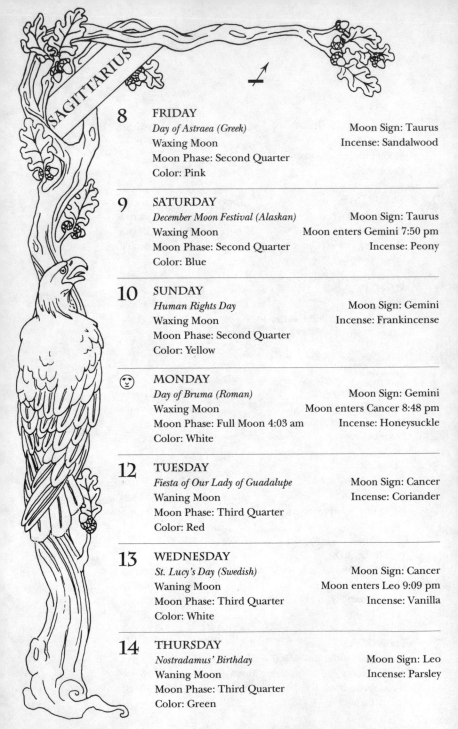

8 FRIDAY
Day of Astraea (Greek)
Waxing Moon
Moon Phase: Second Quarter
Color: Pink

Moon Sign: Taurus
Incense: Sandalwood

9 SATURDAY
December Moon Festival (Alaskan)
Waxing Moon
Moon Phase: Second Quarter
Color: Blue

Moon Sign: Taurus
Moon enters Gemini 7:50 pm
Incense: Peony

10 SUNDAY
Human Rights Day
Waxing Moon
Moon Phase: Second Quarter
Color: Yellow

Moon Sign: Gemini
Incense: Frankincense

☺ MONDAY
Day of Bruma (Roman)
Waxing Moon
Moon Phase: Full Moon 4:03 am
Color: White

Moon Sign: Gemini
Moon enters Cancer 8:48 pm
Incense: Honeysuckle

12 TUESDAY
Fiesta of Our Lady of Guadalupe
Waning Moon
Moon Phase: Third Quarter
Color: Red

Moon Sign: Cancer
Incense: Coriander

13 WEDNESDAY
St. Lucy's Day (Swedish)
Waning Moon
Moon Phase: Third Quarter
Color: White

Moon Sign: Cancer
Moon enters Leo 9:09 pm
Incense: Vanilla

14 THURSDAY
Nostradamus' Birthday
Waning Moon
Moon Phase: Third Quarter
Color: Green

Moon Sign: Leo
Incense: Parsley

15 FRIDAY
Festival of Alcyone (Greek)
Waning Moon
Moon Phase: Third Quarter
Color: Peach

Moon Sign: Leo
Moon enters Virgo 10:30 pm
Incense: Basil

---

16 SATURDAY
Festival of Sophia
Waning Moon
Moon Phase: Third Quarter
Color: Gray

Moon Sign: Virgo
Incense: Cedar

☽ SUNDAY
Feast of Babaluaiye (Santerian)
Waning Moon
Moon Phase: Fourth Quarter 7:41 pm
Color: Orange

Moon Sign: Virgo
Incense: Sage

---

18 MONDAY
Waning Moon
Moon Phase: Fourth Quarter
Color: Lavender

Moon Sign: Virgo
Moon enters Libra 2:01 am
Incense: Lilac

---

19 TUESDAY
Waning Moon
Moon Phase: Fourth Quarter
Color: Black

Moon Sign: Libra
Incense: Maple

---

20 WEDNESDAY
Mother Night (Odinist)
Waning Moon
Moon Phase: Fourth Quarter
Color: Peach

Moon Sign: Libra
Moon enters Scorpio 8:12 am
Incense: Thyme

---

21 THURSDAY
Yule • Winter Solstice
Waning Moon
Moon Phase: Fourth Quarter
Color: Violet

Moon Sign: Scorpio
Sun enters Capricorn 8:37 am
Incense: Lavender

22 FRIDAY
Pryderi's Birthday   Moon Sign: Scorpio
Waning Moon   Moon enters Sagittarius 4:57 pm
Moon Phase: Fourth Quarter   Incense: Nutmeg
Color: Rose

23 SATURDAY
Chanukkah begins   Moon Sign: Sagittarius
Waning Moon   Incense: Eucalyptus
Moon Phase: Fourth Quarter
Color: Brown

24 SUNDAY
Christmas Eve   Moon Sign: Sagittarius
Waning Moon   Incense: Thyme
Moon Phase: Fourth Quarter
Color: Gold

☽ MONDAY
Christmas Day • Solar Eclipse   Moon Sign: Sagittarius
Waning Moon   Moon enters Capricorn 3:54 am
Moon Phase: New Moon 12:22 pm   Incense: Clove
Color: Silver

26 TUESDAY
Kwanzaa begins • Ramadan ends   Moon Sign: Capricorn
Waxing Moon   Incense: Dill
Moon Phase: First Quarter
Color: Red

27 WEDNESDAY
Feast of St. John the Evangelist   Moon Sign: Capricorn
Waxing Moon   Moon enters Aquarius 4:25 pm
Moon Phase: First Quarter   Incense: Juniper
Color: Yellow

28 THURSDAY
Bairns' Day (Scottish)   Moon Sign: Aquarius
Waxing Moon   Incense: Cinnamon
Moon Phase: First Quarter
Color: Green

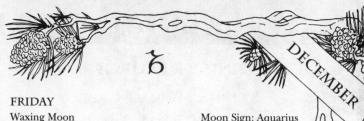

♑ DECEMBER

29 FRIDAY
Waxing Moon
Moon Phase: First Quarter
Color: Peach

Moon Sign: Aquarius
Incense: Ginger

---

30 SATURDAY
Chanukkah ends
Waxing Moon
Moon Phase: First Quarter
Color: Indigo

Moon Sign: Aquarius
Moon enters Pisces 5:27 am
Incense: Maple

---

31 SUNDAY
New Year's Eve
Waxing Moon
Moon Phase: First Quarter
Color: Peach

Moon Sign: Pisces
Incense: Sage

❧

SEASON TO TASTE

Why don't seasons start on a regular schedule—December 21, March 21, June 21, and September 21 of each year? Why do the equinoxes skip around between the 20th and the 22nd?

Because the Earth takes more than 365 days to orbit the Sun. A year is actually 365 ¼ days long. As a result, the first day of each season starts six hours later than it did the year before.

To keep the seasons in their place, we add a leap day every four years. Otherwise, we'd wind up with some springs starting in September and some autumns falling in March.

DEVELOPING THE MAGICAL WILL

BY JOHN MICHAEL GREER

O ne of the lessons of authentic magical training is that the real tools of magic are within the self. Wands, athames, altar bric-a-brac, and similar occult hardware simply provide anchors for the magician's own inner capabilities and focal points for the magical energies of the cosmos. Collecting hardware may make a fashion statement, then, but it doesn't make a magician. What does make a magician is the work of developing the inner potentials of the self. The most important of these is the magical will.

What is the magical will? In simplest terms, it's the power of choice that all human beings possess, restored to its full strength through training. To act on the basis of will is to choose freely, instead of following the unthinking patterns of automatic behavior that dominate so many lives. To become a magician is to learn to will strongly and skillfully, to accomplish the freely-chosen purposes of the self.

It's wise to take a moment, though, to clear away another common misunderstanding. Will has nothing to do with the teeth-gritting inner struggle that many people associate with the word "willpower." Aleister Crowley used to tell an anecdote about a student who failed to grasp this, and tried to project his astral body through "willpower," tensing his physical body in the process until it was as stiff as a board. As anyone who has experienced astral projection knows, this is exactly the wrong way to go about it! The acts of a truly strong will are effortless. It's when the will is weak or divided that tension and struggle come into the picture.

How does a magician strengthen his or her will? The same way an athlete strengthens his or her body—by using it. Just as there are exercises for the body, there are exercises for the will; just as pushups and yoga postures look pointless to those who don't understand them, many of the exercises magicians use to train the will seem pretty strange at first glance.

For example, one exercise for developing the magical will is to stand at one side of a room, choose a point on the opposite wall, then cross the room and touch that point. Turn around and repeat. This may seem silly, but it involves making a choice and acting on it and thus teaches the use of will.

Another effective way to develop the magical will is to take up a magical practice and do it every day. Over and above the fact that you'll become very good at the ritual you've chosen—no small point for a practicing magician—you'll find that your ability to make choices and act on them, in and out of magical practice, will grow dramatically over time.

There are any number of other exercises for the magical will, and a few of them have been listed here.

EXERCISES FOR THE MAGICAL WILL

1. Sit in a position where, without moving any part of your body, you can see a clock. Keep perfectly still and silent for five minutes. Don't move a muscle except to breathe. When you can do this easily for five minutes, try it for fifteen.

2. Do the same thing, with your body in some unusual position. Change the position each time you do the exercise.

3. Choose an activity you don't like, and do it as often as possible for a week, paying careful attention to the experience. Then do the same thing with an activity that you enjoy. Compare notes.

4. Look at a watch or clock with a sweep second hand, and see how long you can keep your eyes fixed on the movement of the second hand without looking away even for an instant.

5. Put a small, brightly-colored object somewhere in plain sight in a room. Spend at least fifteen minutes in the room. During this time, do not let yourself look at the object.

6. List the routes you take to get from place to place on a regular basis. Choose one route you use often, and abandon that route completely for a month, using other routes to get to the same place.

7. At least a week in advance, choose a specific place you've never been, and set a precise date and time to be there. There should be no other reason for the trip. Be there on time.

8. Choose some complex and unfamiliar task. Again, there should be no other reason for doing the task. Work out a detailed plan for accomplishing it, and then carry it out. Then choose a different task of the same sort, and without making any plans at all, carry it out. Compare notes.

9. Pick a subject about which you have strong feelings. Choose the point of view that you disagree with most strongly, and write a short essay defending that point of view. Make it as serious, logical, and convincing as you possibly can.

10. Pick a subject about which you know absolutely nothing—the history of Paraguay, the structure of your spleen, the names of all the weeds that grow where you live, or anything else—and learn about it in detail.

11. Similarly, choose a skill or craft that you've never tried before and never thought of doing—juggling, soapmaking, or anything else—and learn how to do it competently.

12. Invent an exercise for developing the magical will on your own, and work at it until you've mastered it.

Cosmos Kids

By Bernyce Barlow

When Hopi children are very young they are given a rattle representing many of the Hopi ideals. The rattles are made out of round gourds that represent the Earth. A circle is drawn in the center of the gourd with rays emitting from it, representing the Sun. In the middle of the circle is a swastika symbol, called the rolling logs. If the rolling logs are depicted clockwise they represent the rotation of the Sun, counter clockwise represents the Earth. The handle of the gourd represents the Earth's axis aligned north and south. The Milky Way is sometimes shown by side markings that look like a railroad track crossing. Inside the rattle bone, corn, seeds, or small pebbles are placed to create a sound that represents the vibration of the Earth's axis. The shaking of the rattle signals an event or a warning. After a child comes of age, around seven or so, the rattle is replaced with another type of rattle without markings,which is similar to what the kachinas carry.

Another learning toy of Hopi children is the kachina doll. Traditionally, the dolls were hand carved from cottonwood tree roots, then delightfully painted and ornamented. The doll itself is not empowered with magic as the true kachinas are. They simply are given as gifts to teach the children what different kachinas look like in the ceremonies they will see and what those kachinas represent.

Kachinas are not gods. They are helpers, like angels, if you will. They are said to come from the stars and represent the forces on Earth like rain, reproduction, harvest, animals, the Sun and Moon. They can also represent human attributes as the kachina clowns do. Their purpose is to help the human family to evolve in harmony with creation. In Hopi ceremonies and dances the kachinas are represented by members of the Hopi tribe, painted, and sometimes masked.

Blue Corn Girl Descends into Summer

By Elizabeth Barrette

Sky quickens with heat
Air shimmers thick,
melting on horizon's edge
Earth turns wet and ready.

Dancing on delicate feet
She comes,
Heel and toe and
swirling shawl,
Drumming Her way
into summer.

Hear the People singing on the hill
High over the fields, over the farms
Chanting an ancient blessing.

Into the silken tassles She comes,
Into the turquoise kernels She comes,
Blue Corn Girl descending to earth.

Into their hearts the People take Her,
Into their souls the People take Her,
Chanting and dancing an ancient blessing.

Sacred before and behind Her now,
Sacred above and below Her now,
Sacred to left and to right and within Her now—
The People pour Her a path of pollen,
Golden and holy, blessing the ground as She goes
Blue Corn Girl whose bounty feeds the tribe.

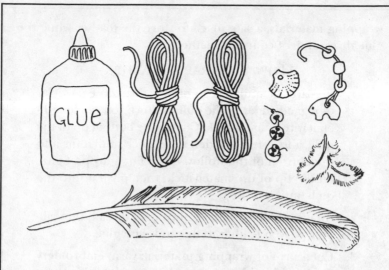

Feather Wrapping

By Breid Foxsong

More and more people within the Pagan community are working with shamanic techniques. These are not necessarily Native American techniques. Every culture in the world used some form of shamanism, but many people associate the term with Native American practices. One of the most common of the shamanic techniques involves smudging, or blessing a person, space, or item with sacred smoke. Once again, most cultures had some form of ritual involving sacred fire or smoke, usually associated with air. As a method of controlling the motion of the smoke, something was waved over the bowl containing the incense. As part of the association with air, that something was usually a feather. This brings us to the topic at hand.

Although feathers are commercially available, they are often not prepared for extended use. Most of us have some kind of animal in the house and they like nothing better than to get into the ritual gear and wreak havoc. You should wrap any feather that you wish to keep. Wrapping enables you to hang the feather up and away from cats and other small beasties and will help keep it from blowing away or getting ragged. To wrap a feather, you will need a few basic supplies, such as glue, wrapping materials, a safe place to store the feather while the glue dries, and, of course, a feather.

How to Wrap a Feather

1. Prepare the quill. Clean off any dirt, loose particles or ragged edges. If the quill is short, you can lengthen it with a matchstick. Cut off the bottom tip of the quill, and pare a wooden matchstick until it fits into the bottom of the hollow quill. Put a drop of glue on the tip of the matchstick, then push it into the quill until it is snug.

2. Attach a loop of yarn, embroidery thread, thin ribbon, or thin leather to the quill with glue.

3. Cut a strip of wrapping material: yarn, embroidery thread, thin ribbon, or thin leather. Make this about twice as long as you think you'll need. If it ends up too long, you can always shorten it, but it's difficult to add more later. Fold the yarn in half, place a tiny dot of glue in the middle, and attach it to the part of the quill just below the vane. Wait for the glue to dry (about twenty-four hours).

4. After the glue has set, pull both ends of the yarn to one side. Wrap the yarn around the quill in a spiral pattern until the quill is entirely covered.

5. Place a dot of glue at the bottom of the quill. Make sure that the yarn wrapped around the end of the quill is embedded in the glue. Wait for the glue to dry, then cut the loose ends.

Elaborations

A. Before wrapping the feather, glue some additional down fluffies of a harmonizing or contrasting color to the base of the vane. Then wrap over the bottom of the fluffies as you wrap the quill.

B. Wrap the quill in a variegated yarn or a very thin patterned ribbon.

C. Use two pieces of yarn in different colors to wrap.

D. Add beads or other decorations to the loop before attaching it to the quill. You can also attach the beads to the ends of the wrapping material after finishing the wrap.

TIPS: Super glue and other fast-drying synthetics work well because they dry quickly. Elmer's takes longer, but is made of natural substances. Try and use an applicator with a fine tip, or use a matchstick to place the glue. That way you don't end up with large blobs of glue where you don't want them.

EDITOR'S NOTE: If you find your feathers in the wild rather then buying them you may wish to disinfect them before wrapping them. Bird feathers often carry mites that can cause lung damage in humans and pets, as well as spreading to pet birds. Commerical mite killer comes in a spray-pump bottle and is available at most pet stores that carry bird supplies. Before bringing them into the house, spray your feathers and enclose them in a glass jar with a tight-fitting lid. You may also want to add some cedar to the jar; it helps kill mites. After a couple of days, remove the feathers, wipe them off gently with a soft cloth or paper towel, and wrap!

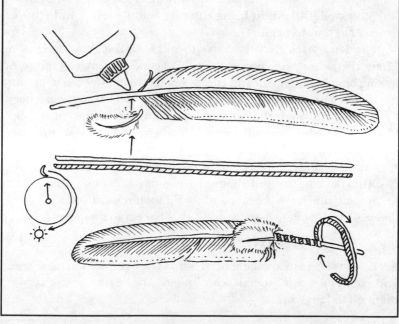

FAIRIES IN THE GARDEN

BY ANNIE REDWING (CARRY WALL)

Sometimes the world seems an empty place, but that's only when we have become unbalanced and have not been in touch with nature. We have also perhaps been remiss in making our gardens welcome spots for the fairies and elementals.

Once you become aware of the nature devas and become adept at getting close to them, you'll wonder why you ever felt so down, because their loving energies are merely waiting to help you fulfill your desires to have an abundant garden. They'll help you weave the magic spell to grow lush vines and heavenly flowers of many different colors and hues—for their delight is in helping the plants to develop and fruit or flower. But how to begin?

Garden fairies are very active throughout the growing season. There are many ways to attract them. Two good ways are soft music, or leaving bits of good bread and cheese out for them. An even better way to attract them is to plant a fairy garden with plants that have been found down through the centuries to be favored by the "little folk." Plant your garden carefully, tend it lovingly, and call out and make their welcome known. Soon, you may see on a moonlit summer night (especially as Midsummer night nears), a group of laughing and merry sprites dancing around a fairy circle in or near your garden. Make them some tiny frosted cakes and they'll soon reward you with a garden you won't believe—and your work will seem to disappear!

FAVORED FAIRY PLANTS

APPLE TREES: An ancient belief states that fairies inhabited these trees and could enchant mortals who lingered beneath them, carrying them off to fairy land.

ELDER BUSH: It is believed that the elder helps one to see the fairies. Stand beneath an elder on midsummer night's eve and you may see a fairy procession.

FERNS: Grown near thyme beds with plenty of soft moss around to make soft fairy beds, ferns provide plenty of hiding spots for the shy sprites.

FORGET-ME-NOTS: An old belief is that if you hold the blue flowers and wishes, and if you are pure and true, the keys of fairy land will come to you.

FOXGLOVES: Also called fairy caps, fairy gloves, fairy bells—the little folk use this plant to make their wardrobe up.

HEARTSEASE: Used by fairies to make love potions.

LILY OF THE VALLEY: The tiny flowers and fragrance make for a perfect bouquet for the little folk.

MALLOWS: The fairies use the seeds of these plants as their "cheese."

OAK TREE: Holes near the bottom of old oaks lead to fairy land. Fairies love oaks and love to live in them.

ROSEMARY: Called the elf plant, it is believed that fairies are entranced by their scent.

THYME: The absolute favorite of the fairies, its color and fragrance delight them. They often lie in it.

TULIPS: The flowers of the tulip create the perfect fairy baby basket. The babies rock away in these colorful petals while the elders dance.

Sacred Medicine Sites of
Ka-maka-nui-'aha'i-lono

By Bernyce Barlow

There were many Kahiki (Land Far Away) islands in the sea that came and went like step-
ping stones across the Pacific. Nobody knows for
sure which island Kihiki Ka-maka-nui-'aha'i-lono
came from, but they knew that he followed the
strangers who looked like him. They were pale
skinned with blue eyes, and they carried a disease
that spread throughout the islands. Ka-maka-nui-
'aha'i-lono followed the strangers, healing those who got sick with
the disease. He knew the medicine ways.

Ka-maka-nui-'aha'i-lono is translated as the "large-eyed or pig
eyed messenger who pursues," and pursue he did, beginning at Ni'i-
hau, then on to Kauai and so on, until he reached the island of
Hawaii. It was there, near a village called Kiala-ka'a, that Ka-maka-
nui-'aha'i-lono met the man who would apprentice his medicine
knowledge and father the first medical practices of Hawaii.

The story goes that Ka-maka-nui-'aha'i-lono was resting on a hill
when the people of Kiala-ka'a extended their hospitality. He gra-
ciously accepted their invitation, and while eating noticed a man
with bright red skin working in the Taro fields. He asked about the
man and the villagers said he was their chief, Lono. Ka-maka-nui-
'aha'i-lono warned the villagers to take care of their chief because
he was ill. When the reports reached the ears of Lono, he became
angry that such a thing be said about him! So angry, in fact, that he
raised his pointed digging stick and slammed it into the ground, accidentally piercing his foot. The injury was severe and Lono passed
out due to loss of blood. The villagers were frantic. Finally one ran
to find Ka-maka-nui-'aha'i-lono. He carried a pig offering with him.
The healer returned to the village, gathering medicine plants along

the way, especially the young leaves and seeds of the *popolo* (black nightshade). When they arrived at the village, Ka-maka-nui-'aha'i-lono pounded salt and the popolo into a poultice secured in coconut mesh (a fiber-like material found at the bottom of coconut leaf clusters). He placed it over the wound and the blood stopped.

Lono remained under the watchful eye of Ka-maka-nui-'aha'i-lono until he was well. When it was time for the healer to leave, Lono asked permission to go with him as his apprentice. In acceptance, Ka-maka-nui-'aha'i-lono spit in the mouth of Lono, acknowledging his request with the recognized sign of power. Lono then became Lonopuha, *puha* meaning sore.

As Lonopuha traveled with his teacher from district to district he became proficient in the methods of healing. After a great deal of study, it was time for Lonopuha to begin practicing on his own, as well as teaching others the medicine ways. While Lonopuha went to Wai-manu, Ka-maka-nui-'aha'i-lono went to Kukui-haele. Both established schools of medicine. Lonopuha was considered the first medical Kahuna with rank, and the founding forefather of the Kahuna Hala. The land surrounding both Kukui-haele and Wai-manu was declared sacred ground. Kukui-haele became known as the land of many heiaus. Schools of medicine were established at these sites, as were the rites and rituals of the healing Kahunas of the future. By right and power, the holy ground of the first birth sites of medical Kahuna knowledge imprints the essence of the One Who Pursues from the Land Far Away. The above established sites became places of mystery and magic, as well as universities of technique and diagnosis. As years passed, new schools of thought and purpose were aggregated, but the old ways were never thrown aside, only added to, for better or worse.

It is important to remember that the history, imprint, and physics of the site combine to create its spirit of place. Even though there may be many healing sites, the character of each site will remain individual.

THE CEREMONY AND RITUAL OF HULA

BY YASMINE GALENORN

When most people think of hula, they think of ukuleles, grass skirts, and women whose hips move faster than a propeller blade. They think of luxurious hotels and luaus, and movies like *South Pacific*. But the art of hula is far older than Hawai'i's entrance into statehood, and far more sacred.

An integrated combination of movement, *mele* (poetry), and rhythm, hula originated as both a tribute to the gods and a way to preserve history. Seldom used as entertainment, the dances were passed down through generation after generation in strict form, for this was the way of recording the past; this was the way of paying honor and respect to the Gods. If you altered the dance, if you performed it without utmost devotion or concentration, you would change history and also show the gods your lack of concern.

The dance was also used to commemorate specific events, such as the birth of a royal child or the undertaking of war, and there are indications that hula was used in magic, such as for fertility or abundance. Hula is taught within a *halau* (school) by a *kumu* (teacher). There are both *'olapa* (the dancers) and *ho'opa'a* (the chanters and percussionists). While the hula may be performed without instruments, in history the dance was never performed without chanting or singing.

When Christian missionaries arrived in Hawai'i in the 1820s, they were scandalized by the Pagan rites and rituals. Hula was seen as a sexual practice rather than a ceremonial practice, and was branded as sinful. The missionaries couldn't accept the scant clothing or uninhibited nature of the Hawaiians and quickly set out to abolish the hula. When Queen Ka'ahumanu, widow of Kamehameha I, was baptized a Christian, she passed an edict outlawing public performance of the hula, which broke up the stronghold of the halau and effectively started the destruction of one of the oldest practices on the islands.

When David Kalakaua took the throne in 1874, however, he instigated a resurgence of interest in Hawaiian culture. Nicknamed the Merrie Monarch, he rescinded the edict forbidding the hula and encouraged the renewed pursuit of the dance. He built the 'Iolani Palace and instituted an orchestra that played every day for the public's enjoyment. Though fifty years intervened between the hula of the past and the hula that now rose to prominence, the dance was alive once more.

However, now hula had become more of an entertainment. Ritual and ceremonial roots were ignored and Westerners began utilizing it as a tourist gimmick. As the century turned and Hawai'i's monarchy was overthrown by the United States, the dance was co-opted and practically turned into a burlesque format. Through the machinations of Hollywood, the beautiful and backward Hawaiian hula girl became the staple for such movies like *South Pacific,* Elvis' *Blue Hawai'i,* and numerous other films.

Luxury hotels promoted all forms of Polynesian dance as hula and lumped them all together in Westernized versions of luaus, taking the hula down to the level of pure entertainment.

Still, underneath all the cellophane skirts and plastic leis something of the old form remained. Then, in the 1970s, a renewed interest in the culture and religion of Hawai'i brought the ancient form of hula, the kahiko hula, back into the spotlight. As foundations and organizations rose to document, preserve, and perpetuate Hawaiian history, hula halaus once again rose up and the ancient traditions, modified for this century, were reinstated. Today, the debate still rages, however, on whether kahiko hula should stand as it once stood without alteration or change, or whether some of the new dances, created in the kahiko style, are acceptable additions to the ever-growing body of legend and mele behind the form.

In Hawai'i, there are specific goddesses to whom the hula is sacred. Laka, the foremost goddess and creatrix of the dance, demanded strict *kapu* (or taboos) regarding certain actions during training. The breaking of these kapu resulted in swift and direct punishment, and students were taking the chance of offending the goddess should they succumb to temptation. Laka's kapus included sex, unhygienic practices, sugar cane, disrespect to the kumu, and other infractions. Rituals to purify the student after breaking kapu would have to be performed before the dancer would be back in good graces with the kumu, the halau, and the goddess.

While Laka is considered the primary patroness of the hula throughout many of the legends, Hi'iaka embodies the spirit of the dance. There is a tremendous body of work recounting the sagas of Hi'iaka and her older sister, Pele. More than 300 songs and chants record the epic struggle between Pele and Hi'iaka over the ho'opa'a Lohi'au.

The primary story of Pele and Hi'iaka told through hula centers around a young man, a chanter named Lohi'au, with whom Pele had fallen in love. Lohi'au was a mortal who resided on the island of Kaua'i, and Pele missed him dearly. She asked Hi'iaka to fetch him for her and Hi'iaka agreed, asking in return that Pele protect her 'ohi'a lehua groves while she was gone. Pele gave Hi'iaka forty days to complete the journey.

The meles tell of Hi'iaka's exploits as she sets about her task and all those she meets along the way. Using cunning and magic, Hi'iaka manages to field her way through the various evil spirits that dwell throughout the island chain to reach Lohi'au's side. Unfortunately, a rift occurs between the two sisters when it takes Hi'iaka more than forty days to complete her task and, though she is loyal to her sister and refrains from sleeping with the attractive Lohi'au, Pele suspects the opposite and flies into a jealous rage. She sends her fires and lava down to destroy Hi'iaka's sacred groves.

As Hi'iaka and Lohi'au return to the Big Island, Hi'iaka sees her groves charred and burned, and in revenge, retaliates by embracing Lohi'au in front of Pele. Pele attacks, covering them with lava. While her sister cannot be harmed, being the goddess she is, Lohi'au is burnt to a crisp. A witness to this battle, one of Pele's brothers catches hold of the spirit of Lohi'au and returns him to his body. Lohi'au and Hi'iaka are reunited and return to Kauai.

Another primary story of hulas dedicated to Pele surrounds her volatile love affair with Kamapua'a, the Hawai'ian pig god. Insatiably in lust with Pele, he follows her everywhere, wooing her even as she calls him a pig, among other insults. Their arguments build until a fight erupts. Kamapua'a rages forth with torrential rainstorms while Pele opens the earth and pours rivers of lava over his forests. Eventually, Kamapua'a's storms begin to quench her sacred fires, and fearing that she will lose the battle, her brothers order her to sleep with him. After that, they become on-again off-again lovers, always fighting, always arguing, and yet passionately embracing one another as their lust fills the islands with energy and vibrancy.

The hulas that retell these stories are beautiful to watch, yes, but when performed with devotion and concentration, the energy and mana that the dancers raise is noticeable even through a television set.

Every year, there are numerous hula competitions that one can attend. The Merrie Monarch, named after King Kalakaua, is probably the most prestigious and famous one in the world. Performers are judged on not only their performance, but on costume, expression, and the mana they bring to the dance. If you ever have the chance to attend, you will not regret it.

A Rite for Connecting with the Healing Essence of Hypericum

By Janina Renée

St. John's wort (*Hypericum perforatum*) is a plant that is familiar to the folklorist because it has been used in all kinds of Midsummer celebrations. It has also been of value to herbalists in treating nervous conditions, insomnia, stomach and intestinal complaints, congestion, and many other maladies. However, these days hypericum is getting a lot of attention as an antidepressant that can rival Prozac. Some impressive scientific studies have verified its effect in relieving mild to moderate cases of depression. In fact, the majority of depressed patients in Germany are treated with this herbal remedy, where it "outsells Prozac by more than seven to one" (Carper, 45). It's interesting to note that one of hypericum's names in German is *jageteufel* because it was believed to chase the devil away.

This useful plant can be bought from herbalists, but it is widely available in pill form, sold at ordinary stores like Walmart and Rite-Aid, as well as at health food stores. For those taking pills from standardized extract, the recommended dose is 300 milligrams, taken three times a day (to equal 900 milligrams), for six weeks. This medicine has a cumulative effect, which is why you should take it for at least six weeks in order to determine how well it works for you.

St. John's wort is also available as a flower essence. Though not one of the original flower essences discovered by Dr. Edward Bach, it has been developed by the Flower Essence Society, and is included in their professional kit. Patricia Kaminski and Richard Katz describe the essence of hypericum as having the positive qualities of "illumined consciousness, light-filled awareness, and strength." They say that it helps correct "patterns of imbalance" by circulating light that "works within the self as a spiritual force that can illumine and anchor consciousness"(172).

It is important to honor the "essence" of a plant, whether it be in its natural state or converted into a tea, pill, or flower essence form. As a result, the following rite for connecting with the essence of hypericum can be performed when you wish to take St. John's wort in any form. When you are ready to take hypericum medicinally, hold your harvested plant, tea, pills, bottle of flower essence, or other herbal preparation before you and say:

I greet you herb of the Sun, you who are called hypericum, St. John's wort, amber, herb-john, penny-john, klamathweed, sol terrestis, and by many other names. The herbals extol your power to give calm and comfort, and freedom of mind. You are especially praised for your power to bring light and energy into mind and spirit.

Now visualize the living plant if you've seen a picture of it. Then visualize a warm, bright yellow light glowing and growing within your herbal preparation, and extending its rays to suffuse your body and being, until you are entirely awash in the light of a golden yellow sun that pulses within you. Now, take your medicine and say:

Hypericum, I honor you now, and affirm your power, asking that you join with my spirit and convey your healing essence. I give you thanks and gratitude. Blessed be!

Incidentally, you can extend your spirit in greeting to the living hypericum plant (or any plant) when you encounter it in the wild. You don't have to pick the plant, and you also don't have to memorize the lines above; it is enough to give it an appreciative nod in order to make a beneficial connection. Although an old-world wild flower, St. John's wort has spread to all states east of the Mississippi, and the entire Pacific Coast. It is found in Australia as well.

REFERENCES

Carper, Jean. *Miracle Cures.* New York: Harper-Collins, 1997.

Kaminski, Patricia, and Katz, Richard. *Flower Essence Repertory.* Nevada City, CA: The Flower Essence Society, 1986, 1992.

Lust, John. *The Herb Book.* New York: Bantam, 1974.

MINTS

By Therese Francis, Ph.D.

What is the only square you find in nature? The stems of plants in the mint family! The mint family is probably the most well known herb family. From the Romans who crowned themselves with peppermint wreaths to the modern wintergreen-flavored Life Savers, mints have been and still are important plants.

MYTHOLOGICAL ORIGINS

Upon discovering Pluto with the beautiful nymph Menthe, Persephone turned the nymph into a lowly plant. Unable to undo Persephone's spell, Pluto softened it so that each time Menthe was tread upon, the sweeter she smelled. Mints have since been anything but lowly.

CULINARY USES

From jellied mint for lamb chops to mint juleps, many varieties of mints have been used in cooking and baking. The best known mints for culinary use are spearmint, peppermint, and European water mint. The best mint for candies is Japanese mint, which most peppermint-flavored candies are made from.

There are several interesting mints. The fruit mints, apple mint and pineapple mint, actually taste like apples and pineapples. They make good jellies. Chocolate mint tastes like, well, chocolate mint. It makes a great breakfast tea!

To feel cooler on a hot day, steep a handful of mint leaves (any variety) in a quart of hot water for ten to twenty minutes. Strain and refrigerate. Wash your face in the infusion. Mint cools the body.

AROMATHERAPY USES

The mint smell is a stimulant that soothes. Add it to bath water after a rough day to bring your energy up but at the same time smooth the edges.

Medicinal Uses

The active constituent in mints is the menthol. Some mints, such as peppermint, have a high level (up to 75 percent) while other mints, such as catnip, have a lower level (around 20 percent). Pure menthol burns, so high-menthol mints, such as peppermint, are not recommended for infants or children.

Catnip is traditionally used for colic in infants. Make a weak tea and let the infant drink some from a bottle. Catnip tea is good also for stomach aches in older children and adults.

Peppermint has a great settling effect on motion sickness, and some people prefer it to ginger. Since menthol burns, peppermint is not recommended for children or infants. Use spearmint or one of the fruit mints instead.

The next time you do a cleansing fast, make a tea of peppermint and alfalfa. (This tastes better than it sounds.) This tonic cleanses the blood but should not be used by anyone with kidney problems.

Don't forget the after dinner mint or mint liquor. Menthol aids digestion, especially of fatty foods.

Cosmetic Uses

Mint is not added to cosmetics just for the scent. Mint water smoothes the skin and works as a toner. Also, mint can be added to green clay to deep cleanse pores.

Tea Readings

The proper way to drink a mint tea is to first deeply inhale the scent, savoring the smell. If you leave the tea leaves in the hot water, the scent will increase with time. Slowly drink the tea, breathing deeply between sips. When a small amount of tea remains, think of a question and quickly tip the cup over onto the tea saucer and then back upright. Some of the tea leaves will fall out onto the saucer and some will stay in the cup. Read the leaves that remain in the cup like you would find pictures in clouds. Let your imagination run. The pictures you find are significant for the question. The leaves that are closest to the top of the cup indicate what will happen soon, and the leaves at the bottom of the cup are further in the future.

THE MAGICAL MALLOW PLANT

BY ANNIE REDWING (CARLY WALL)

Take a walk down an old-fashioned lane and discover the mystical magic of a forgotten branch of the flower family. It's the large family called the mallows, with more than a thousand different species claiming membership.

You may ask why you should bother. In fact, the mallows hold secrets long forgotten. They are important medicinal herbs, as well as being allies for us humans to help us see into the astral world.

A LONG HISTORY

Old-fashioned gardens favored the many varieties of mallow: the hollyhock and the hibiscus for beauty, and the marsh mallow and the musk mallow for medicinal virtues.

Pliny once said, "Whosoever shall take a spoonful of the mallows shall that day be free from all diseases that may come to him." In fact, they are quite healing. The leaves, roots, and flowers of the marsh and musk mallow are useful in fighting inflammation and irritations of the urinary and respiratory systems. By boiling them in wine or milk, you can make a very useful drink for one who has a chest cold with coughs or bronchitis. The powdered root, made into a poultice, will take infection right out of any wound. If you have inflamed eyes, you can bathe them in an infusion of mallow leaves.

BEAUTY AND MAGIC

The hibiscus produces gigantic blooms to surprise and delight anyone. Few garden flowers can match their size. Their five-petal blossoms last only one day but bloom prolifically, so you will never miss the show. Some even produce twelve-inch flowers, but more common are the flowers reaching six inches in diameter, like the Chinese hibiscus or Rose of China.

Who can deny the charm of a row of hollyhocks blooming along the fence row? Their delicate, ruffled blooms in pastel colors are sure to charm your heart. If it's magic you seek, the hollyhock has a long history of it. Apparently, this family of flower is a favorite among the fairies. They love the nourishing seeds and often the seed has been called "fairy cheese." The blossoms are said to be used by the wee folk as boats to float across the creeks. They are also said to make pretty dancing dresses from the blooms and tie the skirts on with strands of thyme. Because of their love for this flower, it is said that you can see into the other realm and glimpse the faeries' world if you soak the blooms, along with thyme and marigold, in wine. Set this in the Sun for three days and on the third night rub it onto your eyelids, and it is said that your eyes will be opened.

Another old remedy says that you can predict the future using the blooms. Pick three flowers and three buds, and gather some twigs and a shallow pan of water. On the night of a Full Moon, turn the blossoms upside down to make the body of a doll. Take one of the buds and pierce it longways so that you can insert the twig down into the body of the doll, leaving the bud at top to form the head. Now insert another twig crossways through the calyx to make the arms. The frilly bloom will appear as a party dress. Take the other blossoms and do the same. Now float them upon the shallow dish of water. As the wind blows, the ladies will swirl. Ask questions about the future. Watch how the ladies turn. If it is to the left, the answer is no, but to the right, yes. If the ladies refuse to dance, the answer is undecided as of yet.

Whatever way you plan to use the mallow plant, you're sure to get great enjoyment from them, so don't forget to plant a few different types and kinds this year. Not only will it brighten a corner of your garden, but also you'll find it a magical plant in many ways.

THE SCENT OF SAFETY

BY THERESE FRANCIS, PH.D.

Throughout the world there have been plants recognized for their potency at keeping evil at bay.

FROM THE MEDITERRANEAN

I sometimes wonder if old Italy had more than its share of ghosts and goblins. Almost every herb we associate with Italian cooking may also be used for psychic safety, including rosemary, basil, bay, and thyme.

Grow a rosemary plant near the door. Its odor will keep evil from entering the house and will discourage mosquitoes from coming in. (Does this make mosquitoes evil spirits?) Use the fresh leaves in salads and spaghetti sauce.

Basil, bay, and thyme can be grown outside of the house, preferably under windows to keep bogeymen from entering. Basil is used to make pesto sauce, and thyme and bay are used to flavor soups.

Another Mediterranean herb is rue. During Medieval times, a rue leaf would be carried by someone who had committed a sin and was feeling "rueful" of having done so. The leaves could also be secretly sent as an indicator that one knew the person had done something unacceptable. The growing plant was favored as a psychic defense against committing a sin (possibly as a reminder that one would rue the day the sin was committed as opposed to actually preventing any actions). Be aware that some people get a poison ivy-like rash from touching the leaves.

FROM THE NEW WORLD

There are many herbs native to North and Central America that are used to drive evil away and keep it away. You've probably heard of many of them since they are very popular: sage, sweetgrass, life everlasting, cedar, and copal.

Although sage grows in the old world, the idea of burning sage for psychic protection and cleansing is a new world one. Many tribes throughout the North and Central American continents use white or mountain sage as an incense. (Both of these types of sage taste very strong and were probably never eaten.) The smoke cleanses the invisible bodies of lurking evil and other people's energies, and strengthens the invisible (ethereal) bodies. Some people use shells to hold the burning leaves and feathered fans to fan the smoke around people and council areas before important decisions are discussed. (Sage is earth, fire is fire, the shell represents water, and the feathered fan air. Thus the four elements, the four seasons, the four phases of life, and the four cardinal directions are combined with intention/spirit.)

Many of the northern tribes follow a sage cleansing with sweetgrass. The pleasant smell attracts allies and other invisible protectors, calms the spirit, and clarifies thought.

In Central America, where sage does not grow and is not always readily available through trade, copal is popular. Copal is a resin grown from one of several varieties of tropical trees. A little bit of hard resin is thrown into a fire or onto charcoal, and the smoke fanned around a temple or council area.

Cedar, juniper, or pinion branches (depending on what is available in the immediate area) are frequently used in sweats and bathing rituals to cleans the physical and etheric bodies. The needles are smeared on the body, burned on the fire, and/or used to strike the skin. This idea is also found throughout northern Europe (saunas, etc.).

A lesser-known plant is called life everlasting, or "evil's bane." The small white flowers of this northern plant are used against many illnesses and conditions, including asthma.

MIDDLE EAST

Many of the protective incenses used in the Catholic church are based on Middle Eastern tradition, which is reasonable when you consider that the Byzantine Empire established Catholicism. Frankincense and myrrh are burned to create a thick, heady incense to repel evil.

Using roses for protection also comes out of the Middle East. Rose petals under the pillow keep nightmares at bay, and rose water in the bath ensures soft skin and pure thoughts untampered by the evil intentions of others.

Rosemary: The Marvelous Magical Herb

By Edain McCoy

I f there was ever a must-have herb for any magical cabinet it is rosemary. This versatile herb is frequently mentioned in grimoires and spellbooks. It is inexpensive, easy to cultivate, and can be used for a vast array of magical needs. Whenever another herb cannot be found to complete a magical recipe, rosemary is often a perfect substitute.

Ruled by the Sun and by the element of fire, rosemary's greatest strength is its transformative powers. This makes it a natural for use in healing magic. The volatile oil from the plant was once cultivated in the Mediterranean region and used as an antiseptic and as a purification oil in religious rites. It is often called for in magical healing formulae. Try adding a drop or two of medicinal ointment to add a magical healing touch, or blend rosemary oil in a base of olive oil and use it as an anointing oil to promote total body/mind healing.

Incenses with rosemary can create an atmosphere conducive to almost any magical need, depending on how the outcome is visualized and what other herbs are included the mix. Alone it can purify the area, raising the vibrational rate to be a boon to the most sacred of spiritual rituals. Mixed with herbs for love, lust, mental prowess, or healing, it can be a boon to these efforts as well.

Rosemary is used frequently in spells to induce romance, particularly if the goal is a lusty relationship. Burning red candles doused in rosemary oil is a great way to add a passionate atmosphere to romantic encounters. Sprinkling the dried herb around areas where you expect a potential lover to walk can turn his or her heart toward you. Inhaling the scent of the pure oil just before bedtime can help curb insomnia, promote peaceful sleep, and prevent nightmares.

For spells of healing, mix rosemary with comfrey or eyebright. For spells of love, mix it with yarrow. For creating lust, mix with cinnamon. Mix with dragon's blood to undo the harmful intent of an enemy, and blend with dill to increase powers of concentration.

The Aztec Flying Pole Ceremony

By Bernyce Barlow

Los Voladores, the flying pole dance, was performed by the Aztecs as a rite of spring. A tree was selected and ritually cut to serve as a pole. Then a small platform was attached to the top of the tree. The pole was securely set in the ground after an offering had been placed in the hole. Often a chicken or food offerings were given, asking the tree to nourish the flyers and see to their safety. Four ropes were tied to the top of *el volador,* or flying pole, and wound around its trunk thirteen times. The thirteen revolutions were believed to represent the four cycles of thirteen years that made up the fifty-two year cycle of the Aztec calendar.

After the pole was raised, a man climbed to the top of the pole with a drum and a flute and settled in on the platform. There he played seven songs, each one seven times, honoring each of the four directions. The songs represented the seven Aztec universes. When the singer was through, four men who had tied themselves to the ropes and climbed the pole threw themselves from the top, screaming like eagles, and unwound around the pole thirteen times. The flyers were adorned with hawk or eagle feathers and were sometimes painted black and red.

Los Voladores was usually performed at the base of the temple mounds during the Spring Equinox. As it is globally with the rites of spring, the Aztecs believed the sacrifice of a living tree, as well as the willingness of a human sacrifice, would hopefully bring on a prolific seasonal cycle from planting to harvest.

Curanderismo: Mexican Magic

By Edain McCoy

Catholicism has probably endured more blending and branching off from its basic tenets than any other major religion. This is not because there is anything inherently wrong with that faith, but because it is one of the oldest and widest spread Christian sects. As Catholicism spread across the world, people blended it with their existing traditions. The syncretic religions resulting from this blending retained the local folkways. These old ways were further blended with the folk magic of other peoples whose cultures influenced the region. In the southwest this process continues to the present day.

The American southwest is one of the most ethnically diverse regions of the world, where the lines of demarcation between various cultures are blurred at best. In contrast to many of the modern magical traditions whose practitioners strive to live in balance with the rest of creation, practitioners of several of the southwestern traditions do not strive for balance, and magical manipulation is commonplace among them. Some argue that this trend is changing slowly, but it appears to be a long way from complete. Part of the reason for this is the traditional Latino or Hispanic perceptions of the modern magical traditions and the names they choose for themselves. For example, the word *Witch* has not undergone a large-scale reclamation as a name for a positive, nature-based religion as it has in Anglo-Amercian culture. This is why we can find a number of magic texts written in Spanish but virtually none about the new Witchcraft traditions that are so popular among other cultures in modern North America.

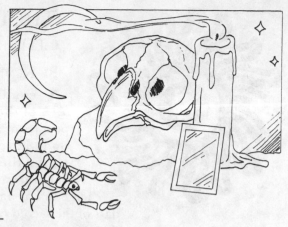

To the Latinos, Witchcraft does not have the Satanic, anti-Christian connotation it has for many other Americans, but to call someone a *brujo* or a *bruja* conjures up an image of someone who practices negative magic and throws curses around like used tissues. *Brujeria,* which in Spanish means "witchcraft," is still felt by the majority to be not just a negative path, but one to be actively feared because it is accepted—rightly in some cases and wrongly in others—that a brujo will curse anyone if the price is right.

In contrast to Brujeria is the gentle art of the *curanderos* and *curanderas,* the wise men and women, shamans, and healers of the Latino community. I was introduced to a gifted curandera through a close friend, and had the pleasure of learning from her and sharing with her some of my own magical traditions. She practiced ancient magic acts, but she considered herself a devout Catholic and all her efforts were done in tandem with various saints and with prayer to the Christian god. No money was charged for her services. There was an adamant refusal by many Latinos to call any of what she did "magic." *Latina Magazine's* August 1997 issue carried a short article on a curandera of New Mexico that emphasized her healing skills, but the idea of *magico* was never even alluded to.

Curanderismo has its deepest roots in the healing arts. In one leading Spanish language dictionary the practice is clearly defined as "folk medicine." In Spanish the word *cura* means "to cure," and in some Spanish speaking cultures the word *curandera* is associated with "Witch Doctor." The most common reason the aid of a curandera is sought is for healing treatments to replace or augment medical treatment.

213

THE LEGEND OF THE FIVE SUNS

BY KENNETH JOHNSON

According to the mythology of the Aztecs and other peoples of ancient Mexico, the Gods have created and destroyed the world four times. Each world was called a "Sun," and each Sun was named for one of the days of the sacred calendar. This calendar, known throughout ancient Mexico and Central America, is the same one we usually call the Mayan Calendar, even though they may not have invented it.

The first world was called the Jaguar Sun, and the people of that early time were devoured by jaguars when their world was destroyed. The second world was called the Wind Sun, and its inhabitants were all transformed into jabbering monkeys before great hurricanes blew their world to pieces. The third world was called Storm Sun, and when a rain of fire destroyed it, only the birds were saved, for they alone could fly to safety. The fourth world was called Water Sun, and it was destroyed by a great flood.

After the end of the fourth world, the gods gathered to create a new one. To do so, one of the gods would have to sacrifice himself upon a funeral pyre. There was a particularly boastful god among them who believed that he could bring light to the new world through such a sacrifice, and that he could do it alone.

The other Gods knew that he was wrong, though. It would take the sacrifice of two deities to bring light to the new Sun, and so another god was chosen: a sickly fellow with a skin disease who was so badly afflicted that he didn't mind sacrificing himself.

The flames were lit and blazed high. The boastful god prepared to fling himself into the inferno, but lost his courage and turned back. What would happen now? How could the new world begin?

Gladly and without hesitation, the sickly god threw himself into the flames. So beautiful was his sacrifice that the boastful god became filled with shame, and thus followed him into the fire.

The sickly god became the bright and beautiful Sun we see above us, and the boastful god, a lesser light, became our Moon.

This world that we live in, this Fifth Sun, received its own name according to the sacred calendar. It is called the Earthquake Sun, and the Aztecs believed that it would someday be destroyed by a series of cataclysmic earthquakes. But when?

The Aztec legends are not at all clear regarding a time frame. Many Native peoples of Mexico and Central America shared the Aztec belief in a succession of worlds, including the Maya, and it is believed that the so-called Mayan Great Cycle of 5,125 years was originally meant to chart the life and death of the Fifth Sun. The Mayan Great Cycle began in 3114 B.C., right after the destruction of the Water Sun by flood, and it is due to end on December 21, 2012. Does this mean that the world will be destroyed once and for all by a terrible earthquake?

It is more likely that the Maya thought of the world-shattering "earthquake" in terms of consciousness rather than in terms of a physical event. After all, they themselves made predictions concerning dates several thousand years beyond the end-date of 2012. We can only assume that they meant for us to survive. In fact, each successive Sun or world can be seen as a step forward in the evolution of human consciousness. If this is so, then we can expect a quantum leap in consciousness when the Sixth Sun begins.

Cactus Magic

By deTraci Regula

Overlooked among the soft, delicate plants that comprise much of herb lore, the magnificent variety of cacti and succulents can contribute to the safety of your household as well as inspire your magic.

While cacti (the proper plural of "cactus") require some special care to thrive, most of them prefer neglect, making them ideal companions for today's busy lifestyles. Water them when they are dry. They hate wet feet, and most cacti that fail do so because of overwatering.

Mammillaria Species

These cacti reproduce by budding off miniature versions of themselves, and a mature specimen may have a dozen or more "babies" clinging to the central stalk. Resembling the multi-breasted statue of Diana of Ephesus, it's easy to see why these were called *mammillaria* by an early classifier. Cacti of this type are perfect fertility symbols, and can serve as a living image of any of the fertility-related goddesses.

If you want to propagate these plants, simply snap off one of the small baby plants. The bigger they are, the more likely it is that they will root well. Place it in a mixture of half sand and half potting soil, or use a prepared cactus potting mix. While it is rooting, water it every day, being careful that the soil does not actually become waterlogged.

If the mammillaria represents the Goddess, it's easy to find cacti to represent the God. Jutting phalliform cacti are common, sending up a bold single stalk. Some of these are covered with spines, while others are smooth to the touch. Generally, these will propagate by growing a companion from the same root stock, resulting in a clump of columnar forms.

Some of the mammillaria grow fairly tall, and in this guise, they too can represents the male phallus and its protective power.

SPIRAL SUCCULENTS

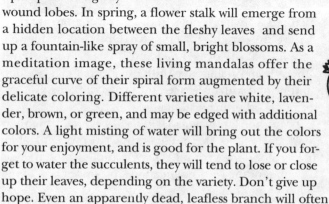

Many of these easy-to-grow plants send up a spiral of tightly wound lobes. In spring, a flower stalk will emerge from a hidden location between the fleshy leaves and send up a fountain-like spray of small, bright blossoms. As a meditation image, these living mandalas offer the graceful curve of their spiral form augmented by their delicate coloring. Different varieties are white, lavender, brown, or green, and may be edged with additional colors. A light misting of water will bring out the colors for your enjoyment, and is good for the plant. If you forget to water the succulents, they will tend to lose or close up their leaves, depending on the variety. Don't give up hope. Even an apparently dead, leafless branch will often begin to bring forth new life with a steady diet of moisture and sunlight, making these excellent symbols of resurrection and new life.

Some succulents are coated with a fur-like material, and unlike their spiny cactus cousins, invite gentle touch. These succulents are excellent stress reducers. A broken lobe will usually produce an entirely new, miniature plant. These succulents are good plants to invoke the qualities of patience, endurance, and fertility.

STONE PLANT OR LIVING ROCKS

These oddly-disguised succulents can be easily thought of as the equivalent of crystal spirits. Growing alone, the pebble-like forms eventually send up a surprising flower. Other forms of succulents have transparent "windows" designed to gather sunlight. Their coolness is reminiscent of the feeling of touchstones and crystals.

WITCH WEED

This quick-growing succulent boasts thousands of finger-like projections, topped with tiny yellow flowers in the spring. Filled with a milky, irritating sap, these plants are physical and magical guardians.

OPUNTIA SPECIES

These species, which are usually paddle-shaped, produce striking large ovaloid pads, called "joints" by experts. At the tips of mature

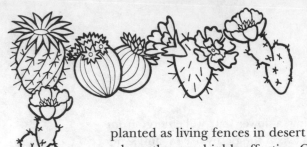

pads brilliant flowers blossom, followed by equally vivid-colored edible fruits. These cacti are often planted as living fences in desert or chaparral areas, where they are highly effective. Opuntia cacti have a great deal of "presence" and it is easy to feel that there is an intelligence in the plant that can be communicated with and asked for protection, inspiration, or many other magical needs.

Another Opuntia is *Opuntia serpentina,* which has long, curving joints that grow in writhing, snake-like forms along the ground. This Opuntia can be used as a symbol of the wisdom, healing, and protection of the serpent kingdom.

SAGUARO

One cactus that grows in solitary glory reminds me of the hermit card in the tarot. This is the saguaro, or *Carnegiea gigantea,* which often stands alone, with a single branch reaching toward the sky as if lifting up an unseen lantern. These are the classic cactus seen whenever an artist wants to convey "desert." You've seen drawings of them in the backgrounds of *Road Runner* cartoons hundreds of times. Unfortunately, these cacti are so treasured by landscapers that in Arizona that they are often rustled. Since the root system of these giants may take hundreds of years to develop, the saguaro generally does not survive transplanting. A few seed companies offer saguaro seed, but be warned that tending it is a task you may pass on to your great-grandchildren.

BARREL CACTUS

Barrel cacti are excellent solar symbols because of their round shape and the decorative spines adorning their crowns. As reservoirs of moisture, these cacti can also be thought of as reservoirs of power and energy. As with all the spined cactus, they too can be assigned a protective function.

Because cactus growth is so variable, individual specimens may take on evocative forms. If your imagination sees a sacred symbol or

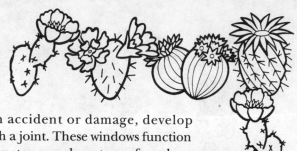

animal in the branches of the cactus, it can be used as a living symbol. Other cacti may, through accident or damage, develop healed holes through a joint. These windows function exactly like the holey stones or hag stones found on the beach. They can be peered through to gain psychic access to other worlds, or to obtain visions.

The sandy soil used for potting cacti is also an excellent home for your crystals, and crystals and cactus seem to have a natural affinity. Mix cacti and crystals of approximately the same size, laid out in a mandala pattern. Meditating on this living garden of rock and plant is calming and will improve your understanding of both kingdoms.

Growing Cactus

Growing cactus from seed is also a magical experience, and a lesson in patience and evocation of the plant spirits. In a shallow dish, place cactus mix with about a quarter volume added washed quartz sand, available from nurseries. Place the cactus seed on the soil and cover with more sand. Keep slightly moist. In about two to three weeks, seemingly out of nowhere, tiny green globes, looking as perfect as if someone spilled some bright green beads onto the surface, will appear. Keep them gently moist and out of direct light under a piece of screening, and, gradually, tiny fuzz-like spines will begin to appear and the miniature cactus will start to take on characteristics of its particular type. Tie in your daily care for these small lives with your meditations or prayers.

Buying Cacti

Flowering cacti are best bought during the spring and summer, when they are revealing their blossoms. Cacti are inspiring in many ways, particularly when a small plant delivers up a tremendous blossom, often three or four times longer than the plant's height.

In cold or wet climates, a cactus will do best as a potted plant that can be brought inside at the change of seasons or weather conditions. Enjoy your beautifuly, sticky, protective cactus garden!

PAGAN TRADITIONS OF ALBA

BY JAMES BROWN

Over a hundred years ago, one of the finest examples of brunnells bridges was erected over the Forth Estuary linking Fife with Edinburgh. The Forth Rail Bridge was then, and still is, one of the most complex feats of engineering ever undertaken, but what many miss on crossing the bridge is the small town that lies directly beneath the south side, The ancient town of South Queensferry.

Many Pagan customs dating from pre-Christian times are still re-enacted all over Scotland to this day, but few customs can prove to be older than the Burry-Man festival that is held annually in this area on the second Friday of August each year, as it has been since Paleolithic times. Proof of this can be gleaned from the various wall carvings in the area, some of which depict the Burry-Man himself.

The actual embodiment of the Burry-Man is that of the Green Man. He is said to symbolize man's affinity with nature. A local man is picked to "go Burry for the year." At the festival time, locals, both Christians and Pagans, help to adorn the man by first making a white linen body suit for him to wear. Once the suit is made, the young local women take to the wild fields and pick the seed pods of the burdock plant, which are basically nature's answer to balls of Velcro. The burrs are then stuck to the suit, covering the man from head to toe completely, with only small holes for the mouth and eyes. The Scottish Lion-Rampant flag is then tied round his stomach, and the Burry-Man is ready for the parade.

Although the festival is a purely Pagan ritual, it also symbolizes yet another fine old Scottish tradition: drinking copious amounts of alcohol! The "Burry" is led around the small town by two helpers. Given the severe heat inside the suit and the large amounts of alcohol he is about to consume, they are well needed.

Once the parade is under way, the Burry visits houses he feels he needs to in order to bring luck to the homes. In order for him to bestow his blessing on the house, the occupants must first give him a large dram of whisky. It is not unknown for the Burry to visit more than fifty houses, but most only manage thirty to forty.

In earlier times, the Burry would have the pick of the women in the village after the festival, but unfortunately for the present day Burry-Men, this part of the tradition is no longer recognized. However, there are still some perks to being the local Burry, apart from the obvious alcoholic ones. The Burry is given the freedom of the city for the first week commencing the festival.

It is thought that the seed pods of the burdock plant were once used to make a very intoxicating wine/mead that may have been produced in the area, and many believe this is the reason for choosing to cover the man in burrs. A more likely explanation would simply be that some early Pagan people had bestowed some religious significance on the plant, given that its seeds stuck to almost everything that touched it.

The whole area of the Forth Estuary and its islands was heavily populated by early Pagan people. At that time it would have been covered in dense woodland, and given the large expanse of calm water, both fresh and salt, the area would have housed an abundant supply of food for the growing villages, one of which was to become South Queensferry.

In most people's opinions, one of the most fascinating aspects of the festival is the involvement of the locals. Like most of the small fishing villages of Fife and its surrounding areas, they now have a relatively high population of Church-going inhabitants who make no bones about speaking out against the "evils" of witchcraft, but during the Burry-Man festival, all the locals join in. It is almost like a glimpse into the past when people could and would work together, no matter what their religious beliefs. It is a strange, yet enjoyable sight to see Pagan

folk working alongside Church Elders and the like, each enjoying each other's company and bearing no malice toward anyone.

The Burry-Man festival also used to share the day with another, more dubious re-enactment of an ancient custom: the climbing of the greasy pole. Although this may sound like a reasonably tame tradition, the custom had to be outlawed back in the fifties due to the fact that many people actually died during the festivities! The custom was basically to grease twenty feet of a fifty-foot pole with cow fat, then erect it, greased end up. It was the job of the young men in the village to take death into their own hands by attempting to climb the pole all the way to the top. Unfortunately, most accidents occurred when the young man would be thirty or so feet up the pole, and on hitting the greased part, would simply plummet to the ground, occasionally breaking his legs and other limbs, but all too frequently dying in the process.

The origins of the custom lay in the finding of a wife. The pole was a phallic symbol like the maypole. It is thought that if a man were to complete the task, managing to get to the top of the pole, he would then be guaranteed a woman to marry. Customs that end in a similar outcome are carried out to this day the world over, though now they usually only entail the buying of a few gin and tonics and the promise of a large house and bank balance. A much safer alternative, I think!

After more than twenty people died in total over the years, the local council decided to ban the greasy pole all together. However, as with most things in Alba, just because it had been banned, it did not mean the custom was stopped. Indeed, to this day people say it is still carried out in secret deep within the woods, but naturally no one knows anything about it, except that on the second Friday in August, the local hospital is deluged with patients needing treatment for broken limbs after suffering "mysterious accidents."

REMNANTS OF PAGANISM IN BRITAIN

BY RAYMOND BUCKLAND

Neo-Paganism, or "new" Paganism, is actively practiced in Great Britain, as it is in many countries around the world. The Wiccan revival, spearheaded by the late Gerald Gardner, spawned a legion of Neo-Pagan religious paths. Britain has many instances of what might be termed "old" Paganism, still alive and well. There are many traditional customs celebrated annually throughout the British Isles that are unbroken practices from pre-Christian times.

Although the early Church did all in its power to stamp out anything and everything that smacked of pre-Christian Paganism, there was a large number of endemic folk festivals that it overlooked. Outwardly they must have seemed to be no more than quaint, innocent folk dances and processions, celebrating the time of harvest or the coming of spring, that were no threat to the new religion. Many simply passed unnoticed because the local clerics were themselves participants in the rites.

One of the best known such Pagan survivals is the Abbots Bromley Horn Dance, which has been well documented both here and elsewhere, but there are many more, lesser known, such celebrations.

In Abbotsbury, Dorset, "Garland Day" is celebrated on May 13, which was May Day in the old calendar. Originally every family in the fishing village would make a garland of flowers and, in procession, carry it to the sea. There they would hang it on the prow of the family boat and take it for a short trip out to sea before returning to shore with it. There it was blessed—presumably originally by a Pagan priest or priestess—today by the village priest, before being taken out again and tossed into the sea. This was a form of blessing the sea at the start of the mackerel fishing season. Today the local school children are the ones who make the garlands. They make just three: one of wild flowers and one of cultivated garden flowers made by the smaller children, and one larger garland made by the older children.

There is an Arbor Tree Day celebration held at Aston-on-Clun, Shropshire, where an old black poplar tree in the center of the village is decorated with ribbons and flags every May 29. The decorations are left on all year, to be renewed the following year. The date is the old Oak Apple Day and almost certainly is a remnant of ancient tree veneration. In the center of Appleton Thorn, in Cheshire, stands a thorn tree that is similarly venerated, this time on July 5, the old Midsummer Day. The ritual is known as "Bawming the Thorn." Bawming is an old word for annointing or adorning.

A remnant of an old fertility rite is still performed every year at South Queensferry, on the Firth of Forth, West Lothian. It features what is known as the "Burry-Man," a man dressed totally in white flannel to which have been attached thousands of the burrs from the burr thistle (*Arctimus bardana*). He wears a cloth helmet with eye-holes cut into it so that even his face is covered with the burrs. On his head he wears a bowler hat (derby) covered with seventy roses. Four roses are also added to both his front and back. A flag is tied about his waist. In each hand he holds a staff topped with many flowers. Two attendants walk beside him, helping support his arms, which he keeps held straight out. They all start out in the morning and walk slowly a total of seven miles around the village, not finishing until evening. As they reach each house, a shout goes up and the occupants rush out to give him gifts. The Burryman does not speak at all and his attendants collect the gifts (which these days are usually money for charity).

Horn blowing and noise-making generally is associated with driving away evil spirits in many parts of the world. The practice is to be found scattered throughout the British Isles. On the Isle of Man, on the night of May Eve, horns are blown just as they used to be for centuries on the lighting of the Beltane fires. The Isle of Man is full of ancient lore about the fairies, some of whom are of evil intent. The horn-blowing is a ritual to keep these creatures away. At Gainsborough, Lincolnshire, horn-blowing plays a part on Oak Apple Day, when huge garlands and crowns of flowers and gilded oak apples are hoisted on ropes across the streets. As soon as the boughs of apples and flowers have been tied in place, all the children will blow horns, creating a cacophony of sound that lasts all day. In Penzance, Cornwall, groups of horn-blowers will pass through the town in the early hours of May Day morning, blowing their fanfares under windows to wake the folk, and receiving gifts in return. Here the horn blowing is to signal the arrival of summer. In all of the above, it used to be that the horns were homemade from cow horns or from shells, though today most of them are cheap manufactured ones.

A whole host of Pagan beliefs was carried into the Christian era by the Morris dancers found throughout the British Isles. Outwardly they were dancing to entertain and to celebrate the seasons, but in actuality many, if not most, of their dances were full of Pagan symbolism. Morris dancing is extremely popular today, both in Britain and many other countries.

The many varieties of hobby horse, for example the Padstow one (which is probably based on the charger of the Celtic sea-god Manannan) and the Minehead one, are associated with pre-Christian steeds and feature in parades, pantomimes, and in Morris dances. In these traditional celebrations, Paganism lives on in modern Britain.

PITTENWEEM: A LAND OF WITCHES

BY JAMES BROWN

Although there is little actual documented information on the Picts of Alba (Scotland), some Roman records do exist pertaining to the language used by our early Pagan forefathers. For example, many place names in Alba have the prefix "pitt" in their names. The word *pitt* was a Pictish Gaelic word meaning "share of land belonging to the Picts." It might also be noted that three farms in Fife share the name "Pittcorthie," meaning "Pictish share of land containing a symbol stone," and indeed, all three have a symbol stone somewhere within the confines of the farm. One town bearing the prefix pitt on the southern east coast of Alba in the Kingdom of Fife is the small fishing village of Pittenweem. It is true that many places all over Europe can lay claim to playing a vital part in the establishment of what we know today as Paganism, but none more so than this small fishing village. Today there is little evidence of the barbaric treatment that was heaped upon this town during the Witch persecutions, but dig a little deeper and you will soon find a history that is second to none in Pagan terms.

One cannot even attempt to recount Pittenweem's full history in one short article, but basically, the name translates to "a Pictish share of land containing caves." Pittenweem itself differed from the many Pictish colonies in Alba at that time in that it is generally thought that there was a strong Celtic presence as well. Many standing stones that can still be viewed to this day contain both Celtic/Druidic and Pictish symbolism on the same face of the stone, and were almost certainly done at the same period of time. Due to an almost constant threat of invasion by Romans from the south, the Scotti from the west, and the Vikings from the east, Fife marked the most southerly stronghold and therefore had to be the largest. It is thought that both the Picti and what was left of the true Pagan Celts (most having been converted to Christianity by this time), worked and lived together in this area. Soon after the various threats disappeared and

the majority of the Pictish people were all but wiped out by the Christian-led Scotti after signing a peace treaty with them (approximately the ninth or tenth century), the inhabitants found themselves with only one belief system. It was a strange blend of the two Pagan cultures. Alban witchcraft had been born.

Throughout the many documented cases of witchcraft practiced in the British Isles, the small town of Pittenweem still manages to stand out among the rest. The aptly-named writer and chronicler Sir Walter Scott wrote that "more people have been executed for the crimes of witchcraft in this most damnable town of Pittenweem in one week than in the whole of Scotland in one month!" He also added, "we must find a way to stamp out this most evil of crimes in this thoroughly evil town!" Of course, what he was mistaking for devil worship was merely the inhabitants of the town going about their Pagan religious duties and ceremonies. To the best of my knowledge, the first use of the word "coven" also comes from the Church records of the East Nuek of Fife in 1642, which is where the town is situated. (It was previously thought the first use of the word was made in 1643, once again in Church records.)

One of Pittenweem's more famous inhabitants was one Grizzie Gairdner, a self-confessed witch (of the real kind) who had something of a reputation for cursing people, places, and in one case, the whole town! Most Witches and Pagans are familiar with the works of Gerald Gardner, but a little-known fact is that he laid claim to old Grizzie being his distant ancestor!

One widely-documented case was when Grizie Gairdner decided to cast a spell that would induce a plague of beetles on the town. This was done in revenge toward a young man who, in his ignorance, supposedly refused the sexual advances of old Grizzie. It is also documented that the curse did indeed work and that year a plague of beetles of every description descended upon the town, ruining the crops and infesting every household. To this day, the inhabitants of Pittenweem still fear a return of the curse. Grizzie herself was eventually burned at the stake for of witchcraft.

One of the best authenticated stories of a Pittenweem Witch casting a curse is also a little-known one. One of the most famous characters in Alban history was to fall victim to a curse, placed by a Pittenweem Witch! We have all heard the story of Robinson Crusoe, but the actual character on whom the story was based, one Alexander Selkirk, found out the hard way that, in that day at least, Witches were not to be crossed. The source of this tale is the closest living descendant of Alexander Selkirk, who to this day still lives in the town. It is not known what the reasons were behind the curse, but it is known that two days after the spell was cast, Selkirk set sail from Lower Largo, a small fishing village a few miles down the road. The rest is, as they say, history.

Many scholars and historians still try to dispute the existence of truly Pagan Witches during the period of time stretching from the thirteenth to fifteenth centuries. One piece of information from the Church records of the East Nuek of Fife proves all these theories wrong. One of the major truly Pagan ceremonies is the "fertility rite of fire," which basically involved the young girls of the village leaping over an open fire with a broom between their legs. One would not have to stretch the imagination too far to see the symbolism behind this rite. It is not hard to imagine an outsider seeing this rite performed at night and imagining that they were actually flying on their brooms. This is exactly what is on record at the St. Monan's Parish Church records. In the year 1638, records show that an outsider of the village witnessed the whole rite and explained it word for word to the local pastor, who then recorded it. It was later adapted to mean that the Witches themselves had been flying on their broomsticks. Thus the legend of Witches flying on broomsticks was born. To many people, this is proof positive that people were indeed practicing what we know today as witchcraft back in the dark ages.

The majority of Pagan folk assume that most people accused of witchcraft were burned at the stake. This is not true of most of Europe, though it was the case in Alba. In England only a handful of witches were ever burned. Most were either hanged or died during

the torturous interrogations. Indeed there were more Witches burned in a day in Pittenweem than in the whole sordid history of England. The simple reason behind this was that burning a Witch was a very expensive exercise. The family and friends of the accused had to meet the costs, which helped give rise to the myth that Scottish people are tight with their money! In one week during 1648, thirty-six people were put to the stake in Pittenweem.

The traditional covens that exist today in the East Nuek of Fife still perform rites that were being practiced hundreds of years ago. This is only possible due to the fact that some original grimoires from the time of the Witch persecutions are still held by the elders. Even though the teachings are recognized and practiced, the books themselves are rarely, if ever, opened. Most of the elders who have these books in their possession prefer to have them photocopied, and the copy is still guarded as secretly as the original. Only certain group members and selected solitaries are privileged enough to view the manuscripts, though few would be able to read them even if they did have access, given that they are written in the old Alban tongue.

It might be useful for a lot of the solitaries out there to note that there are no references in these grimoires whatsoever pertaining to coven work. Indeed it is highly unlikely that the average Witch of that time ever practiced in a "coven" at all! It would appear that actual covens, or at the very least, the word "coven," were invented by the Christian Church of that time and was so heaped on us that we even started believing it ourselves! This is not to say covens are not a good idea. They work well if operated by the correct people.

Lastly, if any readers find themselves visiting Alba, make sure to visit the small, unassuming town of Pittenweem. You can be guaranteed a warm welcome by the locals and all the help you require with your studies. Much of what we call witchcraft and Paganism today is owed to the good people of Pittenweem, its surrounding areas, and the hundreds of other Witches from towns in Britain who gave their lives in order that the religion could survive and flourish into the wondrous and ancient belief system we know today.

Music and Ritual

By Julie Forest Middleton

The chant started low and slow, and as more of us learned it, we joined in. Someone added a high harmony and someone else started a drum beat on the floor and quickly it became rich and full and gathered steam. Then suddenly it caught fire and we were on our feet and dancing as the fire filled us. The energy snaked around the circle like braided silver; it rose through us and around us, and when it reached its peak we shouted it off into the universe, sending it out to our chosen destination. We whooped and hollered as we fell to the floor, and as we calmed down, the priestess grounded the remaining energy back into the Earth.

Music and ritual—how does it work and why? What makes a chant work one time and not the next? What can music do for your rituals? How do you teach songs and use music when your group doesn't like to sing?

What Singing Does and How It Does It

Think about the times you've sung with others around a campfire or at a sing-along during a concert. Remember the feeling of cohesiveness and bonding that happened? When a group sings together, it breathes together, and songs become breathing meditations. Singing together focuses your energy and attention; it gets everyone's energy moving in the same direction; it puts all of you in a "groove" together.

In ritual, music can do many things. It can invoke a greater being and speak to Her or Him in prayer; it can help to raise a cone of power. Music celebrates, grieves, soothes, heals, trances, and connects the parts of the ritual together.

Music teaches. It carries the word (liturgy) and provides both example and role model of how to best live our lives.

Has a song ever spoken to you so truly and deeply of your own experience that you cried? Music touches our hearts and dissolves our defenses. It opens us up and allows Spirit to enter. It speaks to the unconscious parts of ourselves (and to the collective unconscious) and brings about healing and change.

Each song has a unique tune (that opens us up), unique words (that teach), and a unique energy (that stirs us to change and heal). In other words, each song has its own unique intention. When you begin designing a ritual, you first settle on your intention: what do you want this ritual to do? How do you want it to happen?

So when you select songs for your ritual, look at the intention and energy of each part of the ritual and pick songs that will enhance or add to this energy and intention. Songs are like plants—if it's appropriate in its setting it will work; if it doesn't work there, it's a weed. So what do you want this song to do at this point of the ritual? What energy do you want it to bring? How do you want people to feel during and after the song? What is your intention?

CHANTS

In Pagan rituals, chants are the songs most often used. Groups usually sing chants three or four times, then stop. Unfortunately, this gives no chance for the energy of the song to develop and work. Repetitive sounds awaken the inner world of Spirit.

A chant is a short song that needs to be sung over and over and over for a long time, until you're totally bored, then you sing it some more. It's then that the magic happens. If you're using a song to invoke the Goddess, sing it long enough that the Goddess will hear it and come. Don't stop singing it until She does come. (You'll know.)

If you're using a chant to raise a cone of power, sing it until it catches fire and takes off, and then at the height, send it up and out. Or sing it until it doesn't catch fire; in which case you'll simply bring it to a close and ground the energy. Sometimes it's impossible to raise a cone (people are too tired or wrung out and it just won't happen) and that's okay too. Don't force something that's not going to happen.

Some chants are longer songs that insist on being sung many times. There's something so very satisfying that you simply want to keep going. Don't be afraid to sing a song for five or ten minutes, or for thirty. In all times in all cultures people have sung their sacred songs, and the oldest chants are the devotional ones. Think about Gregorian Chant, sung for hours on end in monasteries. Pagans don't have monasteries to live and worship in. We have living rooms and back yards and sometimes parks and, occasionally, dedicated land. We sing our chants wherever we are.

ZIPPER SONGS

A zipper song is one in which a certain key word or phrase can be replaced to change the meaning. For instance Starhawk's song *Snake Woman* goes, "Snake woman shedding her skin / Snake woman shedding her skin / Shedding, shedding, shedding her skin / Shedding, shedding, shedding her skin." That's the way you'd teach it, singing it enough times that everyone's familiar with the tune and words. I might not feel like a snake woman tonight, though. Maybe I feel more like a worm, in which case I might change it to "Worm woman burrowing down / Burrowing, burrowing, burrowing down." Maybe Connie feels like "Eagle woman flying so high," and Jim sings "Mountain man feeling so strong."

Zipper songs give each individual a chance to express where they are in their process, and if you listen to the phrases each person chooses, you can learn lots about them.

One way of making these changes while you're singing is to go around the circle in order and let each one do a verse. You may want to let people put up their hands when they've got a verse and you point to them. You'll probably want to discuss this beforehand if it's a new or beginning group.

ROUNDS

Rounds are songs like "Row, Row, Row Your Boat" where you divide up the available singers into groups, and each group begins singing the song at a different time. The trick to learning rounds is to sing the song many times all together as a group, so that everyone's thoroughly familiar with it before you divide into parts. As a rounds singer you'll learn to listen so you can hear all the parts happening at once. When everyone's comfortable singing it as a round, you can stand up and walk around and sing it, or you can sit in a circle and number off so you're not with the others singing your part. The true test of proficiency is to sing a round with one person on a part.

Rounds are not easy to sing, especially for shy singers. Try teaching a round as a song; when you've sung it for several months and everyone's feeling very secure, then divide up into parts and sing it as a round. Be sure to put a strong singer in each group.

HEALING SONGS

One of the purposes of Pagan ritual is to give a time and place to unburden ourselves of all the emotional muck we collect. That's why I like to start a circle with a check-in: go around the group (either in order, or in popcorn style where people speak when they're ready) and let everyone give a short version of what's happened since last you met. This clears the air, lets everyone feel heard, and shakes off the last of the mundane so you can go between the worlds without stuff hanging on you.

The Emerald Earth Laughing and Drumming Society of Berkeley took this concept a step further and did whole ritual circles this way. Each person got five to ten minutes (depending on how many were present), and when each person finished speaking she either asked for a specific song, or asked the circle to come up with an appropriate song. The only rules were (1) don't interrupt the speaker, and (2) don't try to fix things, just listen. This is a very healing way to run a circle.

Sometimes, during the check-in or during the circle itself, a person will be so overcome with the emotional muck of life that he will explode. This person needs the special attention of an on-the-spot healing. It's best to ask the person what he needs: to be held, rocked, stroked, left alone, listened to.

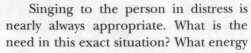

Singing to the person in distress is nearly always appropriate. What is the need in this exact situation? What energy do you want to put out to help heal this person? Which song you select is important. Here's where having many songs becomes essential.

"Having," in this case, means being able to sing the song anywhere, without words or music; studying words of the song as a poem until you grasp the teaching; studying the music until you feel the mode and structure; feeling the energy of the song; singing the song long enough to understand the song's intent; knowing how to change the song's energy; groking the song in other ways; and having a written or taped copy of the song (both is better).

The all-time best healing song I know is by Libby Roderick and it goes "How could anyone ever tell you you were anything less than beautiful? / How could anyone ever tell you you were less than whole? / How could anyone fail to notice that your loving is a miracle? / How deeply you're connected to my soul." This song can be sung in many ways and never fails to care for people musically.

TRANCING SONGS

All cultures in all times have had trance songs: Shaker songs, Indian ragas, certain Japanese music that expands the mind's frequencies, certain Greek chord changes that do something to your consciousness, and certain contemporary Pagan chants that spin you out into ecstacy. There are Shamanic journeying chants in indiginous tribes all over the Earth, and the amazingly primal effects of the digeridoo on us that are not so much learned as remembered.

The repetition of certain sounds is known to promote the experience of transcendent realities. The repeated sound patterns stabilize the breath and movements of the mouth and throat; and that with the volume, all create modifications in the body. Long periods (three minutes or more) of self-produced repetitive sounds bring relaxation, lower brain waves, increased warmth in hands, and a feeling of being centered. When the sounds are long and vowel-centered, the effect is even greater (From Don Campbell, *The Roar of Silence*).

The hard thing to do when you've started a trance-inducing chant is to walk with a foot (or a brain) in both worlds: the trance world and the what-passes-for-reality-at-the-moment world. You must keep a foot in the physical space of the circle in order to shape the energy and eventually to ground it and bring people back. You must. You can let yourself go a little bit out, but you must be able to return at will, and you must be able to look at the clock. Almost any song can be used as a trancing song.

TEACHING THE SONGS

Many of us were told early on, either directly or by implication, that we couldn't sing, so we've been shy about singing in public; the more you sing, of course, the better you sing; chants are easiest to learn and teach because they're short and sweet. "Air I Am" would be my first choice of a song to teach a shy group.

You as the song leader need to do some homework before working with a group. Talk with the Priestess about the intention of the ritual, and where in the order she wants songs and what she wants to do with them. Find a starting pitch in your singing range and practice the song so you can sing it loudly and accurately, and so you can start on the same pitch and sing it the same way each time. Pitch pipes help. If it's a longer

song you'll need to break it into manage-able chunks and practice singing each chunk several times.

Teach new songs at the beginning of a circle, before it starts, so you won't have to break the flow and rhythm of the ritual. Teach only one new song per meeting if you have a shy group. Teach the words first, es-pecially if they're in another lan-guage. Say the words aloud, togeth-er, several times, perhaps in chunks. Clap the rhythm if it's tricky. Then you sing the whole song aloud. If it's a short song, just keep on singing it and people will sing with you when they feel they can. Sing loudly so others can both hear you and hide behind your voice until they become more certain. Teach slowly; don't go on until each chunk is secure. Don't use rattles when you're teaching—they get in the way of hearing. Af-ter your circle has learned the song, keep a steady drum beat so all can feel the song's pulse.

If you're teaching several new songs at once, you might want to write the words down and hand them out. Except in extreme cases I much prefer learning and teaching songs by ear: one per-son knows the song, sings it and teaches it to the group. A song learned by ear will stay with you much longer, and when you sing it, you sing the song. If you use paper, you sing the piece of pa-per. People tend to get addicted to the paper; so if you can teach with the paper, and then make people put it away, that's an ac-ceptable compromise. Some songs in other languages are best learned by ear (African songs), and some are best learned on pa-per (Bulgarian). You can also get a large tablet and write the lyrics for the whole group to see. Another possibility, if the song has been recorded, is to play the tape so the group can hear what it sounds like. Don't use the tape to teach unless it's a clear, clean arrangement, the tempo you want to sing it, and in the pitch that suits you all.

Call and response songs are fun to teach and easy to learn, and many longer Pagan songs have choruses that are easier for the group to learn than the verses. Try to sing the new song at several different places in the ritual; this will help develop auditory memory. Keep a list of which songs you've taught to your group so you can repeat them at regular intervals. I carry around a small book, listing the songs I have by title under various headings: "Earth," "Air," "Healing," "Winter Solstice." Many songs will be listed under several headings because they fit into several categories.

USING MUSIC IN RITUAL

Don't look at music as an add-on to the ritual, but as an integral part of it. Music helps carry the intention of the ritual; helps move, promote, or enhance the energy; and helps bring the teachings to your group. Again, the more songs you have, the more you have to share.

The energy of any given song can be changed in several ways. You can change the tempo of the song; that is, try singing slow songs fast and singing fast songs in a more prayerful manner. Sing a song louder or softer. Change the style of the song: try swinging it or making it into a gospel song. Add drums. Add rattles. Play with it.

Sometimes you'll get a song started and it will take off for parts unknown, dragging you along like a runaway team of horses. "How on Earth am I going to get this stopped?" you'll think. Sometimes if you start singing more softly you'll disperse some of the energy. Sometimes if you repeat the last line or phrase of the song over and over, people will get the hint. Sometimes, if you've got the loudest drum, you can simply beat very loud the last half line of the song and then stop at the end. If you simply don't go on, sometimes people will stop. Sometimes if you rattle really loud and fast at the end you can get it stopped. Sometimes you can put your arms in the air and slowly move them down toward the Earth and people will respond to the visual cue. Sometimes you just have to let the energy wear itself out.

Songs are energy, and when they're combined with your group's energy and the energy of your ritual, you can do magical things! Music helps it happen.

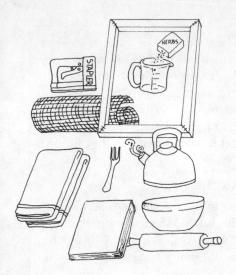

Making Your Own Herbal Paper

By Breid Foxsong

Materials

You will need several sheets of typing paper, a bowl, hot water, a fork, two kitchen towels, a metal screen, a wooden frame, a stapler, a rolling pin, and two tablespoons of ground herbs of your choice.

Procedure

1. Tear several sheets of paper into pieces the size of a penny or smaller.

2. Place the pieces in a bowl and cover with hot water.

3. Stir to make sure all of the paper is wet.

4. Let stand overnight.

5. The next day, tear the paper into pieces as small as possible and then stir with a fork for several minutes. (You have now made pulp.) This can also be done in a food processor if you don't mind adding the mechanical energies, but like any magical tool, you are better off doing it by hand. As you stir, add in the ground herbs. They need to be ground or finely chopped so that they don't create flaws in the paper. Experiment with various herbs, keeping in mind their magical qualities. The pulp should remain a thick mush in texture. If this is part of a spell working, chant or focus on your purpose as you do this.

6. Prepare a metal screen (like those used in windows or screen doors) by stapling screen to a wood picture frame. You can use a small window screen if you like. The dimensions can vary, but it should be larger than you want the finished paper.

7. Smooth out an even layer of pulp (approx. ⅛ inch thick) onto the screen by hand.

8. Let the water drain for a couple of minutes.

9. Flip your screen over so that your paper pops out onto a clean kitchen towel.

10. Cover the paper with another kitchen towel so that you have a "sandwich" of paper between two towels.

11. Use the rolling pin to press out more water and flatten the paper.

12. Carefully peel off the top towel. Turn the wet paper over onto either a smooth counter top or on a piece of glass (you can use a window for this) paper side down, and then carefully peel off the remaining towel

13. Let the paper dry overnight or longer.

14. If you want to smooth the paper for writing on, spray the dried paper with a fine mist of water. Place a clean smooth rag over the damp paper and iron it with a slightly warm iron until the paper is dry.

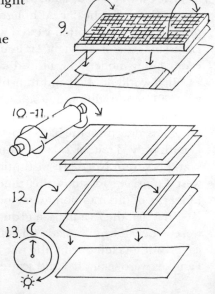

You can use your paper for gifts, for spell work, for stationery or for just plain fun! Enjoy!

TRAITEUR: CAJUN HEALING TRADITION

BY SUZANNE SYNBORSKI

Imagine you are tormented by a never-ending migraine, an incurable rash, or a debilitating nervous condition of unknown origin and your doctors just can't help. You have already availed yourself of all that traditional medicine has to offer. Where do you turn?

In Southwest Louisiana, the answer is simple. You can visit a Traiteur, a Cajun folk healer. Although in many parts of the country folk or faith healers are often viewed with a jaundiced eye, in southwest Louisiana, talk of visiting a Traiteur seldom causes a raised eyebrow, even among modern-day individuals who "should know better."

In a world of MRIs and transplants, the Traiteur is a singular aspect of Cajun tradition that miraculously survived the perilous journey into modern times, along with spicy food and spirited music. A few miles away from the barren prairies and winding bayous of Cajun Country, the Traiteur is largely unheard of despite the fact that researchers from Northern institutions regularly pass through southwest Louisiana to study this time-honored practice. Perhaps the longevity of this tradition is an eloquent testament to its legitimacy.

In 1755, the Acadians, a group of fiercely independent people, were expelled from Canada for refusing to abandon a neutral political position taken during the war between the French and English. Families were separated and scattered all along the Eastern Coast of

America. After suffering extreme hardship, many Acadians, later to become known as Cajuns, found their way to a new homeland in southwestern Louisiana. They were not welcomed with open arms, and Louisiana was not paradise.

To ensure their personal and cultural survival, they formed a tightly-unified clan and set about the task of making a new life in a hostile semitropical wilderness that assailed its inhabitants with blazing heat, oppressive humidity, poisonous reptiles, storms of mosquitoes, hurricanes, and raging fevers. Access to standard medical care was more than hard to find—it was most often totally inaccessible.

Masters of adaptation, the Cajuns compensated for the lack of formal medical care by establishing a unique folk healing tradition. The Traiteur, French for healer, served as an intermediary for God. As channels for God's power, they healed using carefully-guarded secret prayers, the laying on of hands, and remedies acquired from the Indians as well as from sources such as the Spanish, German, African, and Haitian cultures.

Although the legend states that Traiteurs are either born with a veil, after the death of the father, or are the seventh child of a seventh child, most Traiteurs are not born, they are made. In truth, there is only one requirement for becoming a Traiteur—a pure heart. Because survival of the community once made it imperative that the secrets of the Traiteur not be used for selfish reasons, protocol insists that initiates and their intentions must be carefully examined before they are allowed to join the ranks of the Traiteur. The craft is always handed down by an experienced Traiteur to a younger student of the opposite sex, because passing the secrets down to one of the same sex will cause the senior Traiteur to lose his or her powers.

There is great variance in the abilities demonstrated by Traiteurs. Some specialize in treating specific disorders, while others are generalists. Some refrain from treating certain ailments because the symptoms transfer to the Traiteur after they are banished from the patient. Some will only work at certain times of the day, or only on patients of one sex. Since the practices of Voodoo and black magic are alive and well in South Louisiana, some Traiteurs spend as much of their time treating supernatural disorders as they do natural ailments.

Treatment styles also vary. While most Traiteurs work armed only with prayers, some use props such as candles. Others use implements such as knives that, for example, may be held broadside against a wart. Without any cutting whatsoever, the wart disappears.

Traiteurs never advertise or even offer their services; they must be asked for help. To achieve results, all they need is the name of their patient, whether human or animal. The recipient of the Traiteur's services need not be local. Most Traiteurs insist that their powers can travel over great distances, so long as a body of running water does not separate them from their target. Many conditions can be treated over the phone.

Unlike certain healers in other parts of the world, the Traiteur will never ever ask for payment. Even thanking a Traiteur is a break in tradition. Because most Traiteurs are very religious and believe that the healing is actually an act of God, only God may be thanked. However, a donation is allowed if the patient can find a way to leave it without being seen by the Traiteur. Donations do not always take the form of currency carefully hidden where it is sure to be found. A visit to the home of a Traiteur often reveals other heartfelt offerings such as bowls of fruit, handcrafted items, or religious mementos.

Skeptics sometimes try to discount the authenticity of Traiteurs by attempting to ascribe their success to the power of suggestion, to the patient's imagination, or even to hypnosis. These explanations fall short because they don't account for the fact that Traiteurs enjoy great success with children, babies, animals, non-believers, and persons who have absolutely no idea they are being treated.

Today, most Traiteurs are quite elderly, and their numbers are dwindling. Young people are still being trained to carry on the tradition, but not in the same numbers as when Traiteurs were integral to the survival of the insular, enigmatic Cajun community. Unfortunately, there is little doubt that some morning soon the rising Louisiana Sun will obliterate the shadow of the last Traiteur, and like a night-blooming flower, this gentle art will become only a sweet memory.

Finding Sacred Spaces in Wild Places

By David Cumes, M.D.

Most people who use the outdoors for adventure or recreation stress the external part of the experience without necessarily paying much attention to the more sacred aspects of the journey. They yearn to climb the highest peaks, ski the steepest slopes, and kayak the most treacherous rivers. This ego-strengthening behavior may boost self-esteem and increase self-mastery, but it frequently takes us away from a sense of the revered.

Apart from being a wonderful place to recreate and restore our burnt-out psyches, nature can also be a sacred space and a powerful inner tool for facilitating self-awareness and self-discovery. Only when we are aware can we draw nearer to a deeper sense of being or to our higher self. Ancient philosophies have told us that we have to go beyond ego in order to reach for self. The ultimate goal of mystical philosophies is to leave the duality of everyday existence and reach a state of oneness. Ego is the biggest barrier to this realization.

Even without any esoteric practice it is easy to appreciate a feeling of unity and the interconnectedness of all things when one has been out in nature for some time. "Wilderness rapture" occurs because nature makes us humble and facilitates contact with our higher self, our soul, or our divine or Buddha nature. When we experience self we become one with nature's sacred space.

In the West, we have created a separation between ourselves and wilderness. Wilderness has become something to be conquered rather than a sanctified space, and this ethos lies deep within our culture. We look at wilderness as being remote, an area to be approached with preparation and trepidation. We take all sorts of workshops and survival courses to help us face what nature may present. However when people are taken into wilderness, this reality, mainly based on fear, may reverse and the desire to control or conquer vanishes. It is replaced with a sense of harmony and a feeling of letting be, a release from this duality that we are "here" and wilderness is out "there."

Luther Standing Bear said, "It was only when the white man came that wilderness existed. The Native Americans recognized the earth as their sacred mother." The basis of the Native American vision quest is that when one is in wilderness for a sufficient time, in a certain way, and with the appropriate intention, an altered state of consciousness ensues and the seeker's sense of duality disappears. It is then that a special dream, vision, sign, metaphor, archetype, power, or totem animal will appear as a sacred message to that individual to guide him or her in life's purpose. This "fusion" between the quester and the sign occurs in an altered state of awareness.

Nature, by allowing access to spirit or self, can be a way to access our divine nature and our special purpose on earth. Many of us who love nature and use it as a form of spiritual practice acknowledge it as a sanctuary or a sacred place. Those who go into the wilderness to achieve or conquer are less likely to connect with the sacred because of an almost adversarial attitude toward the Earth Mother. Many of the terms used in the wild outdoors are almost militaristic. We may mount an assault on a peak or attack a particular wilderness challenge with great gusto. Other descriptions sound egocentric and imply that we have control over wild places and the elements when we do not. We "bag" peaks we don't own, and "run" rivers that are actually running us. These descriptions seem to exclude a dialogue with the sacred. To connect with the Earth Mother in a consecrated way we should remember she is feminine and receptive and does not take kindly to aggression.

Joseph Campbell described the essence of the hero's journey. "The hero ventures forth from the world of common day into a region of supernatural wonder. Fabulous forces are there encountered and a decisive victory is won. The hero comes back from this mysterious adventure with the power to bestow boons on his fellow man." Implicit in this journey is the entry of the hero or heroine into a sacred space of supernatural wonder. Since the space is sacrosanct the hero cannot remain, but must return to his or her people with the grail that only this space can provide.

Anatomically speaking, the left brain is more masculine, intellectual, and goal-oriented. When we achieve, we feel good about ourselves, and therefore this side of the brain connects us more with the ego. The right or feminine part of the brain is more receptive and intuitive and connects us to the higher self. Certain places may also be described as masculine or feminine depending on their special features and energies. Mountains engender a more feminine, intuitive, and softer mode of being, whereas jungle and bush areas, by virtue of the physical challenges and dangers that abound, are more masculine, harsh, and cognitive. It is much easier to just "be" in the Sierras than in the Amazon jungle. Similarly we can get much more cerebral and technical about how to be safe and comfortable in the African bush with all its predators than when just trekking in the Rockies. Certain regions are more distinctly masculine or feminine, and therefore connect us more or less strongly either with ego or the self.

Peak experiences of awe, oneness, harmony, and inner peace are common in wilderness. According to Abraham Maslow, the peak experience is a change in consciousness during which there is transcendence or at least partial transcendence of the ego. This event may occur when a hiker sees an animal or a vista and for a brief, blissful moment in time there is no separation between him or her (the observer) and that object (the observed). In Eastern traditions, a more profound description of the same event would be called *samadhi*, or nirvana. The peak experience is like a mini-samadhi when observer, observed, and process of observation fuse into one—unity rather than duality. The adept mystic is able to induce samadhi at will and remain in that state as long as desired.

To most of us, however, the peak experience is usually a transient, unpredictable occurrence. When we are mesmerized by a splendid site in nature we develop a special feeling or emotion inside our body. The minute we begin to analyze the experience so that we can hold onto it, it escapes and we lose the wonder of that instant. The cognitive left brain gets in the way of our most intense inner moments. There seems to be a point where an intuitive, empathetic, right-brained fascination that has no ulterior motive becomes a left-brained goal or rationalization and the balance is disturbed, taking us out of the sacred.

The key to entering hallowed space and having wilderness rapture is the ability to balance various polarities. There is no adequate neurophysiological explanation for this sensation and the best we may be able to say about it is that it hinges more on a right, rather than a left-brain phenomenon. It is more of an emotional, intuitive, receptive event than an intellectual or cognitive experience.

There is a certain core truth that we need to take with us if we wish to access the sacred in nature more deeply. This universal belief can also be appreciated by studying ancient energy systems such as the yoga chakras and nadis or the Kabbalistic Tree of Life. These same principles are embraced by the polarities in shamanism and also our modern day neurophysiological concept of left and right brain, the balance of which leads to a "whole" brain experience. To reach rapturous heights in wilderness safely, both left and right or whole brain function are necessary. The left brain keeps us safe in nature by honing our technical skills, the right brain allows us to enter the "softer" dimensions of the wilderness experience. The Yoga model shows the need to balance the Sun and Moon polarity and the Tree of Life demonstrates the idea of equilibrium in the left, or feminine, and right, or masculine, sides of the Tree.

Wilderness rapture occurs when one is in harmony with the different polarities, and nature has countless opposites to help us achieve balance. We cannot have light without the dark, we appreciate food much more after being hungry, we need to be wet to enjoy being dry, there is no rose without a thorn—hence the magic in nature.

To enter the sacred we need to just "be" and our usual Western ego bolstering behavior will neutralize our best efforts unless we remain diligent and aware. Intention and receptivity are key, and when these are directed inward, expanded states of awareness prevail and admittance to the archetype of the Garden of Eden becomes possible.

Some places in the wild are more sacred than others. We may go into a valley and find it dark, foreboding, and anything but holy, and then climb up to a peak that we find uplifting, inspirational, and celestial. Places may appear sacred because of a certain spectacular beauty, a special energy that pervades the area, or because something eventful may have happened there in the past. It may be deemed sacred by others for generations or just by ourselves because of our own peak experience with a sign such as a rainbow, a spectacular storm or sunset, or the appearance of an unusual animal. The ultimate expression of a sacred space occurs when duality disappears and oneness or unity consciousness prevails. When this happens we touch our divine nature and experience the sacrosanct directly.

The importance of polarity is highlighted in the physical characteristics of sacred space. Where high and low, deep and steep, open and closed, dry and wet meet there is an affirmation of the core truth of the importance of opposites, paradoxes, and contradictions. Desert regions can be sacrosanct by virtue of the polarity inherent in sand and sky.

Nature reinforces the fact that in the balance of the opposites we find our center, our equilibrium, and our sacred space. In these areas of contrast, aboriginal peoples were inspired to perform acts of wilderness art. The rocks of the planet are decorated as testaments to the sacred, and when one visits them there is something palpably different in the energy of these sites. The Nazca lines in the southern desert of Peru are an example of a sacred site where, for lack of rocks or cave walls, the art was rendered on the crust of the earth.

If we can balance our masculine and feminine energies, our Sun and our Moon channels, the left and right sides of the Tree of Life, our light and our dark aspects and our ying and our yang forces, we will more easily appreciate the distinct polarity and the sanctity of these unique sites.

How to Navigate a Pagan Festival!

By Silver RavenWolf

E ach year more and more magical individuals pull together to host Pagan Festivals. Many times it takes over a year of planning and lots of hard work to ensure that the magical attendees enjoy a safe and spiritual event. In this article we're going to talk about the inner workings of a festival as they relate to you, the participant, and what you can expect when you set those magical wings down in Pagan Festival Land.

The Rules

At the gate someone will hand you a set of rules (or you may have received them when you sent in your money). All festivals have rules, based on laws of the state and county, requirements of the owners of the land, and past experience of the festival coordinators. You are expected to follow the rules. Most festivals now have security teams to make sure you follow the rules. These teams are there to ensure your safety and happiness at the site. At check-in you will usually be required to sign a form that lists the rules, indicating that you have read the guidelines and that you will follow them. Yes, they can legally throw you out if you don't follow the rules. In the past, some very nice magical people have brought along kindness-impaired buddies. If you think that your friend will not enjoy this new exerience or has a history of dysfunction, it is in your best interest (and everyone else's) to leave him or her at home. Most festivals now require you to wear an identification tag that indicates you belong there. Please wear the tag, and don't be offended if you aren't wearing your tag and a staff member asks you where it is.

Clothing Optional

Okay! You've found where you're supposed to set up your stuff. You've got those tent poles out, and a man walks by you wearing a pentacle the size of your mama's old cook pot and nothing else! Many outdoor festivals are clothing optional. Check this out before you decide to go. If you are taking your children, do not expect the staff to change the policy of the whole festival because you forgot to read the information packet and here you are, 1,000 miles from home, three kids in tow, standing among 239 nekkid Pagans. On the other side of the magical stick, don't get all in a huff you come in the buff and discover that you are at a festival where clothing is required. Rules are rules. I've personally seen both instances and have been amazed at the ruckus one person can cause just because they didn't bother to read their festival packet before they came.

Cameras and Camcorders

Since the vision of the man with the oversized pentacle cannot be missed, you whip out your camera, aim and...someone screeches in your ear, "Stop that!" Some festivals do not permit cameras or camcorders. Usually this rule is in the festival information that you receive before you go. With the advent of the internet, too many people put up pictures they have taken without asking the permission of the individuals in the photo. Remember, not everyone is out of the closet.

Every Festival Has a Nut or Two

Some individuals feel that because they are Pagan, they don't have to follow the rules. I've been to several festivals where people on drugs have ruined everyone else's fun. One man tore through a campsite and destroyed three tents. One woman in a drunken

stupor almost died of hypothermia. True, these instances are downright stupid, but a festival coordinator has no idea who is sane and who is less than human when the registration fees come in. Many festival security personnel will now hand these people directly over to the police. And you know, they *should*.

PEOPLE IN GENERAL

You will meet lots of happy Pagans at the seminars, rituals, vendor row, and musical events. You are not going to like everyone there, and everyone is not going to like you. Get over it and leave the bad attitudes at home. Enjoy yourself. The larger the event, the more unusual people you are going to meet. Not every person who attends a festival is a magical person. Larger events tend to draw a bigger cross-section of individuals. If you are unsure about a festival talk to individuals who have attended in the past. There is also a big difference between an indoor festival (held in a hotel) and an outdoor festival, with indoor festivals requiring stricter control due to legal and social constraints. Festival coordinators around the country are now communicating with one another and do weed out potential difficulties during preregistration. They have your best interests in mind. You will meet High Priestess Kiss-My-Feet. You will meet High Priest Fake-Family-Lineage. You will meet Bubble Witch and Mistress Serious Witch. You will discover interesting souls who don't know who they are or why they are there. You will meet snobs who won't talk to you because you aren't anybody. No kidding. On the other hand, you will meet lots of fun and interesting people who are at the festival to learn, grow, and have fun, so don't let the strange ones get to you. Depending on the event, you will meet well-known Pagans (musicians, authors, publishers, poets, drummers, bards, etc.). Check your festival brochure for the featured speakers and events.

THE VOLUNTEER LIST

Many festivals have you sign up at the gate for a few hours of volunteer duty. Please, if you sign up for any task, do it. Don't forget about your promise and party with your friends. Someone will be stuck with the job you offered to do. I was at a festival last year and one poor man stayed up with the need-fire all night because the people who said they would relieve him didn't bother to show up.

THE FIRE CIRCLE

This is one of the highlights of any festival. Before you march down to that great place in the woods, apply the bug spray and dress appropriately. Fire circles are very hot, so it would be a good idea to layer your clothing. If you plan to take an instrument, like your drum, you might want to carry a small camp chair. Even if you don't have an instrument, many fire circles do not have seating, and you might just want to sit and watch for a while. Don't forget your flashight, as in my experience, most fire circles are well away from the other events of the festival, and even though festival staff come up with marvelous ideas for lighting the path, after about 1:00 AM many of the lights go to sleep. Having a drink in a cup with a lid is a good idea too. Theft is not normally a problem at festivals, but counting on everyone's honesty is not the best idea. Keep your things together. If you plan to walk away and leave your drum or other items for a moment or two, ask the person drumming or sitting beside you if they would mind keeping an eye on your stuff. Don't dance through burning ashes that are as large as a big nosed Pagan's head or whip those long tendrils of lovely hair too close to the flames in dancing frenzy. It is very hot close to a large bonfire. If you really want to dance and it is too crowded, back off for a bit. It's been my experience that the largest number of people leave after the first hour of dancing and drumming, allowing plenty of space for you to enjoy yourself. Even if you've never danced before, don't be afraid that you will look silly. I stood back from a fire circle once just to analyze it, and you know, everyone looked fine and even the most zealous dancers did not look stupid. Warning: All night drumming is usual fare at festivals. Many people just love this (including me) but some first time festival goers find the constant sound disconcerting until they get used to it. Finally, you may not want to take small children to the late night fire circle due to the dancing and falling ash.

SEMINAR AND RITUAL DECORUM

Pagan Standard Time (meaning things don't get started on time) is a common difficulty at festivals, especially if the attendance count is high. Again, get used to it. Coordinators work very hard to make sure things get going and move along quickly, but there will be the occasional time lapse. Presenters forget their time slots, the twenty-ton chicken for the potluck came frozen, etc. It happens. Just go with the flow. Try not to be a whiney-Witch or pompous-Pagan, and do your best to attend the seminars or rituals on time. Excessive talking to your neighbor during a ritual or seminar is rude to the others attending. If you aren't interested in the function, you can quietly go to another place that might capture your attention. If you are very late, you can usually sneak in the back of any lecture, but perhaps not a ritual as the circle may be cast. Smoking and drinking alcohol is usually prohibited during a lecture or ritual. Save your questions or comments until the end of the lecture. Most lecturers allow time for questions or comments after their presentation, or they can walk off to the side and talk to you. This way, the next presenter can begin setting up for his or her time slot without interference. Rituals are a bit different. Sometimes main ritual seems to be more of an exercise in Keystone Cop decorum. With lots of people to coordinate, events might take awhile to proceed. I used to believe that leaving a ritual in mid-stream was the height of bad manners, but I've attended some events that were so long I thought my bladder would bust. If you just can't take it anymore, don't make a big deal about it. Slowly edge your way to the back of the crowd, then run for it!

DAY AND NIGHT VENDING

Most festival coordinators control the number and type of vendors to enhance variety. Don't count your money out in the open. Most people are incredibly honest, but there is always that one or two who are looking to clean up, and in all the cases I've ever known of festival theft, the thief was not a magical person. Many festival-goers look at vendor row like a flea market. Most festival-goers will cruise through vendor row several times before buying

because they are looking for bar-
gains and will check out vendors
with duplicate items. Vendors often barter among themselves,
and occasionally barter with general festival attendees. Several
festivals are permitting night
vending. It used to be that every
vendor shut up tight at around
6:00 PM. Not any more. Some
sites now provide generators for
electricity or allow tiki torches
for night vending. Many festival vendors

are now professionals and competition is stiff, with more vendors
than ever before. In festivals past, when vending was new and not
someone's livelihood, the early close-up time was to ensure that
the vendors could attend evening festival events. Professional vendors have gone to hundreds of evening events and would prefer
to remain at their sites for consumer interaction. You see, vendors
aren't just there to sell stuff. Most festival vendors are a gold mine
of information. They vend at festivals all over the country, meet
lots of interesting people, and are extremely magical. You'll find
that many older vendors are elders in their own clans or traditions and their wisdom is exciting and entertaining. About one
hour before shut down, some vendors with large, heavy items may
be willing to significantly cut their prices, so if you are looking for
a major bargain you just might net that coveted whatever if you
wait until the last minute to purchase. All vendors take cash, most
take checks, and about half now take credit cards.

PHONES

Some sites do have pay phones. Please do not hog the telephone.
I tried to call home once at a festival on a pay phone. I had to
wait behind a woman who gave her complete grocery list to her
husband, a young fellow who was whispering sweet nothings to
his girlfriend at home for over forty-five minutes...you get the
idea. Because of bad phone manners, many festival sites will not
allow you to use the phone on the premises unless there is an
emergency. I now carry a cell phone.

WITCH BALLS

By Amber K

Folklore gives us many ways to protect and bless our homes, from a sprig of rowan fastened near the entryway to the brightly-colored hex signs of the Pennsylvania Dutch, to the inverted horse shoe nailed above the door to "catch the luck" and hold it. The "Witch ball" is one more protective device.

A Witch ball is a hollow glass sphere hung at a window, near the hearth, or in a corner of a room near the ceiling, that averts or traps evil before it can bring harm to the occupants of the home. It may be only a couple of inches in diameter, or large as a pumpkin.

Some writers have said they were called "Witch balls" because they were made to protect a home from Witches. It is just as possible, however, that the balls were used by Witches to ward their own homes, and those of their clients.

No one knows exactly when these talismans first were used. The manufacture of glass and the ability to make blown-glass vessels are very old skills; the Roman Empire had a lively trade in glass two thousand years ago. We know that Witch balls were used in old England, but whether this was a legacy of the Roman occupation or a later custom is uncertain. Certainly Witch balls were common in colonial America.

Many witch balls were coated inside with silver nitrate. It was said that these reflected the "evil eye" or any negative spell back on the sender. Also, any demon seeing his face reflected in the silver ball would be frightened and flee, or maybe seeing the world reflected in a curved, distorted way was enough to confuse him. Other balls are created with slender threads or pillars of glass inside to catch any evil spirit that ventured within. Yet others were simply the glass balls, clear or green or blue, used by fishermen to float their nets. Perhaps these were reflective enough to work in the same way as the silver balls.

Witch balls have also found their way into the garden in the form of the large "gazing globes" on pedestals that adorned many Victorian gardens and are still seen occasionally today. If a flower garden is a place of beauty and serenity, a refuge from the cares of the world, certainly it deserves protection as much as the house itself.

Another place where Witch balls turn up is on the family Christmas tree—or more accurately the Yule tree, as the custom of dragging a tree indoors is doubtlessly Pagan in origin. The tree may be a variant on the Yule log, which was originally a huge dead tree (and phallic symbol), conveyed to the manor house by the men of the village with much singing and ribald horseplay. There one end was placed in the great hearth, and a fire kindled. Over several days of feasting and festivity the Yule log was gradually pushed into the fire as the end was consumed.

The Yule tree may also have been a representation of the World Tree of old Northern Europe. The whole universe was imagined as a great ash tree, called Yggdrasil. Its roots reached down into the Norse underworlds, Niflheim and Muspelheim; its crown stretched up to Asgard and the halls of the gods; and in its branches deer and other wild creatures browsed. This great tree is akin to the Tree of Life of the ancient goddess civilizations of the Near East.

On our Yule trees today we place lights and stars and candy canes, carved animals and elves and Santas and—of course—little glass spheres. Witch balls. Gold for the reborn Sun god, and silver for the Moon goddess, whose blessings and protection we ask for the coming new year. In *Ancient Ways* (Llewellyn, 1991), Pauline Campanelli suggests that the "shiny glass balls catch the light of the new born Sun and send it back as a magical means of enhancing the Sun's energy."

You can have your own Witch ball up year 'round. Buy a large and beautiful Yule ornament, or seek out a glass fisherman's float in an antique shop, or look in a catalog of garden statuary such as Toscano's for a "gazing globe." Give it a special place of honor in your home or garden, invoke the gods of your choice, and consecrate it to its protective purpose. Dust it frequently to remove any negativity from its surface. Perhaps it will make your home that much more of a safe haven.

PAGAN PARENTING
BY SILVER RAVENWOLF

Over the years many parents have written me letters asking me how one should bring up a Pagan child. Like any other parent, I'm not an expert on how to raise children, and I often hesitated in my answers, as every family situation is different. So far, though, we've done okay. Rather than give you instructions on how you should raise your child, I'm simply going to tell you what I did with mine. You can take it from there.

THE EARLY YEARS

The early years were not too bad, as I look back on them. I wrote under a pen name, so we didn't have anybody crashing the door, burning crosses on my lawn, or any other such nonsense. I worked a normal eight-to-five job. I hired a nanny who cared more about the welfare of my children and her soap operas than she did about my choice of religion. We didn't get into major peer problems until the oldest hit fifth grade, and it seems that the fifth year of elementary school for each of my children brought on the insensitive peer pressure that is prevalent for every child regardless of religion. At this age the bullies look for a chink in the armor—in the case of my children it was their mother's religion. My youngest boy handled the bullies entirely different from the other three. Extremely athletic and devilishly charming, he either lied to his peers or beat them up, whichever proved useful at the moment.

During these early years I taught my kids how to meditate, how to do ritual, how to talk to nature spirits, how to pray with the angels, and how to do simple spells. Although I continued to practice my religion, I didn't insist that they do it, too. We talked about all religions and why people believe the way they do.

THE MIDDLE SCHOOL YEARS

These years got very dicey, especially for the oldest three. Kids are volatile at this age anyway. Again, the weak spot in the family fortress was mom's (and now, dad's) religion. My kids were taunted on the bus to such an extent that I had to drive them to school every day.

One boy slammed my oldest daughter into a locker and carved the word "Witch" on that same locker. I called his mother. He was grounded for a month and had to apologize. The oldest was now convinced that her social life would be ruined because of her parents' religion. When her friends came to visit she would tear down my altar. She did not understand how this could possibly upset me because the world revolved around her, and I shouldn't mind a bit since I was to be subservient to her world. After two years of this I had to explain to her how much it upset me that she would rip apart my altar. We came to an agreement—I was allowed to keep my altar as long as I made it innocuous. Although it sounds like I conceded, I realized that, much like my husband many years before, she needed to know that she was more important than my religion. I know it sounds stupid, but the biggest fear that children and spouses have of their practicing Wiccan loved ones is that they will stop loving them. The oldest stopped practicing the religion during these years.

The younger daughter had her share of difficulties, but she handled them in a different way. She was physically attacked the last day of school by a fundamentalist girl and her gang of friends. The school refused to do anything this time around, and the parents turned away. This youngest daughter, usually exuberant and well liked by her peers, turned inward, and came out fighting. Her last year in middle school she single-handedly got a substitute teacher and a teacher's aide fired for religious discrimination.

My son, with his slight build, suffered in silence through his three years of middle school and I was never able to get out of him, what, if any, problems he was having because he didn't want me going into school like the Morrigan incarnate. Don't think, however, that I left him swinging in the wind. The oldest fought back through denial, the next one fought back with her mouth and her fists, and my son fought back with protection magic.

Each child stopped attending regular circle nights during middle school, but in different years. The two boys hung on the longest because they particularly liked the drums. I didn't force them or harass them. Sometimes they would attend, other times they didn't want to

be bothered. During the middle school years I ran the summer playground, building it up from nothing to something, worked for the local newspaper, and put in a few years as a school crossing guard. Since I had not abducted any children, everyone kept relatively quiet.

THE HIGH SCHOOL YEARS

During the high school years it is common knowledge that parents do not, and never will, understand their children. This said, we launched into a new set of pubescent problems, and my faulty memory of my own high school years fled me completely. When the sales of my books skyrocketed and I appeared on local television and in the newspaper, my oldest daughter indicated in high-pitched screeches that her life was now over. Didn't I realize that she had entered the realm of "doomed souls" in the pecking order?

Where the oldest had ceased her interest in Paganism completely in middle school and now looked upon me with disdain, my younger daughter kept it just within reach, but launched into her freshman year ultimately ignoring Paganism in favor of her new friends. This motley crew brought on a whole new dimension in parental nightmares, aided by her elder sister, who thought she had the inherent ability to save the scum of the town from their own demise. Both girls got into big trouble and it took their Witch Mamma and Pagan Papa to get them out of it with a warning that if it ever happened again, they were on their own. Reality struck with true force as both girls realized exactly what their parents were capable of *because* of their religion.

Suddenly, for the eldest girl, it was cool to have magical people for parents, and she slid back into Paganism as if she'd never left it, with her peers cheering her onward. Granted, she put her own twist on it and continued to remain outside the sphere of practicing adults, but such is my oldest daughter. She graduated in good standing and now took every new boyfriend on a tour of the local bookstore that had an end cap presenting my latest books. If the boy didn't keel over from heart failure she deemed him acceptable for a date or two.

The younger daughter handled it differently. She turned to academic and physical excellence, which wasn't a bad deal, with a healthy respect for the Wiccan religion, which she now occasionally practiced. It took a dirty deal in an athletic competition and a friend in the hospital for her to turn to her own magical practice.

TODAY

We're still working through the school system and the trials and tribulations are not over. The system itself, so far, looks upon me with a wary eye, but has made no move to harass, though a few teachers have been especially rude to my children. I have never insisted on special treatment for my kids, nor have I made an issue of our sacred holidays. In truth, it would have made matters worse for them, not better, and I felt they had taken enough abuse over my books. A few of the teachers in this particular system (as in every other system) are themselves in-the-closet Pagans. They have tried to help my kids in their own way, but the hatred of children raised by fundamentalist parents is more than they can bear. These teachers have families who rely on their income.

The biggest realization I've gotten out of these years with my children is that each kid processes the ups and downs of life differently, and you have to tailor your actions to each individual child. There is no blanket response to the question, "How do I raise my child in the Pagan Way?" I think a better realization is "How can I raise this child in the best way suited for him or her?"

Were there times over the years when I considered giving up my career and my religious choice because of my children? Absolutely. After contemplation, however, I realized that my family was not alone in the world of discrimination. If I were black, I couldn't choose to change the color of my skin. I have suffered discrimination because I am a woman, but I never considered changing my gender. Why, then, should I choose to switch religions due to the uneducated and ignorant pressures of others? My husband and I stuck to our religious choice, and I believe that in the end, when we are dead and gone, we will have given our children the foundation of the Wiccan philosophy itself: To know, to dare, and to will. The to be silent part is a bit difficult for me, but we're not all perfect.

RELIGION IN THE SCHOOLS: A PAGAN GUIDE

BY CREIDE STEWART, ESQUIRE

Contrary to claims of certain church groups, the United States is not a Christian nation. However, in recent years, there has been a serious attempt to override all of the law under the First Amendment on the subject of prayer in schools and to allow the word "God" into the Constitution for the first time. So far, none of these attempts have been successful, but with or without legal basis, prayers are being said, rules are passed forbidding the wearing of our religious symbols, and Pagan children are ridiculed and harassed in our public schools.

The law on this subject is very clear. Public schools may not support the teaching of one religion's beliefs. While certain aspects of different belief systems may be taught in a comparative religions course, the schools and teachers are not permitted to preach, pray, or otherwise suggest to the students in any way that one religion is superior to another. If the school district allows the students to form a Christian club, students who wish to form a Pagan club must be permitted to do so. In no case may teachers participate in, sponsor, or otherwise endorse religious clubs. School children may wear symbols of their religions provided that these symbols do not otherwise violate school dress codes.

It sounds so simple, doesn't it? This is the law and it should be enforced. Students are allowed to pray, to read religious materials, to wear crosses or star of David necklaces, or to gather together before school around the flagpole because they choose to do so. What more do those who would change the Constitution want? To be very blunt, what they want is a Christian theocracy where their religion is the only one recognized and all other practices are forbidden and scorned. Under the current law, they are unable to achieve that goal.

In many small, rural communities around the country (and in some that are not so small), attempts have been made to silence the Pagan school child's freedom of religious expression. Pentagrams are forbidden as "gang symbols." Prayers are said before class and before graduation ceremonies in direct violation of the law. Children of non-Christian faiths have been physically accosted in some schools to force them to pray. This is not just a Pagan problem either. Many of the discrimination stories that come out of our schools nationwide are tales of Jewish or Muslim kids being put into the very uncomfortable position of being a minority because of their religious beliefs. It is illegal and there are solutions.

The very first step for a Pagan parent who has children in the public schools is to become involved. It is no easy task to blend a career, other children, and caring for a home, but spending a few hours a month in your child's school as a volunteer or room parent is a great place to start. If you are an active presence within the school, you will be able to see warning signs of discrimination at a point before they become a problem. If volunteering is too great of a time commitment, promise yourself that you will stop by and observe your son or daughter's class for a morning. Make sure that you attend all school functions at which parents are welcomed, like concerts, back-to-school nights, and parent teas. By being a parent who is involved with education, you will gain a stronger voice if a problem arises and you have to deal with it.

If a violation of the separation of church and state does occur, the best way to deal with it is through personal contact with your child's teacher or principal. Make an appointment to discuss the situation and be prepared to do so quietly, thoughtfully, and in a non-aggressive manner. Remember, the law is on your side if one religion (not your own) is being favored in a public school. Do not go into this meeting threatening a lawsuit against the district. It may come to that point eventually, but only on rare occasions is it necessary to bring one of these cases to the courts.

Explain to the teacher or principal that you are concerned by something you heard from your child or saw during your visits to the school. State why you feel this action or classroom lesson was not appropriate under the First Amendment's rules about religion in schools. Ask politely if the person you are speaking to is aware of the problem

and/or the law, and then request a resolution to the problem or for the activity to cease. What is important here is not that you go in with the "I am Pagan, hear me roar" attitude, but that you remind the school that there are certain laws on the subject and that you would like to see those laws obeyed. You do not even have to tell the teacher or administrator that you are Pagan—just that you are a believer in the Constitution.

If your child chooses not to participate in the Pledge of Allegiance, send a note to the school's office about this before school starts. Something simple like "Johnny does not choose to recite the Pledge of Allegiance," with your signature is legally sufficient. No one may be forced to take part in this daily ritual with its newly-added recognition (1954) of the Judeo-Christian deity.

If you have attempted reasonable steps like those outlined above and do not receive satisfactory answers, or are told that you do not have valid concerns, there are several more extreme measures that can be taken. Bear in mind that as you move up through various remedies, the stakes get higher and pressure can (and probably will) be applied to you and your child. You can contact the school board in writing, outlining your concerns and requiring a response. You can contact a local attorney. You can contact the ACLU or Witches' Anti-Discrimination League. All of these steps tend to make the school administrators feel threatened, but so long as you have tried to solve the problem logically and calmly first, the problem will be resolved in the end.

As with all Pagan legal issues, the school discrimination problem is one that is being slowly but surely addressed. It is hard to remain patient when your child is the victim of this sort of harassment or forced religion, but only the calm and common sense approach is truly successful in the long run. Being an advocate for your child means accomplishing a goal in the least intrusive way possible. Do not go to war unless it becomes necessary.

Spiritual Burnout

By Cerridwen Iris Shea

Burnout is a condition of physical and emotional exhaustion as a result of repeated and long-term exposure to high levels of stress. It happens when one overzealously engages in an activity to an extent where, on physical, psychological, and emotional levels, one can no longer adequately function. It is a result of imbalance. A person who is "burned out" has used up all resources and often suffers from depression, anxiety, short temper, lethargy, mood swings, loss of or increase of appetite, loss of interest in sex, and inability to interact well with others.

Add the spiritual factor to burnout, and there's really big trouble. The spiritual level encompasses one's personal connection to the divine, and one's way to make sense of how each individual's web of life interweaves with the lives all around us. Spiritual burnout magnifies all the symptoms of burnout. The loss of the connection to the divine spirit can send a person into a destructive spiral. It is especially forceful if the burnout was caused by an overload of spiritual activity.

Spiritual burnout can cause feelings that divinity is not listening, not appreciating all the work being done, and ultimately, can cause anger and/or depression. Why honor a divine spirit that doesn't give a damn? Does that mean divinity doesn't exist?

When people are devoted to a cause, activity, or belief, they tend to throw themselves into it to the exclusion of everything else. When the devotion isn't returned in the same fashion, then resentment, anger, and depression often result. Sometimes, the person burning out will intensify his or her efforts, and this becomes a destructive spiral. What can we do?

Everyone needs a break once in a while. Academics have sabbaticals, a practice I wish would be common throughout all professions. Taking a "time out" occasionally is important. It allows one to reassess goals, desires, and affirmations. It also allows time to reflect on the past, to find where the patterns are, how those patterns fit together, and which ones need to change.

Books on magical study emphasize the need to work every day. This is a fact. In order to truly live a magical life, one must work each day to integrate spiritual beliefs into daily living. However, that does not mean that one can never, ever, take a break, or that taking a break will force one to start again at Wiccan Square One.

The most common types of spiritual burnout that I have witnessed among magical people are as follows: the overzealous student, the overworked high priest or priestess, and the person who has a tragedy occur and feels unsupported.

The Student

When you start down a new path, you want everything *now*. You want to have a complete set of beautiful, charged, fully operational tools *now*. You want to be adept at a hundred spells with a hundred percent success rate *now*. You want to be able to glide through life and receive acclaim for your grace, prowess, and shining light *now*. The truth of the matter is that it takes time. If you do not master the basics, you cannot master the higher levels of skill. There is no substitute for hard work, study, and experience. There is also no substitute for mistakes. Threw a spell and it bounced back? Why? Couldn't be bothered to learn how to cast a spell properly? Well, what did you expect?

When you make a mistake, take the time to trace back the ritual. Break down the elements and see what didn't work. It could be carelessness, it could be unfocused intent, it could be you were misleading yourself. Re-work the spell over and over until you get it right, but don't feel you have to do it all in one day. Spread it out over a period of weeks or months. It's like coming up with a new recipe in cooking. You've got to test it.

Read as much as you can, talk to people, and correspond with people. Take a class. Maybe you need a new teacher.

Keep your studies balanced with your mundane life. Remember, eventually you won't be leading two separate lives. They will be integrated. Enjoy time with non-magical friends and family. We live in a magnificent, diverse world. Take advantage of it.

THE HIGH PRIEST/PRIESTESS

If you're leading a group, it's terribly easy to fall into martyr syndrome. I've done it myself a few times. I've watched several high priestesses around me do it, and crash and burn. Yes, teaching is an enormous responsibility. These people have put their trust in you, but they are also still responsible for themselves.

The best way of working that I've found is to allow students, coveners, etc. to participate in all aspects of the ritual. Let them help plan. Let them take on specific tasks such as calling in directions, consecrating the elements, and walking the elements around the circle. Teach them and let them do. Have the feast after the ritual be a potluck. If you're having an open circle, tell everyone who's invited what to bring. Most people are honored by an invitation to ritual and they are delighted to bring a covered dish. It makes them part of things.

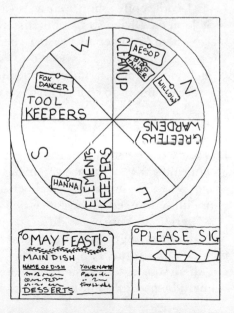

The most important thing is: if you are feeling overworked and under-appreciated, communicate. Don't accuse your students or coveners of being ungrateful. Simply state what you are feeling, without judgment toward them, and ask for help. I think you'll be surprised at how quickly they will rally around you. If certain members continue irresponsible behavior, consider asking them to leave. There is nothing wrong with following different paths.

A Person Dealing with Tragedy

Terrible things happen to good people. It doesn't mean that you've done something to deserve it, or you're being paid back for something done in a past life, or that God hates you. I don't have a pat answer for every situation, and I know that saying "there's a reason for everything in the web of the universe" is no comfort.

The most important thing to remember is that you are not alone, be it on the spiritual plane or the physical. There are counselors, clinics, support groups, the Internet—whatever you're going through, if you reach out, you will be able to find someone to help.

Find places that make you feel calm and comforted. If you can't create a section of your home that is a sanctuary, find someplace close by where you can retreat. Depending on what sort of sanctuary I need, I have several different places in New York where I go: a favorite coffee shop, a corner in a book store, the Cathedral of St. John the Divine (yes, a church), and Central Park. These are places where I can get my bearings, hear divinity speak, and feel safe while trying to make sense of the world. Once you get grounded and centered and start to get things in perspective, you can consider active options to change what you need to change.

Ego

In every instance, stop and take a long, hard look at yourself and how you are behaving in the world. Where is your ego involved in an unhealthy way? What are you trying to prove and to whom by trying to be the ultimate magical person? Why do you think the entire universe needs to be concerned with you right now?

There is an enormous difference between healthy self-esteem and ego. Ego often hides under a martyr syndrome or goodness syndrome. Ego also hides within insecurity. Separate out where your ego is causing you more pain and more burnout. It might be painful, but, in the long run, it will serve you well.

Take a look at what motivates your actions and what responses you need to change.

TAKING TIME OUT

There are times when you simply need to take time out from everything, no matter what. You may feel that you want to re-think how you relate to divinity, or you want to commune with divinity once a week instead of on a daily basis. There is nothing wrong with that, as long as it is done in an honorable fashion.

Time outs can be ritually begun and ritually ended. First of all, figure out what you are getting away from. Then figure out what you want your time period to be. If you belong to a working group, ask for a leave of absence or ask to be cut out completely from the group if you're fairly sure you won't come back. Don't just stop attending events and abdicate or ignore your responsibilities. Especially once you've been initiated, this is a breaking of your oath, and there are consequences. You need to leave in an atmosphere of love and trust.

If you are part of a group, participate in a a leaving ritual. Whether you are on your own (solitary) or working with a group, do your own ritual, even if it's just lighting a candle and explaining to divinity that you need to take a break.

While you're on your break, do things that you enjoy. Do things that you've denied yourself, as long as they don't hurt you or anyone else. Most of all, listen. Divinity has unusual ways of communicating, and you may receive the answers you seek when you least expect them. Use the mindfulness that you learned in your work to enhance your rest and appreciate everything around you. It doesn't have to be a burning bush to have a message.

How to Avoid the Evil Eye

By Jim Weaver

The evil eye is one of the oldest and most widespread magical beliefs in the world. Simply put, the evil eye is the belief that a person can bring misfortune to another human or animal by giving a jealous stare or envious glance. The misfortune may take many forms: a sudden illness, business may go bad, crops may fail, or an animal may go lame, to name only a few.

What isn't so simple is understanding just how the evil eye works. It is believed most people who have the power to cast the evil eye aren't even aware they possess this unfortunate ability.

Since most cases of the evil eye are caused by this involuntary power, no one can be certain from who or when the evil eye may strike. This makes it one of the most feared of all magical powers.

Over the centuries, many cultures have developed folk methods for taking precautions against the evil eye before it occurs. It seems the best way to deal with the evil eye is to avoid it in the first place.

In Greece for example, preventing the evil eye is a daily part of life for many, and is taken quite seriously. Here the evil eye is called *to mati,* which means simply, "the eye."

These are a few of the folk methods popular in Greece and the Near East used to protect against the evil eye:

- If someone is staring at you and you become uncomfortable, move or step aside. It is believed you are literally getting out of harm's way and letting the negativity pass you by.

- Spitting, which is a widely accepted form of defense against the evil eye, is also used in Greece. When you feel someone is secretly wishing you bad luck, spit in their direction three times. (Please, use a dry spit, or blow your breath through your lips.)

- Babies are thought to be especially sensitive to the curse of the evil eye. When a newborn yawns, it is the custom to make the sign of the cross over the little open mouth to prevent the evil from entering.

- Garlic, a universal cure-all for many types of hostile magic, is also believed to guard against the evil eye. In Greece however, it is used in a different manner. Instead of actually using the plant or bulb of garlic, many Greeks believe by saying the word "garlic" quietly will form an invisible shield of protection around you. If you think someone is envious of you, mutter "skortha" under your breath, which means garlic in Greek.

- In Greece beautiful charms are made by jewelers to be worn as a safeguard against the evil eye. One of the most popular is known as an "eye bead." These amulets are about the size of a pea and have the shape of a human eye painted on them. This type of charm probably dates back to ancient Egypt, where the eye of Horus, which appeared on jewelry and art, was used to ward off evil of many types. The eye bead will stare back a curse and return it to the sender before harm can come to you. I have a beautiful eye bead set in gold that I purchased from a Greek jeweler in New York City. They are not expensive and can be found in Greek or Middle Eastern jewelry stores in this country. As with any charm, it has no power in itself alone. You must charge it with your own belief system.

As we enter the twenty-first century, the belief in the evil eye is as strong today as it was thousands of years ago. Even though understanding how the evil eye works may remain somewhat of a mystery, by drawing on ancient ways of protection, we can prevent ourselves from becoming victims of one of the world's oldest forms of negative magic.

FACING YOUR FEAR

BY DIANA OLSEN

You have your candles picked out and a place away from distractions. You have your book of ritual. You're ready to go except for one little thing that keeps gumming up the works: you haven't dealt with your fear.

Fear is that emotion that made you wait six months until you felt comfortable buying a black candle. Fear made you hide all your altar materials, even though you live alone and only entertain your cat and your goldfish. Fear led you to store your tarot cards in the freezer.

Since this article assumes you're new to experiments in spiritual development, we'll also assume that you haven't crossed the maxim "let it flow and let it go" when dealing with any really strong motivating or un-motivating emotion.

This essay isn't about psychology and facing old resentments toward parents—leave that to professionals. This is about finding a way to ease into ritual so you can start experimenting within your chosen path. Reading about magic and earth worship is all fine and well, but if you don't add experience, a lot of that learning can go for naught.

Fear can prevent you from exploring rituals. For some, it even prevents reading about Paganism for fear of "going to hell" for witnessing "forbidden" information. Fear can prevent people from finishing rituals in process. Worst of all, it can prevent you from working through a valid learning experience.

The reason why this happens is similar to the reasons most of us survive a bed-wetting phase as children. We're afraid of the unknown; crossing into ritual practice means possibly raising the monster that used to live under our beds—and he doesn't just want toenail clippings anymore. We fear failure: what if disaster happens when we mispronounce a syllable? Will the cat turn into a puma and the house burn down? Will we have to face the embarassment of doing this silly ritual only to find it doesn't work, and end up feeling even more foolish? These fears can't be blamed on all the times we had to wake our

parents to change the sheets—they can be roundly and cheerfully blamed on society. Once you're finished blaming your favorite targets and feel better, go on to the next paragraph.

Getting rid of fear doesn't do much good. Facing and conquering fear or ignoring it like the pestiferous child it is probably creates more productive results, magically speaking.

Examine your fears and choose a method of coping. The methods generally involve emotional management. For example, when I first started practicing, my fear came from the strange sensations I felt from the energies I raised. I had to develop a way to find out if these energies were normal or something that I should, as a matter of self preservation, avoid.

I handled my problem by practicing circle casting. I got to the point where I can meditate on the type of circle I want surrounding me and the same energy sensation that used to spook me surrounds and satisfies me, since it's exactly what I want.

Other methods of handling fear of performing ritual involve slow immersion, short rituals, and protection spells. The method depends on the person. If adjusting to energy sensations is the problem, try shorter rituals—even just casting a circle, calling the quarters, and promptly dismissing them. Once you are more comfortable, move on to actually "doing something" while in the circle. If you feel you have to do a ritual because some emergency arises where you have a driving need to use magic, a protection spell as a preliminary is the best "quickie" way to conquer fear available. Many protection spells are easily located both on the Internet and in Pagan material published. A protection spell gives reassurance to the subconscious mind that what you are doing is safe, and reinforces, too, that you have made it safe for yourself.

If these suggestions don't give you the motivation you need to take that first step, then commune with your deity to face this problem, or in the words of a beloved pugnacious three year old, "Get over it!" Ritual involves experience. Experience includes fear. To grow spiritually and psychically, you must experience fear and somehow work with it. Ritual could be the first step.

The Natural Way to Psychic Self-Defense

By Marguerite Elsbeth

Invisible forces are all around us. They exist as a spiritual part of nature, and make a deep and lasting impression on our psyches or subconscious minds, even though we cannot always perceive their existence. Unusual or unfamiliar energies are not necessarily evil in and of themselves. Still, because invisible forces tend to shape-shift according to the physical, emotional, and mental constructs of our ordinary world, they are not always pleasant or even vaguely hospitable to us when we happen to fall under their spell.

The Nature of Psychic Attack

We are protected from disruptive psychic influences because we commonly dwell in a state of mindful oblivion, a by-product of the routine frenzy produced by our fast-paced, high-tech society. However, the unseen remains alive and well in the persons, places, and things we encounter every day, and we are psychically affected by it nonetheless.

During our daily travels, we may meet individuals who embrace a woe-is-me attitude, are prone to attracting the darker side of life, or who are deliberately handling these forces in an unscrupulous manner. Occasionally we may enter office buildings, homes, or wilderness areas that are tainted by emotional discord or haunted by malevolent spirits, or we may touch items that hold the gloomy impressions of unfortunate past events.

There are times when we may bring the more challenging elements of the invisible world upon ourselves. This occurs when our magical inclinations lead us out of our depth of knowledge and understanding, or when we inadvertently fall victim to a vulnerable chink in our emotional armor. Now, with radio, television, and the relatively new addition of computer interaction, we may even reach out and touch the unseen in cyber-space!

All of the above are examples of situations that bring us into contact with invisible forces that overwhelm the psyche, and trigger the instinctual, uncontrollable fear-reaction known as psychic attack.

PRIMAL FEAR

The primal part of the back brain, called the *medulla oblongata,* is responsible for automatic bodily functions such as breathing, substance assimilation, digestion, elimination, and various involuntary physical movements. It is the control center for the central nervous system, which is also in charge of our habitual emotional responses. When we feel threatened, anxious, or fearful, the primal brain reacts by stimulating a big-chemical reaction called "flight or fight." Neurotransmitters release a rush of adrenaline into the bloodstream, which then floods the vessels of the back brain. As a result, we may experience any number of uncomfortable physical and emotional sensations: heart palpitations, cold sweats, hot flashes, numbness, shock, anger, sadness, fear, panic, feelings of dissociation, and even thoughts of impending death.

Obviously these are legitimate, natural responses to real-life crises—violent crime, accidents, relocation, childbirth, divorce, disease, or the passing of a loved one. However, an encounter with hostile, invisible forces can produce the exact same symptoms, with one exception: it is difficult to explain to the average person with little knowledge of the esoteric side of life that you are experiencing these symptoms for no apparent reason.

First, rule out any material causes in a logical, systematic manner. Alcohol and substance abuse, physical, emotional, or mental conditions, stress, or a predilection to hysteria or panic must all be taken into consideration when attempting to make an honest diagnosis. Next, see the following checklist to determine that what you are experiencing is the real thing.

√ Strange dreams or nightmares, sometimes accompanied by night sweats, the sensation of weight on the chest or body, or actual physical bruising upon waking up.

√ A hallucinogenic home environment, including "breathing" or undulating walls and furnishings. Unusual pet-related antics, like seeing the family dog or cat repeatedly stare at a particular spot on the ceiling or in the corner of a room, chasing invisible objects, or manifesting sudden fearful behavior such as cringing or shaking.

√ An atmosphere filled with dread, fear, and oppression, or cold spots in sunny or warm areas of the house.

√ Marked nervous exhaustion leading to extreme physical weakness, loss of appetite, insomnia, and possible mental/emotional breakdown.

√ Evil odors that come and go, slime marks on the floors, walls or counter-tops, or unidentifiable footprints in odd places, leading to and going nowhere.

√ Noise and other sound materializations, including ringing bells, creaks, clicks, whispers, laughter, singing, or moans.

√ Inexplicable fire outbreaks, moving objects, and appliances or lights that turn on and off by themselves

√ Shiny floating balls of light, sometimes carrying a distorted face or image in their midst, or shadowy figures standing in doorways or passing through walls.

Your first inclination might be to take flight and head for the hills upon experiencing these eerie occurrences. However, it is far better to stand your ground and fight for your right to peace and privacy. Whether the psychic attack is a result of human interference, mischievous spirits, elemental astral forces, disconnected thought-forms of your own creation, or a magical experiment gone wrong, you are being violated by an intruder and you must treat the unwelcome invasion as such.

Every culture and spiritual tradition has a unique way of dealing with the phenomena of psychic attack, but what if you are a novice magical practitioner, or simply an open-minded person who happens upon an unruly hidden force? If you can't get help from someone with experience, no one will believe you, or you dare not tell anyone for fear they'll think you're crazy, following are ten natural psychic self-defense methods that really work:

1. Discontinue your association with any person, place, or thing that may be suspect in causing the attack.

2. Head for the nearest herb shop and load up on St. John's wort, valerian root, kava kava, and an amino acid called GABA. All of these natural remedies will calm your nerves, allow you to get some rest, think clearly, and stop you from being afraid.

3. Go into a wilderness area and find a hilltop clearing encircled by trees. This type of landscape brings you closer to the higher spiritual realms, and provides you with a naturally protective magic circle. Lie on the earth in the center of the circle and listen to the sounds of nature. Watch the clouds drift across the sky, feel the warmth of the sun on your skin, and the vast energy of the earth beneath you. Stay there until you feel centered and grounded. Repeat as necessary.

4. Clean your house from top to bottom, including drawers, closets, and storage areas. Throw or give away anything you have not used in a year.

5. Light up your life. Replace low wattage bulbs with halogen lights. Open the curtains and let the sun shine in.

6. Keep moving. Hiking, running, biking, walking, swimming, and dancing are all activities that express life and uplift your spirits.

7. Breathe. Fear cannot exist where there is breath.

8. Drink purified water, eight glasses a day and then some. Add one cup of sea salt and one cup of baking soda to your bath water. Soak twice a day.

9. Make a phone call to the perpetrator of the attack if it is a living person and you are relatively certain of his or her identity. Tell them that you are aware of what they are doing, and demand that they stop or you will report them to the proper authorities. Dark magicians and their ilk usually prefer to work in secrecy, so blow out their circuits by blowing their cover, and return the attack to its sender in the process.

10. Help those in need, take comfort in prayer to your personal gods, and call out to the universe for aid.

PSYCHIC ATTACK

BY ESTELLE DANIELS

Psychic attack is the most frightening psychic phenomenon one can experience. Many claim to have been victims, and some feel they were scarred badly. Others were able to fight and win.

What is a psychic attack? It is the feeling that something is "out there" after you, intent on doing harm. Very rarely, it is a conscious working on the part of someone else. Most commonly you feel something is out there and won't leave you alone.

Psychic attack is a common cry wolf in the magical community. "I walked by his house yesterday and I felt something watching me." "I was out with this group and now I feel run down and drained. They attacked me and took my energy." These statements are the usual type of "proof" one gets describing a psychic attack. Psychic phenomena are highly subjective. Not everyone has the same level of abilities, nor do they manifest in the same ways.

When a person is relatively new to psychic work, they experience the phenomenon of "opening up." Their latent abilities are awakened. Before, when the person was not psychically aware, they noticed little of the "other worlds." Opening up can be good, but it can also lead to some uncomfortable experiences. Imagine being deaf. You cannot hear music or conversation or traffic noise. Then you suddenly can hear. Now you are hearing, but you have yet to be able to filter or distinguish the pleasant from the unpleasant or harmful. You hear everything: that which is relevant to you, that which is incidental, and that which is not meant for you. Being newly psychically aware is quite similar. You pick up on everything and have yet to be able to filter out that which has no relevance to you. The natural psychic background noise that many have learned to deal with can be deafening until you learn to shield and protect yourself. You can become a bit paranoid because there is so much and it takes time to gain the skills.

In my opinion, ninety-nine percent of the time what is perceived as a psychic attack is no more than background noise. Like a psychic backfire, it is loud and startling, but does no harm. If a person is newly aware, they may hear it and wonder, "what was that, where did it come from, was it directed toward me, can it hurt me," and so on. When a person worries and wonders, they start straining to "hear" more and start to pick up on more stuff until they are perceiving the psychic mice running across the floor and freaking out. Another analogy is a city person moving to the country. There is no traffic noise, no hustle and bustle of people, but they hear the wind in the trees, the crickets chirping, and the animals at night. Those sounds can be strange and startling to someone not used to them. The country person moving to the city jumps at every car horn, siren, or screech of brakes until they learn to tune it out.

Because psychic phenomena are subjective and personal not everyone is going to hear what you hear. You might pick up on something that nobody else does. Does that constitute a psychic attack? Not really.

WHAT CAN YOU DO?

The bad news is that you can never totally block some stuff. The good news is there are simple and effective techniques for grounding and shielding that can make life quieter and more comfortable.

Some people have an amulet or talisman that does the shielding, grounding, and centering for them, but this can become a crutch. If you lose it, you are defenseless.

The best way to protect yourself is to learn techniques to ground, center, and shield yourself. Grounding and centering is a way of restoring emotional and psychic equilibrium. You concentrate on your body, the here and now. This diverts your attention and you can disconnect from the creepies. Shielding allows you to block some or most of the psychic stuff until and unless you want to open up. These techniques are simple and effective, and when learned make life as a psychically-aware person more comfortable.

GROUNDING

One effective exercise is the Lesser Banishing Ritual of the Pentagram, LBRP for short. (see page 36 for more information.) The first part of it is effective to help a person regain equilibrium. The full ritual will help block out most psychic noise.

Another grounding technique is to eat a heavy meal. Fast food, meat and potatoes, or something filling and substantial or greasy. Red meat or lots of butter and cheese are good grounding foods. If you feel jumpy, avoid stimulants like coffee, caffeine, or alcohol. Physical activity, from taking a walk or doing light chores up to a full workout can also effectively ground and center. A bath or shower can do the trick. Laughing helps. Watch a funny movie, read a funny book, or just swap jokes with friends. Most psychic critters are not comfortable around laughter. Become mentally absorbed in something active, not passive like watching TV. Doing long division, income tax, or other pencil and paper math can be absorbing, and possibly frustrating, but will also get your mind off the stuff "out there."

SHIELDING

Shielding can be elaborate like the LBRP, or simple, like visualizing yourself inside a glowing energy shield, like a spaceship. Any psychic energy will hit the shield and be deflected away from you. These shields can be anchored to the zenith (heaven) and horizon by energy rays if you want extra stability. Shields can be like an outer set of energy clothes.

Shields need periodic attention. If you work at keeping them, they will stay. In a creepy situation, giving them an extra dose of energy, strengthening your shields, can be helpful. If you want to perceive something you can open a hole in the direction you want to feel, you do not have to drop them.

There are many other techniques, but these are simple and effective. Hopefully they will help.

Dealing with Elementals, Ghosts, and Other Spiritual Beings

By Cerridwen Iris Shea

D o you ever hear funny noises in the night and you know it's not the heater or the cat? Do you ever discover that something is missing or has been moved? Does a place suddenly fluctuate in temperature, or do you feel like you're being watched? No, you're not on the newest version of a Fox real-life TV show. You probably have some spirits around your place.

Contrary to many literary and Hollywood stories, having spirits in your home is not necessarily a bad thing. In our path, we often work with spiritual beings, especially around Samhain. They can be elementals, element energy, totem animals, spirits of the deceased, guardian angels, lost souls, the guardian spirit of the place, or an energy you forgot to thank and release the last time you were in circle. The list goes on and on. It can get downright crowded if you're not careful. How do you deal with such visitors?

First of all, do your research. Stop groaning. I know, I know, I'm always talking about research, but research is important. Know what it is you're dealing with. Read up on the history of your town, your street, your property. Find out what happened to the people who lived there before you. It doesn't have to be anything as dramatic as a murder or a madwoman in the attic. It could be something as simple as an unfortunate dog hit by a car who died on your property last week.

During a waning Moon, do a major housecleaning, top to toe. Then take two white candles and a green candle. Set up an altar in your usual fashion, only do it in the place where the disturbance is usually the strongest. Cast your circle, creating a safe space between the worlds. Call in guardians for each quarter and ask them

specifically to do just that, guard. You want to make sure you are inside a protected space. Burn some spirit incense. I usually use a combination of rosemary, sage, patchouli, frankincense, and just a dash of mugwort.

Then, invite in the spirit, making it clear that it can only enter the sacred space with good intention, sort of like going to Switzerland. The circle is neutral territory. Your fears and the spirit's crankiness need to be left outside. Sit down and have a chat with the spirit. Find out who it is, and what it wants. Does it need your help in some way? Is is attached to the house? Can you work out some arrangement to co-exist in peace and trust? Ask questions and really listen to the answers. Usually, you can work out some sort of agreement, such as "I will leave out a libation for you or include you in my circle work if you don't scare the guests or smash the china."

I cannot emphasize enough how important it is to listen. Don't assume that you know what the spirit has to say. Don't assume it will be the same as the research that you've done. Perhaps the history is incorrect, or perhaps the spirit is lying. Just because it's a spirit doesn't mean it's telling the truth. Rely on your intelligence and your instincts. You're dealing with an individual, and it is important to give this individual spirit the same attention you would if it was in material form. Many spirits are lost, confused, angry, lonely, and frustrated that they're not understood. Also, the spirit's value systems may be different than yours. If you need something specific, explain what it is as clearly as you can. This can take several days, or even weeks. Be very patient. Usually, after the first conversation, things quiet down a bit, at least until you can work things all the way through.

If you work things through, terrific. You now have an extra roommate. I have yet to get any of the spirits I know to do the dishes and vaccuum for me (darn it), but they do often help. They are terrific at letting me know when something is wrong, whether it is someone trying to illegally enter via the fire door, or someone who left a burning cigarette in the hallway.

What happens if it is not a particularly nice entity and you can't come to an agreement? This is rare, but it does happen. Then you need to get out your banishing tools and do a full-scale banishment ritual. I've found the dark of the Moon to be the most useful for this. Read several banishment rituals, and come up with your own from the inspiration. Use the strongest banishing incense and oil that you can come up with. Call on your guardians and totems to

come into the circle and help you. Cast your circle for your entire home and property. Starting in the north, moving counterclockwise, perform the banishing. Make sure you go into all cupboards, closets, nooks, crannies, crawl spaces, tool sheds, etc. Once the banishing is done, start in the north again, and move clockwise throughout the entire space to seal it.

When the New Moon begins the next day, do the strongest protection ritual you can find and enforce it every day until the Full Moon. You will need to re-cleanse and re-seal the space every month. It won't need to be as complicated a ritual, but it needs to be done.

Even in a banishing, however, treat the entity with respect. There doesn't need to be high drama hocus-pocus, just firmness and clear intent. It is your home and you have the right to make it a safe, magical place. Most spirits will respect and enjoy that. If not, it is now your space and you must secure it.

What about if and when you move? Cast another circle and invite the spirit(s) in. Explain why you have to move and where you are going. Some spirits are bound to a place, and will stay where they are. Make sure you take the time to bid them a respectful goodbye, and thank them for everything. Some spirits may use this as a reason to continue their journey separate from you. Again, thank them and wish them well. You can always reconnect at Samhain. Some may wish to go with you. Discuss it with them and come to a mutual understanding.

When you move into a new place, preferably before your belongings arrive, take some time to get to know any spirits that already reside there. Include them in your cleansings and consecrations. Talk to them about their place in your life and whether they should stay or go. Help them feel respected and real.

Work with spirits, respect them, and enjoy an unusual and fulfilling relationship unlike anything you could share on Earth.

THE MOODUS CAVE

BY BERNYCE BARLOW

On Mt. Tom near Haddam, Connecticut, is a cave that has been the source for stories and legends for thousands of years. The cave is called the Moodus Cave and it is best known for the noises it makes. Single booms, multiple booms, rifle rat-a-tat-tats, pops, roars, and sounds like thunder often roll out of its mouth! The first written accounts of this strange cave were penned in the early 1700s by settlers to the region. In 1791, the sounds were so loud they were heard in New York and Boston. Newspapers reported that toppled chimneys, bouncing boulders, and flattened walls were caused by the Moodus noises.

One popular story about the cave was created and circulated by the earlier settlers of Haddam as an attempt to explain the mysterious sounds. It was said a great war among the Witches of Haddam East and Haddam West carried on beneath the two districts in the Underworld, and the cave carried the noises of their battles to the surface.

Their battles were noisy and sometimes unnerving, but nobody dared to silence them. Night after night the Witches would throw lightning bolts and thunder claps back and forth, and night after night the townsfolk of Haddam would lie awake wondering if the battle would ever be won by one side or another. Sometimes the sounds would go away for a decade or so, but they always returned when the story of the Witches of Haddam East and Haddam West was no longer being told, as if the Witches were reminding the town's people they were indeed still there.

The Wagunk tribe called the region *Matchitmoodus,* meaning "land of many noises." They held rowdy, earsplitting ceremonies there imitating the spirit of place, who they called Hobomko. It was believed when Hobomko was irate he would boom and sputter his displeasure across the land. The louder the noises, the madder he was. When Hobomko was exceptionally angry the ceremonies became intensely boisterous in hopes to appease his ire.

What causes the sounds at the Moodus Cave? I am so glad you asked...it's really an interesting freak of the norm! There are a number of earthquakes that originate from a spiracle area 4,560 feet deep and 760 feet in diameter beneath the cave. In and of itself this is not unusual, as earthquakes often generate from deep spiracle centers. What is unusual is that for some unknown reason there are very few filters between the ground and the atmosphere at the cave site, so if the ground moves just a teeny tiny bit you can hear it. On the Richter Scale -2 is a hundred times less ground motion than a human being's senses can detect, but at Moodus a -2 reading can cause a great big boom that can be heard for quite a distance. Can you imagine a Moodus Cave in Los Angeles?

Cauldron Magic

By Gerina Dunwich

In contemporary Witchcraft, the cauldron is an important magical tool that symbolically combines the influences of the ancient elements of air, fire, water, and earth. Its shape is representative of Mother Nature, and the three legs upon which it stands correspond to the three aspects of the Triple Goddess, the three lunar phases (waxing, full, and waning), and to three as a magical number. Additionally, the cauldron is a symbol of transformation (both physical and spiritual), enlightenment, wisdom, the womb of the Mother Goddess, and rebirth.

Since early times, cauldrons have been used not only for boiling water and cooking food, but for heating magical brews, poisons, and healing potions. They have also been utilized by alchemists and by Witches as tools of divination, containers for sacred fires and incense, and holy vessels for offerings to the gods of old.

If a large cauldron is needed in a ritual, it is generally placed next to the altar, on either side. Small cauldrons, such as ones used for the burning of incense, can be placed on top of the altar.

In the Middle Ages, most of the population believed that all Witches possessed a large black cauldron in which poisonous brews and vile hell-broths were routinely concocted. These mixtures were said to have contained such ingredients as bat's blood, serpent's venom, headless toads, the eyes of newts, and a gruesome assortment of animal and human body parts, as well as deadly herbs and roots.

In fourteenth-century Ireland, a Witch known as Lady Alice Kyteler was said to have used the enchanted skull of a beheaded thief as her cauldron. Also in the fourteenth century, a male Witch by the name of William Lord Soulis was convicted in Scotland for a number of sorcery-related offenses. His peculiar form of execution was death by being boiled alive in a huge cauldron.

According to an old legend, if a sorceress dumped the vile contents of her cauldron into the sea, a great tempest would be stirred up.

Ancient Irish folklore is rich with tales of wondrous cauldrons that never run out of food at a feast, while an old Gypsy legend told of a brave hero who was boiled in a cauldron filled with the milk of man-eating mares.

It is said that bad luck will befall any Witch who brews a potion in a cauldron belonging to another. If the lid is accidentally left off the cauldron while a magical brew is prepared, this portends the arrival of a stranger, according to a superstitious belief from Victorian-era England.

The cauldron and its powers are associated with many goddesses from pre-Christian faiths, including Hecate (the protectress of all Witches), Demeter/Persephone (in the Eleusinian mysteries), the Greek enchantresses Circe and Medea, Siris (the Babylonian goddess of fate and mother of the stars, whose cauldron was made of lapis lazuli), the Celtic goddess Branwen, and others. Perhaps the most well-known and significant goddess with a connection to the cauldron is the Celtic goddess Cerridwen, from whose cauldron bubbled forth the gifts of wisdom and inspiration.

Although the cauldron has traditionally been a symbol of the divine feminine since the earliest of times, there exist a number of male deities from various Pagan pantheons who also have a connection to it. Among them are the Norse god Odin (who acquired his shape-shifting powers by drinking from the cauldron of wise blood), the Hindu sky god Indra (whose myth is similar to Odin's), Bran the Blessed (the Welsh god of the sacred cauldron), and Cernunnos (the Celtic horned god who was dismembered and boiled in a cauldron to be reborn).

Depicted on the famous Gunderstrup cauldron (circa 100 B.C.) is the stag-horned Cernunnos in various scenes with different animals. Believed by many to be of Celtic origin, this large silver cauldron may have once been used in sacrificial rites.

The use of sacrificial cauldrons can be traced to the ancient religious and magical practices of various European cultures, as well as to some shamanic traditions. Human and animal victims would first be beheaded over the cauldrons and then have their blood drained out into the cauldron, where it would be boiled to produce a mystical substance. Among the Celts, a potion of inspiration was said to have been brewed in such a manner by the priestess of the lunar goddess.

The cauldron is linked to the Holy Grail—a chalice that is believed by Christians to have been used by Jesus Christ at the Last Supper. However, prior to its incorporation into Christian myth in the twelfth century, the Grail belonged to British Paganism as a symbol of reincarnation and the divine womb of the Goddess.

THE CAULDRON OF CERRIDWEN

Cerridwen, a deity associated with the feminine symbols of water and the Moon, is the shape-shifting Celtic goddess of inspiration, wisdom, and the magical arts of enchantment, divination, and prophecy. She possesses the three aspects of the maiden, mother, and crone, and is a goddess whose invocation is a significant aspect of both the initiatory and mystery rites of Celtic magic.

In her mysterious cauldron, according to ancient Celtic legend, Cerridwen prepared a potion of enlightenment for her son that consisted of the yellow flowers of the cowslip, fluxwort, hedgeberry, vervain, the berries of the mistletoe (a plant sacred to the Druids), and the foam of the ocean. It was warmed by the breath of nine maidens, and required brewing for a year and a day.

A youth named Gwion drank three drops of the potion, causing the rest of the brew to turn into poison and destroy the cauldron. To hide from the angry goddess, he used his newly-acquired shape-shifting powers to change himself into a grain of wheat. However, Cerridwen transformed herself into a black hen and devoured him.

CAULDRON SPIRIT

Many Witches pour a bit of ordinary surgical spirit (rubbing alcohol) into their cast iron cauldrons and light it by carefully dropping in a lit match. This is often done as part of healing rituals, invocations to the elemental spirit of fire, scrying divinations, sabbat fire festivals, and various working rituals. (Note: A quarter cup of rubbing alcohol will burn for approximately three minutes.) Be sure that the cauldron is resting securely on a fireproof stand and is not close to any flammable substances. Do not touch the cauldron while it is hot unless you cover your hands with protective oven mitts. If the fire must be extinguished before it burns itself out, smother it by covering the cauldron with a lid or by sprinkling salt or sand over the flames. Remember, whenever working with the element of fire, use caution and common sense, and respect the spirits of the flame.

The sight of a cauldron blazing with fire can be very magical and mesmerizing, and when the alcohol has been steeped in aromatic herbs, a sweet but gentle incense-like fragrance is produced. To make an herbal cauldron spirit, put a small bunch of any or all of the following into a glass bottle: fresh lavender flowers and leaves, fresh mint leaves, fresh rosemary flowers and leaves, and fresh thyme flowers and leaves. Fill the bottle to the top with the alcohol, cap it tightly, and then give it a good shake. Keep it in a cool place for thirteen days, shaking it twice daily (every sunrise and every moonrise). Strain it through a double thickness of muslin into a clear bottle. Cap it tightly and store it away from heat or flame. Cauldron spirit will keep indefinitely.

CAULDRON DIVINATION

Divination is an art that has been practiced in one form or another since ancient times and in all levels of culture.

There are a number of ways in which a cauldron can be used for divining. One method is to fill the cauldron with water or wine and place it between two burning candles or under the bright silver rays of the Full Moon. Relax, clear your mind of all distracting thoughts, and then gaze into the cauldron as you would a crystal ball. As with other forms of scrying, your vision will begin to blur after a while and a slight haze will begin to materialize. Keep your gaze focused and eventually a vision, either of an actual or symbolic nature, may be revealed to you.

To determine good or bad omens, according to an old Pagan method, place a cauldron on the ground and burn some incense (traditionally frankincense) or a handful of dried herbs in it. Mugwort, rose petals, vervain, and yarrow are popular herbs of divination among Witches. If the smoke rises straight up to the heavens, this indicates a good omen. If it does not rise or if it touches the ground, this indicates a bad one.

Mayan Days of the Dead

By Kenneth Johnson

Throughout Mexico, the Days of the Dead are celebrated at the beginning of November. So popular has this ceremony become that it is now common in North America as well, especially in Florida, Texas, and California. During this time, we honor our ancestors and departed relatives with food and festivity. In Mexico, people have picnics in cemeteries, bake little cakes in the form of skeletons, build livingroom altars to their ancestors, and lay paths of marigold flowers from the graveyard to the home to help the guide the spirits of the departed back to the altars erected in their honor.

But where did these customs originate?

While it is true that the Spanish who came to the New World brought with them many Pagan folkways honoring the dead, and that a number of these traditions have found their way into the present-day ceremonies, there are also many aspects of the Days of the Dead that have their roots in the ancient civilizations of Mexico.

The Mayan peoples perceived the universe as a great tree with its roots in the Underworld and its crown in the world of the gods. After death, the souls of the departed traveled to the "pool of souls" that lay at the base of the great World Tree. The sacred well that forms part of the ceremonial complex at Chichén Itzá was regarded as an earthly manifestation of this pool of souls. Many Mayan rituals from the ancient days were designed to call forth the spirits of the ancestors from the pool of souls so that they could speak to their descendants and provide wisdom for the living. In those days, a king was called an *ahau* or "lord," and a departed ancestor was referred to in the same way, as an ahau. The rituals that brought the lords back to the land of the living were performed on special days of the sacred Mayan Calendar, called Ahau Days. Even now, some traditional Mayan people visit cemeteries to pay their respects to the dead on Ahau Days. We celebrate the Days of the Dead at the beginning of November because this is the Christian All Souls' Day, which in turn has its roots in the Samhain rituals of Pagan Celtic times. The original Mexican Days of the Dead were celebrated several times a year on Ahau Days, and in some very traditional communities they still are.

When souls were ready to reincarnate into the human world again, they blossomed as flowers on the upper or heavenly part of the World Tree. The marigolds that are set out as a path for the dead to follow are a symbolic remembrance of these soul flowers.

To the Maya, the souls of the ancestors are everywhere. They especially like to manifest themselves in the form of butterflies. If you ever have the chance to visit Yucatán or some other Mayan region, make a trip to the local cemetery. Chances are good you will discover that the place is just filled with butterflies.

THE DAY OF THE DEAD

BY LYNNE STURTEVANT

From wildly-costumed revelers in fashionable Mexico City "discos of death" to simple family observances in rural villages, the ancient pre-Columbian past is alive and well. The Mexican Day of the Dead, or *la Dia de los Muertos,* is a vibrant blend of old and new. Death is accepted and honored as a part of life, and those who came before us are invited to join in the fun.

The Day of the Dead has its roots in pre-Columbian times. The exact origins of the ceremony are unknown, but it was well-established when the Spanish conquistadors arrived in the sixteenth century. The ancient Mexicans saw life and death as interrelated, as inextricably linked as night and day.

At the time of the Spanish conquest, Mexicans recognized and honored the dead once a year by cleaning and decorating graves, preparing ritual foods, playing music, and dancing. The Catholic priests were horrified. They interpreted the celebration as a dangerous Pagan rite with overtones of ancestor worship. They tried to suppress the tradition, but they failed. Eventually, the Catholic establishment accepted the festival and combined it with All Saints and All Souls days on November 1 and 2.

Today, community observances include fantastic decorations, elaborate costume parades, music, street dancing, and fireworks. Although Day of the Dead festivities vary from region to region, the celebrations generally occur between October 31 and November 2. Special markets open during the last few weeks of October. Stalls overflow with bread loaves shaped like bones, sugar skulls, toy coffins, lacy cut paper banners and other necessary holiday supplies.

Although the public festivities are quite popular, the most important aspects of the celebration take place at home. Families prepare offerings, called *ofrendas,* to attract the dead. All spirits, from recently deceased family members to ancient ancestors, are invited to the party. The dead visitors are neither feared nor worshipped. They are welcomed back to the family and are included in the celebration as the guests of honor.

Depending on the family's means, the ofrenda may be a table containing a few modest items or an expensive, showy display. Important elements include beeswax candles, copal incense, flowers, breads, fruits, and sweets. Family members make sure the deceased's favorite foods are on the ofrenda table. If the spirit's favorite food was barbeque potato chips, so be it. Bland foods are prepared for the ghosts of babies and young children.

Dead spirits are especially fond of the scent of marigolds, so petals are scattered from the front door to the ofrenda table. A path of marigold petals leading in the direction of the cemetery is sometimes placed outside the house. This helps the spirits find their way home when the party is over.

When the dead guests arrive, they consume the food and drinks by absorbing their essences. After the deceased finish enjoying the feast, the family eats the food or shares it with neighbors. In some locations, the ofrenda is set up in the cemetery and the party takes place there.

Day of the Dead decorations are the most delightful and fanciful aspect of the holiday. Skulls and skeletons abound. European cultures tend to view skeletons as creepy and unsettling reminders of our mortality. Mexican Day of the Dead skeletons are energetic caricatures. Grinning skeleton figurines have springs in their necks, and their arms and legs bob and bounce in even the slightest breeze.

The skeletons mock death by engaging in humorous or wickedly ironic activities. They are shown wearing evening clothes, dancing, participating in sporting events, riding bicycles, driving cars, and playing musical instruments. Skeletal priests, politicians, and brides and grooms are perennial favorites. Artists create particularly vivid images of the fusion of life and death by decorating the skeletons with plants and animals. Flowers sprout from eye sockets. Lush green vines twine up bony legs.

The Day of the Dead has evolved and changed with the times, accepting new elements while preserving its past. The joyous Mexican celebration encourages us to honor our ancestors and to embrace the reality of our own eventual deaths with humor rather than fear.

Day of the Dead Decorations

½ cup salt
¾ cup hot water
2 cups flour (do not use self-rising flour)

Stir the salt and water for about one minute. Add the flour. Work the dough with your hands until it is soft and pliable. The dough should have the consistency of modeling clay. Place a wet cloth over the dough to keep it moist while you're working on your creations. Dip your fingers in water if the dough feels dry and crumbly. If your dough still seems too dry, add a little more water.

Create skulls and bones. You can make flat, cookie-like ornaments, or rounded three-dimensional forms. For a skull, make a ball, then use a knife or your fingers to give it features. Bones are easy. Think of a cartoon dog's bone. If you intend to hang your finished ornaments, make a hole with a nail or toothpick before baking. Remember the hole will get smaller as the ornament bakes.

Put the ornaments on a cookie sheet and bake them at 325°F for an hour to an hour and a half. The ornaments are easier to remove if you cover the cookie sheet with aluminum foil. Let the ornaments cool completely then decorate them with acrylic craft paint. Add the flowers, vines, insects, and other animals that give them their special charm. It's not necessary, but if you want to protect the finished ornaments, coat them with clear varnish or spray them with an acrylic sealer. These ornaments are not edible!

ROSEMARY FOR REMEMBRANCE

BY DENISE DUMARS

I t is always hard to lose a loved one. It is doubly hard, I believe, in contemporary American society, where death is often viewed as a taboo subject.

People who belong to earth religions, such as NeoPaganism and Wicca, may also feel left out of family observances for the deceased that take place in traditional religious settings. Until recently, there were few contemporary sources that provided an alternate view of death and funeral and memorial services. Ed Fitch's *Magical Rites from the Crystal Well* was the first book I found detailing a ritual for a Pagan funeral. Leilah Wendell's landmark study of Azrael, the Angel of Death, culminated in a one-volume edition titled *Our Name Is Melancholy,* which provides a whole other viewpoint on "death energy," which is very different from the viewpoint of modern American society. Finally, Starhawk and M. Macha NightMare, together with the Reclaiming Collective, have brought about the most comprehensive guide yet in print, titled *The Pagan Book of Living and Dying.*

I recently found myself in mourning for a relative of the Catholic faith who lived across the country. Since I could not participate in the family funeral mass and memorial, I wished to conduct a ritual for my dear cousin that would help me with the grieving process and would honor my departed loved one.

I took some of the suggestions from the books and performed some of the suggested rituals. Then, together with other lore, I created the following remembrance ritual.

MATERIALS

Place on your altar two purple tapers (unscented) and a black votive (unscented or patchouli scented); rosemary and patchouli

oils (easily found where aromatherapy products are sold); a fresh sprig of rosemary—preferably in flower—in a small vase, or a handful of dried rosemary leaves; an incense burner and rosemary and sage incense or any purification incense such as sage, cedar, or lavender; and photo(s) of the deceased and/or other objects associated with him or her. Optional items may include a glass candle of Oya/St. Therese, a piece of black velvet, tarot cards, or a crystal ball.

THE RITUAL

Saturday, Saturn's Day, is a good day to begin this ritual; alternate days include the day you find out your loved one has transitioned or the day of the funeral. Place a photo of the departed next to the vase of rosemary or sprinkle a circle of dried rosemary leaves around it. Place your cards or objects of meaning to the deceased on the black velvet. Play simple meditation music or any music that you find appropriate; I especially like the selections "All Soul's Night" and "The Old Ways" from Loreena McKennitt's *The Visit* and "Samhain Night" from her album *Parallel Dreams*. Take several deep breaths to ground yourself; see a cone of white light surrounding you protectively, as you are very emotionally vulnerable at this time. Light the incense. Call the four directions, placing special attention on deities that rule the afterlife. Anoint the candles with the oils. Light the candles. Now say these words:

> *Rosemary is for remembrance, and I shall not forget.*
> *You are with us always, (Name), forever in our hearts.*

Now say anything loving to the deceased that you wish you could have said when he or she was still on this plane of existence. Don't worry if you feel very emotional or need to cry. Do what you feel you need to do to make the ritual one of cleansing, healing, and swift passage for the deceased into the next realm of this adventure we call "life." Do not encourage your loved one to "hang around" or wail over his or her loss; you want to help him or her with this transition! You may want to read a prayer from the books listed here, or sing a hymn or say a prayer from a tradition of your childhood. You may want to ask a specific goddess, god, or saint to watch over your loved one who has passed over. Allow yourself grief. Feel safe within your circle and allow the feelings to come.

When you feel ready, you may scry or shuffle the tarot deck and pick a card. Set the card out onto the black velvet and look at it, but do not think too hard about its meaning. Do the same for whatever you see in the crystal ball. Now close the ritual, and extinguish the candles.

The next evening, light the candles again and sit in meditation. Sniff the rosemary oil, and repeat the words, "rosemary is for remembrance." Now look at the card you have chosen, or think about what you saw when scrying, and try to determine the meaning as it relates to you and to the departed. Repeat this for at least one more night; you may continue this ritual for seven or nine days if you wish.

References

Fitch, Ed. *Magical Rites from the Crystal Well*. St. Paul, MN: Llewellyn Publications, 1989.

Starhawk, M. Macha NightMare, and the Reclaiming Collective. *The Pagan Book of Living and Dying*. San Francisco, CA: Harper San Francisco, 1997.

Wendell, Leilah. *Our Name Is Melancholy: The Complete Books of Azrael*. New Orleans, LA: Westgate Press, 1992.

Naming the Passages of Life

By Phoenix MacFarland

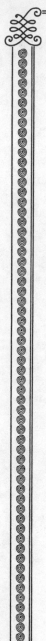

Most people experience some name changes during their lives. We sometimes are given nicknames, for better or worse, by our schoolmates. Our lovers give us special pet names. Most women change their last names when they marry, and they still go from Miss to Mrs., despite the feminist movement and the push toward Msing everyone together in one big, feminine group. As Wiccans, when we set forth upon our spiritual path, we often take a magical name to signify the internal changes that have occurred.

We take magical names for more reasons than just to bear a "cool" name. We do it because the path of Wicca is a transformational one. As we walk along it, we change, we grow. We evolve into new people many times over as we progress through the degrees. Each step requires a new name because we no longer fit the names originally given to us. After having met the challenges the Goddess gives us; after having studied and developed our power and wisdom; after learning to work the magic, the healing of the sick, the divination of the future; after having been the vessel of the very Gods themselves, we just are no longer a Cathy or a Dan.

In some traditions, with each degree's elevation ritual, the Witch takes a new name, but what about all those other times in our lives? We go through so many passages in our lives that go unacknowledged. These stages of life are mileposts of our progress through life. Here are what I see as the ten most significant life passages:

1. **Childhood.** Childhood is the point at which one is no longer a baby. There could be a new name given upon being weaned onto solid foods or completing toilet training.

2. **Teen.** This is a great passage, usually indicated by the beginning of menses in girls. Since boys do not have a marker that is as apparent as menses, parents of boys can help choose what event will mark the passage for them.

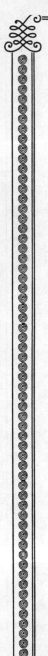

3. **Post Virginity.** Losing one's virginity is an unquestioned landmark event. It's about first love, youth, innocence, broken hearts quickly healed, and the passions of the young.

4. **Adulthood.** Adulthood is an achievement rather than an age. Not everyone who is eighteen or twenty-one should be considered adult. Some people in their forties are not yet adults. Some think one of the reasons this is so is that there are no longer rituals that outline expected adult behavior, responsibilities, and rewards to transform the rebellious teen into an honorable adult.

5. **Career.** When one embarks upon a career, beginning usually with a graduation ritual and ending with a retirement party, one does more than earn a paycheck and bring home the tofu. A career is one's life's work.

6. **Marriage.** I used to think that committed unmarried couples are as much a couple as married people. Then I got married. The wedding ritual is the most profound ritual of your lifetime. It changes you. I see marriage as an initiation into the world of real relationships.

7. **Parenthood.** Creating and giving birth to a child constitutes the initiation into this new realm of life's experiences. Over the long haul is where the real parenting takes place.

8. **Change of Life.** The children move out, the eggs stop sliding down those tubes, the baby machine shuts down, and women get power surges. For men it involves physical aging, grey hair, balding, widening around the middle, and sometimes an hysterical rebellion against these things with a comb-over, a bottle of Grecian formula, and a red Corvette.

9. **The Elder Years.** The elder years are marked by silver hair, the wrinkles, complaints about

how small they are making the print on the aspirin bottles, not being able to get up without grunting, the post-menopausal energy, retirement, and grandchildren.

10. **DEATH.** This is the final passage. The time for reflection about all that you accomplished, all the people you were, all the love you shared, and the people you touched in this incarnation. The cycle ends and begins again.

Life is a circle, the Wiccans sing. It's a dance. Using naming rituals, we can mark the transition past each passage. When the baby achieves its first milepost and becomes, instead, a child, this is the time to retire the baby names you cooed at them when they were at the breast. Consider a tender mother-daughter ritual upon your daughter's menses? Talking about her experience, and yours, teaching her what she can expect, what she needs to know, and honoring that change in her life's path with a magical name. It need not be a public name change. Driver's licences need not be altered. It could be a pet name between mother and daughter, or simply a name change in her diary to help mark the passage and make a memory.

Adulthood and career names are usually given to us when we are first called by the title Mr., Miss or Ms. A young person will giggle when first addressed this way, thinking perhaps that you mean his or her father or mother. When they realize that they have grown up enough to bear that title, it is a profound moment. You can use that feeling in your coming-of-age rituals. At the end, when the supplicant has overcome challenges and achieved the honor of adulthood, call him Mr. or her Ms.

Parenting comes with automatic name change to "Mommy" and "Daddy," and even affecting other members of the family to aunts and uncles or grandparents and great-grandparents. As they grow, your child's names for you will change from ma-like syllables drooled out of a baby's mouth to the "Mama" and "Mommy"of small children, giving way to the "Mom" of older kids and the scornful "Mother" of teens. Mothers can also take the names of mothers they admire,

perhaps from films or literature, and use them in hopes of being as good a mother as those characters were.

It is in the passages of change of life and the elder years that magical names can have the most profound effect upon your state of mind. We are culturally preconditioned to see life's marks upon our faces as signs of decay rather than marks of wisdom. We live in a culture that embraces only the virgin, and to a lesser extent the mother. The crone has little value except as the only alternative to death. It is unfortunate that this is so. Other cultures revere their elders, and perhaps as the Baby Boomers silver, society's priorities will shift.

One way to embrace our eldering is to name it and so claim it. Consider a woman going through her change of life time. She is leaving off the role of mother and is heading toward...? That's the problem. Those little mysterious, unknown dots traipsing off to who knows where and making a fifty-something person uneasy. Try a ritual that marks the time, or that not only marks the ending of the parent years, leaving behind the problems of birth control, the discomforts of menses, and the issues around raising children, but that celebrates the freedom the future. Look forward to the goals we have planned for that time in our lives.

As one enters the elder years, why not take a name to celebrate? We can weave positive magic into the names by choosing names that are imbued with health, strength, wisdom, and respect—whatever is needed. In my book, *The Complete Book of Magical Names,* I have included an "Index of Names by Characteristics" that you can use to choose the names for all your passages, according to what characteristics they will bring into your life.

I was at a Wiccan handfasting (wedding ceremony) in which the couple used all the magical names they had ever had. In effect, marrying all the aspects of themselves to the other's complete self. The end of our lives could be like that. We could look back over a lifetime of names, each marking our significant passages, and reflect on all that we have been, all that we have acomplished, and all the names we bore so proudly along the long, strange trip called life.

TANTRIC DREAM YOGA

BY KENNETH JOHNSON

When most people hear the word Tantra, they think of "sexual yoga." Although this is an important part of the Tantric tradition, it's not the whole story. Tantra is the "magic" of India, and includes ritual, mantra, talismanic magic, and a whole universe of Goddess mythology in addition to the sexual techniques. By way of example, here is a "dream yoga" from the Tantric tradition designed to help you access the Goddess or God, who will appear to you as your inner Dream Lover.

Begin by making sure that your sleep will be as restful as possible. Make your final meal of the day a light one, and get some mild exercise before bed. Best of all, release your daily anxieties through reading, listening to peaceful music, or meditating. Try to sleep in a clean, quiet, well-ventilated room decorated in soft blues or greens.

Lie down on your back with your hands folded over your solar plexus. If you still feel too restless to fall asleep, visualize a blue flame burning at the base of your spine between your genitals and your anus—the psychic center or chakra that is called the *muladhara* or root chakra in Hindu occultism. Allow the light of the blue flame to spread out in all directions through your body. When at last you are perfectly restful and calm, affirm that your dreams will contact the higher powers whose guidance you seek. Then silently repeat the words "dream lover, dream lover, come to me now." Do this several times.

Try to fall asleep lying on your right side with your knees slightly bent, the left leg on top of the right one, and the right cheek cupped in your right hand. Your left arm will lie on your left leg. Traditionally, you should be facing north, although this isn't absolutely necessary.

When you wake up, record your dreams before doing anything else. If you remember only vague fragments, then record the fragments. If you remember absolutely nothing, record the first thought that was in your mind when you woke up. If you wake up during the night, record whatever you may remember from the dream state, though in general, the most important dreams will be those that occur just before waking in the morning.

After a week or so, examine your dream journal, paying special attention to dreams that take place in another time period or in unusual surroundings as well as meetings, conversations, or activities involving people whom you do not know in ordinary life. Pay special attention to sexual symbolism. Be creative. Sexual symbolism is everywhere, if you know where to look for it. Don't be afraid of being naughty or feeling like a Freudian.

In time the sexual symbols will constellate around a relationship with a particular dream character. Hindus and Tantric Buddhists regard such a dream lover as a goddess or god, one of the divine sexual beings called *dakas* (if masculine) or *dakinis* (if feminine). As a Westerner, you are more likely to meet your dream lover in the form of a movie star, casual stranger, the boy or girl next door, or some mysterious, unknown personage.

When you finally meet your dream lover, the process leaps to a whole new level. Every time you encounter him or her during sleep, you must remember to meditate on the dream as soon as you wake up. Re-create the entire dream in your mind. As you replay the dream, examine its content and its symbols with as much conscious awareness and detachment as you can muster.

Repeated contemplation of the important dreams wherein you meet your dream lover will in time lead you to yet another level. According to Tantric tradition, your meditations will eventually guide you out of yourself, traveling along the silver cord that attaches your astral body to your physical body. You will be guided into a whole new universe. There, in that other reality, you will come face to face with the magical being who has brought you this far, and who has chosen to act as your initiator and spirit guide in the other world.

IS THE POWER ON?

BY MARGUERITE ELSBETH

Our destiny on earth is governed by the divine power that placed the stars in the heavens. Every form of creation is here as a result of this mysterious cosmic influence. Cosmic influence runs in cycles, alternately coming and going. The circle, the spiral, and the ellipse are all figures that show us how cosmic energy flows round and round. All of life's processes are cyclic, enabling us to recognize movement in space, the passage of time, and changes in our life experiences.

BODY CYCLES

If you are a woman, you are probably very aware of the body cycles occurring within you, because of your Moon or menstrual cycle, while men may find interpreting their body cycles a little more difficult. As our bodies are comprised mostly of water, a lunar element, both men and women are equally sensitive to the Moon, and can track bodily responses via the lunar phases. You can also look to the physical, emotional, mental, and intuitive big-rhythm cycles that began on the day of your birth. However, just listening to your body is the simplest, most natural way to understand what it's trying to tell you.

Find a comfortable, quiet setting. Lie down, relax, close your eyes, and begin deep breathing. Scan your physical body, beginning with your feet and continuing to the top of your head. Note any discomfort. Does a particular part of your body begin to throb or ache when you come to it? Look at your emotions. How do you feel in general? Are you happy, sad, or angry? Don't worry about why just yet.

Now, allow your intuition to take over by watching the mental images that pop into view. No matter how ridiculous or far-fetched, these pictures are associated with that body ache or pain as well as your feelings.

Use your intellect to put it all together; for example, if your head hurts, you feel angry, and you imagine a plane or vehicle of some sort, it may be time to change jobs, or take a vacation.

The Star Connection

Ever feel like you are running on empty, or have so much energy that you feel awake even when you're asleep? If so, you may be experiencing a cosmic power surge, a time when universal cyclic energies increase or lessen, but are not necessarily in harmony with your own way of going with the cosmic flow.

While there are a variety of times when power surges are unusually strong or apparent, the zodiac, with its twelve fixed stars, and astrology, the doctrine of the stars, are inextricably connected with cosmic ebb and flow. These ancient sky-maps help us to interpret nature, and to realize our natural purpose on earth. We can create certain results from the cosmic vibrations set in motion in and through us by watching how cosmic energies shift with the planetary cycles.

Cosmic Power Surges

Whether you are familiar with astrology or not, you still may instinctively know when the cosmic energy just isn't right, or is too good to be true. This is due to shifts in planetary cycles—how the planets in space today are challenging or enhancing your own personal planetary energies. See if any of these planetary power surges are happening in your life:

MERCURY: Are you experiencing travel delays and mix-communications? Did you send a letter to England and have it returned addressee unknown via Sumatra? Mercury may be cycling backward. Do NOT sign on the dotted line during this time.

VENUS. These days you are the honey luring bees from the hive. Falling in love, looking good, enjoying nature, redecorating your environment, creating something beautiful? What's bringing out the Aphrodite in you? Venus.

MARS: You want to be out and about—playing, not watching, sports. There may be too many projects demanding your attention, or too many men in your life telling you what to do. What? You need to call the mechanic or repair service again? Mars.

JUPITER: You hit the right slot at the local casino and you never gamble, or that raise or promotion finally comes through. Are you having fun, over-indulging and/or gaining weight to boot? Jupiter cycles can bring too much of a good thing.

SATURN: Everything requires hard work and plenty of it, with no help in sight. Oh, well, you haven't been very popular lately anyway. You are re-evaluating your whole life, and everything's changing! Desist your desire to resist, and this Saturn cycle too shall pass.

URANUS: You want to ride off into the sunset via motorcycle, study metaphysics, drop your tried, true love for someone strange, or drop-kick your computer out the window after too many real time power surges. The bizarre, high-tech leap off a cliff—that's Uranus energy.

NEPTUNE: While you're not accomplishing much in the real world these days, your spiritual aspirations are soaring. Meditation, yoga, magic, astral love, and out-of-body experiences are spell-binding your attention right now. What are your dreams telling you? Can you remember? Hello, is this planet Neptune?

PLUTO: Sudden blow-ups over long-forgotten slights, brushes with authority, and too many secret love affairs impel you to seek analysis, or begin an alternative health regime. Self-control is Pluto energy at its best, and this is the time to use it, or lose it.

PROPITIATING THE COSMIC ENERGY SPIRITS

All cosmic energies are living spirits, the gods and goddesses of myth. They are awake, aware, and sentient! Therefore, when certain planets cycle your way, it behooves you to make nice. This means giving the energy spirits their due. Below are deity, color, herb, stone, and animal correspondences for the energies.

MERCURY: Hermes and Thoth; yellow; mace and vervain; opal, agate, and clear quartz; swallow and ape.

VENUS: Freya and Aphrodite; green; sandalwood, myrtle, clover, and rose; emerald and turquoise; dove and swan.

MARS: Aries and Athena; red; tobacco, oak, hicory, and nettle; ruby; lizard.

JUPITER: Jupiter or Zeus; violet; saffron, oak, poplar, and fig; amethyst and lapis; eagle.

SATURN: Saturn or Chronos; black and indigo; frankincense and ash, onyx, crocodile.

URANUS: Uranus; pale yellow; peppermint and aspen; topaz; eagle and man.

NEPTUNE: Neptune or Poseidon; deep blue; myrrh, lotus, and water plants; beryl; dolphin.

PLUTO: Pluto or Hades; deep scarlet; hibiscus; obsidian; Scorpion.

Once you have acquired the necessary items, you may:

- Create an altar and decorate it accordingly; example: for Venus use a green table covering and green candles, set up pictures of Aphrodite or beautiful women, burn sandalwood incense in her honor; supply her with roses, turquoise stones, or jewelry, and a dove or swan feather. Use your imagination.

- Adorn yourself with the colors, scent, and/or stone of the energy spirit in question; example: if Saturn has come for a visit, wear a necklace set with onyx or black beads, and dab on a little frankincense oil.

- Pray or talk to the energy spirit or god/dess who has decided to stay for a spell. Share how his or her presence in your life makes you feel, ask what is expected of you, and be sure to say thank you when finished.

RITUAL OF THE TWINS

BY ELIZABETH BARRETTE

Use this ceremony when you need to put an end to "Witch wars" or other pernicious practices. The ritual draws on Persian mythology featuring twin gods of darkness and light. It works best in situations where two or more parties have been tangled up in conflict for some time and several of the participants now want to stop it. The process incorporates an acknowledgment of past problems, a purification, and an affirmation of future improvement.

For this ritual you will need a brass brazier, self-lighting charcoal, incense, a lighter, a flammable symbol of the discord or pens and paper to write out a description of it, a white bowl, some rosewater, and a bell.

Begin by casting a circle in your usual way. Place the charcoal in the brazier and light it. Add a pinch of incense. I recommend amber (for healing), frankincense (for forgiveness of past ills), or sandalwood (for spirituality). Once the incense begins to burn, talk about the problem, its history, how you got involved, and why you want to put an end to it. Now bring out the symbol of discord, or pass out the pens and paper, inviting everyone to pour all their negative thoughts and emotions into this vessel. Allow five to fifteen minutes for this. Next, read the first invocation:

Angra Mainyu, Demon Prince,
Spirit of Darkness, Serpent Great,

> *Death and trickery are your watchwords,*
> *Deception your every breath.*
> *Rumor and lies leap from your double tongue.*
> *Doubt goes before you, destruction hastens behind*
> *And you, evil twin, laugh in the aftermath.*
> *Enough!*
> *We have worshipped you with our ways before,*
> *But now we turn our backs on you.*
> *We close our ears to your whispers*
> *And our hearts against your hatefulness.*
> *Take this and go away.*

Drop the symbol of discord into the brazier and let it burn. Then fill the white bowl with the rosewater. (You can buy roseflower water at a Middle Eastern grocery store, or make your own by adding three drops of rose oil to plain water.) Sprinkle participants with the fragrant water, or pass the bowl around to everyone so they can dip their fingertips into it. Concentrate on making your thoughts and energy as clean and sweet as the rosewater. After this purification, return the bowl to the altar and ring the bell once. Next, read the second invocation:

> *Ahura Muzda, Master of Heaven,*
> *Universal Law, Light of Day's Breaking,*
> *Turn your bright face to us*
> *And reveal the truth.*
> *May your goodness fill our hearts to over-*
> *flowing*
> *And grant us the peace of*
> *purification*
> *As we make our way toward*
> *enlightenment.*

Meditate on this fresh beginning for a few minutes, and ring the bell three times. Finally, dismiss the circle in your usual manner. After the brazier has cooled, dispose of the ashes in running water (flushing them down the toilet works) or in a deserted place far from your home.

RIVERS

By Rachel Parti Raymond

The rivers of the world have provided life and inspiration since human beings first figured out the benefits of having fresh running water. Rivers were most commonly considered as benefactors of life and prosperity. This makes a great deal of sense since an agricultural society could hardly expect to flourish without a good source of fresh water.

Rivers were also seen as metaphors for the waters of life produced by the womb of the Great Goddess. Sometimes water was seen as menstrual blood, but it was also symbolic of the amniotic fluid that is released at the onset of labor. However, rivers have been described as every type of divine bodily fluid, including breast milk, semen, blood, urine, and tears. The mouths of rivers are highly charged with symbolism. Sometimes they are the vulva of the Great Mother, sometimes they are the entrance to the underworld, sometimes they are both. Other symbolic meanings for rivers include danger, divine messengers, fertility, invasion, life, peace, succor, and wealth. Rivers have also been used as metaphors for the ceaseless passing of time that flows endlessly in one direction.

The image of a tree of life from which four rivers flow is very common and can be found in Buddhist, Christian, Jewish, Muslim, Nordic, and Hindu myths of paradise. In Greek mythology there are five rivers in the Underworld kingdom of Persephone and Hades. There is Acheron, the stagnant river of woe; Cocytus, the icy river of lamentations; Lethe, the river of forgetfulness; Pyriphgethon, the fiery river of rage; and the river Styx, which surrounds the realm and must be crossed after death. It is navigated by Charon the ferryman, who must be paid if you are to cross. This is why coins were placed in the mouths of the deceased.

The Ganges, the Yellow River, the Indus, the Tigris, the Euphrates, and the Nile each had incalculable importance to the development of the civilizations that sprang up around them. The Ganges is the holiest of Hindu rivers. According to tradition, it springs from the feet of the God Brahma. Bathing in the Ganges is supposed to cleanse your life of karmic impurities. Dying on the bank of the Ganges will bring you release from the wheel of karma altogether.

In China, the Yellow River was said to descend from the heavens as the rays of the sun. Like most sacred rivers, the dead were buried in it in order to insure rebirth. The Tigris and the Euphrates were said to have been poured out of a giant pot in heaven by a Babylonian sky god. However the river that had one of the most profound effects on human history is the Nile. Hapi, the God of the Nile, was a hermaphrodite. The river's yearly inundations of the Nile valley carried with it the rich silt, which allowed Egyptian farmers to produce the tons of grain required to keep the massive Egyptian empire fed.

Having nurtured us since the dawn of time, the rivers of the world now need our assistance. Many have been harmed through development and pollution. Still more have been infested with dams and power plants like giant ticks.

The act of just sitting by the banks of a healthy flowing river is deeply moving. The joy of immersing yourself in its waters or riding on its back can be life-changing. If you are fortunate to live near a healthy river, make the most of it. In times of trouble let it absorb your tears into its rushing flow. In times of joy allow your happiness to celebrated by its exuberance, and feel the power of river magic.

MEDICINE WHEELS AND ASTROLOGICAL SITES

BY BERNYCE BARLOW

Throughout the history of the North American continent, the medicine wheel was used as a teaching tool, a star chart, and even a blueprint. One wheel could represent all these functions or simply one of them. The Bighorn Medicine Wheel in Wyoming is a good example of how a muti-faceted wheel functions.

First of all, it is said the Bighorn Medicine Wheel was the initiation site of the first Sundance, a Native American spiritual ceremony. The Sundance lodge was said to be constructed around the arrangement of this wheel. Both a Sundance lodge and the medicine wheel have twenty-eight poles, representing the twenty-eight lunar cycle days. The four directions are represented in the wheel, as are the teachings that accompany them. These teachings were part of the Sundancer's initiation rites. The traditional Sundance lodges were aligned to certain stars—the same stars that were aligned by cairns within the Bighorn Wheel. When a certain star passed a backsite cairn, it was time to start the dance. There was also a Summer Solstice alignment that marked the traditional time of the Sundance ceremony.

The Bighorn Medicine Wheel was also constructed to highlight the dawn stars of the Summer Solstice. The star Aldebaran in the constellation Taurus rose heliacally around 1500 A.D. to match a side cairn within the circle. This is no longer true because over long periods of time stars change their positions in the sky. Nevertheless, Aldebaran was an important star in the pre-historic teachings of the Lakota Nation, who claim to have originated the Sundance. That is why its alignment was included in the Bighorn Medicine Wheel. The star Regel from the constellation of Orion is also represented in the Bighorn Medicine Wheel by a backsite cairn, as is the star Sirius. If the Hopi would have built the Bighorn Wheel the Pleiades would have been one of the alignments because the Pleiades are a part of their teachings.

Although the Bighorn Medicine Wheel is one of the best known astrological sacred sites, there are literally thousands of these wheels dotting the high ground of the Great Basin, the Southwest, the Great Plains, and Canada. Actually, the Bighorn wheel is a newcomer on the scene. The Moose Mountain Wheel in Canada was built 1200 years before the Bighorn and was probably the prototype for it!

Most wheels are built on high ground with a clear 360-degree view of the horizon. Not all medicine wheels are as complicated as the Bighorn wheel. Some are very simple, depicting a circle marked only with the four directions and nothing else. These circles were usually used for ceremony, protection, or teaching.

Medicine wheels were not the only type of astrological calendars built by the ancient dwellers of North America. Rock and boulder alignments were also constructed for similar purposes. At Blue Mounds State Park in Minnesota, the grassland prairie hosts a 1,500 foot line of quartzite boulders that align a Northeast sighting of the Summer Solstice. Another boulder alignment site was recently bulldozed over in Carson City, Nevada, by a private land owner who was aware of what he was doing and didn't care. This site was referred to as Arrowhenge and consisted of a group of large boulders in the form of an arrowhead aligned to both the Summer and Winter Solstices. Some of the boulders had been painted with red ochre dating back a few thousand years. This site was quite spectacular and was ruined by a jerk who is going to get a personalized note and autographed copy of this book!

There are also horizon calendars, used most often in the West, Southwest, and Big Sky Country. Horizon calendars simply used different landmarks on the horizon to mark months, Moons, Solstices, and Equinoxes. Distant mountains and large rock formations were the landmarks of choice. Sometimes large boulders would be moved to a horizon lookout point and notched to show where the Solstice sun would rise or set. Sun temples, like the one found at Mesa Verde, Colorado, used horizon notches as one way to mark astrological events. The notches were carved into the temple walls and still serve their purpose. Generally, the calendar keepers of the tribe sought out landmarks where the Sun rose and set during Solstices and Equinoxes, but some horizon calendars marked star placement as well. When the sky changed, the landmarks were changed accordingly, especially if the calendars sighted a night sky.

You can actually create your own horizon calendar by employing the same methods that the ancient calendar keepers used. On the morning of Summer or Winter Solstice look toward the rising Sun and pinpoint the location or landmark it rises over. Trees work, but they sometimes get cut or burned down or die. One year a tree might be there, the next year it might not. This is why mountains, boulders, islands, and rock formations are usually chosen as horizon calendar landmarks.

Another type of astrological site can be found at a place lovingly referred to as Woodhenge or Cahokia in Illinois. Instead of using boulders or rock circles to mark astrological sightings, wooden poles of red cedar were erected. Just as England has its Stonehenge, the United States has its Woodhenge. At Cahokia, at least five "Woodhenge" calendars have been excavated. The cedar pole calendars were built in concert with the ceremonial mounds that remain on site, particularly Monk's Mound.

As you can see, the ancient calendars of North America were not only ingenious but practical. Their accuracy was based on observation. It is a part of human nature to mark time, so if you have some time to spare maybe you could plan a visit to an astrological site during a Solstice or Equinox date. Mark it on your calendar as a day of celebration!

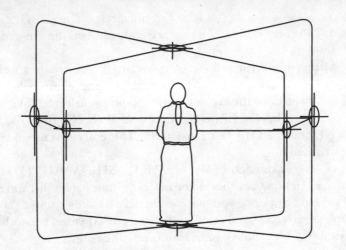

THE ROSE CROSS

BY ESTELLE DANIELS

The Rose Cross is most effectively done with a stick of sandalwood incense. This can also be done silently or audibly, or visualizing only. It can be done either alone or after performing the Lesser Banishing Ritual of the Pentagram (LBRP; for more information seen page 36). If you can't use incense, hold your hand as if you had incense in it.

PART 1

The Rose Cross is done on the cross quarters. Light the incense. Ground and center with three cleansing breaths if you didn't do the LBRP. Start in the southeast. Face outward. The movements that you will perform at each cross quarter are identical. The crosses you will make are equal-armed, in gold, with a red "rose" at the center. Each cross is connected to the adjacent ones with a blue cord.

DRAWING THE CROSS

Holding the incense in your right hand, start in the center, chest height, and move your hand up, then down past the center, then back up to the center. Then move right and back left through the center, then back to right and pause at center. Then draw the rose with a clockwise spiral of at least two full circles. The cross is established. The rose "cements" it in place and connects the cross to the blue lines forming the web.

When you perform the rose cross ritual, you create a web of energy lines anchored at the cross quarters, above and below. To make the web draw the crosses in the following order: SE, SW, NW, NE, SE, ABOVE, NW, BELOW, SE, SW, ABOVE, NE, BELOW, SW, NW, NE and then the last cross at SE. There are seventeen in all (see diagram).

As you make each cross, say "YE-HE-SHU-AAAH" (*YHShA*, Joshua, in Hebrew, another name of God). Intone it loudly. You may feel strange, but once you are comfortable, it adds energy. As you complete each cross and move to the next cross quarter, say nothing, but draw the blue energy lines connecting the roses.

For the last cross at SE you say "YE-HE-SHU-AAAH-YE-HE-VAH-SHAA" (Joshua, and another tetragrammaton). When drawing the last cross and sealing it, move up and down, right and left, and also in and out in three dimensions before drawing the last rose. The rose binds the whole thing and "fires" the net, activating the protective web, lighting all a bright luminescent silver. Take a breath and relax.

Part 2

Put the incense aside, but keep it burning for the healing aroma of sandalwood. This part calls down the light into the circle and yourself or another person who needs healing energy. It is adaptable to most any healing purpose: physical, spiritual, and psychic. It should only be done inside the energy web, as it's not effective otherwise.

When healing, the person to be healed sits on a stool in the center facing east. Draw the energy web, above, below, and around both of you. If you do the LBRP first, the person can sit in the center for that also.

Facing east, stand behind the seated person. If alone, just stand in the center of the circle. Relax, with your feet shoulder width apart.

With your arms straight out to the side right hand up, left hand down, visualize the cosmic lemniscate of energy looping through your body, shaped and directed by your hands, like a figure eight on its side. Intone the words YOD-NOON-RESH-YOD (*YNRY* in

Hebrew, Latinized *INRI*). This is another tetragrammaton, an acronym for "The beginning, life, death and the end."

Then, with your right arm straight up, your left arm straight out, making an L, head tilted left, say "Virgo, Isis, mighty mother."

With both arms wide upward in a V, head tilted back, looking up, say, "Scorpio, Apophis (ah-pahf-iss), destroyer."

With both arms crossed over your breast, hands on shoulders, head bowed down, say, "Sol, Osiris, slain and risen."

While opening your arms upward to full extension above your head, tilt your head back until you are looking up, and intone "Isis, apophis, Osiris, eeeeeeee, aaaaaaaa, ooooohh." (Resonate the vowels. It adds energy.)

When the resonances have died down, move your arms to the Virgo position (in an L) and say "L," then move to the Scorpio position (in a V) and say "V," then move to the Osiris position (in an X) and say "X." (This should be done relatively quickly). Then repeat the arm and head motions and say "L-U-X." Then raising your arms above your head, you say, "Lux (Luke's); light; the light of the cross; let the light descend!"

As your arms are raised you should grab ahold of the golden energy shining down from above and draw it down over the top of the head of the person seated in front of you. If doing it on yourself, pull it down over the top of your head. Do not push or force the energy. Just let it flow down.

This energy is to be taken as needed, just poured, like honey. You will also get some energy, and this is okay. Once done, you might do a cleansing breath, and maybe let your hands rest on the person's shoulders. You and the person seated may feel warm, energized, or a bit buoyed up. This is normal. Ask and make sure the person is okay and centered afterward. You are done.

The Rose Cross is another circle that is not taken down, but allowed to dissipate in its own. For healing, this can be done up to three times a day, morning, noon, and night; theoretically it's most effective at dawn, noon, and dusk. Twice a day is also good, and even once a day is helpful. Try to do it at regular times each day. The healing effects may at first be only temporary, but over time it can be very effective.

THE KEY TO MAGIC

BY ELIZABETH BARRETTE

Key magic is an ancient and honored form of folk magic, often handed down within families and rarely committed to print. It dates back to the invention of lock-and-key devices, but the ever-evolving complexity of security technology has raised an interesting conundrum: modern keys do not work nearly as well as antique keys when it comes to magical applications. Why could this be?

At first glance, it seems logical that modern keys should work better in this regard because they offer much greater security in terms of keeping things locked up. However, the mystery clears when you compare an antique key and a modern key side-by-side: they have quite different shapes. An antique key has a little notched head for turning the tumblers, a long body, and a round, open handle. A modern key has a flat, notched blade for turning the tumblers and this blade attaches directly to the handle, which is usually solid rather than open. Also, antique keys typically consist of brass or iron, occasionally silver; modern keys almost always consist of aluminum, tin, or similar light metals.

The antique key serves as a miniature magic wand, and indeed some tarot decks depict keys on some of the wand cards. The long body of the key represents the masculine principle while the round, open head (often decorated with ornate, curling patterns) represents the feminine principle. When taken together, the parts of an antique key express the union of these two powerful forces. Also, iron offers protection while brass captures solar/fire energies, and silver responds readily to any magical energy. Modern key materials possess much less magical receptivity. The short, flat blade and plain, solid handle of a modern key poorly express the original male/female dynamic that gives antique keys so much of their power. Therefore, the serious practitioner of key magic prefers to use antique keys for most purposes. You can find these easily and affordably at resale shops, auctions, even yard sales.

So what can you do with a suitable key? Keys offer cradle-to-grave service. In Germanic and Celtic cultures, an iron key placed in a baby's crib would keep the fairies from stealing the child. Several cultures recommend secreting a key in the coffin before burial so that the deceased can unlock the gates to the next world. Midwives may use a key, preferably the key to the nearest house of worship, to "unlock" a pregnant woman's womb and thereby ease childbirth. Another health-related application suggests that to cure a nosebleed, you should string a brass key, knot the string and put it over your head, and then drop the key down your back: the key "locks up" the flow of blood. This extrapolates well to other situations where one wishes to stop blood flow as fast as possible, and makes a very discreet solution because you can keep the key in your pocket and simply project its power where needed just as you would project any other type of energy. Alternatively, put one antique key on the same ring with your car and house keys, so as to have one readily available at need.

Key spells and lock spells also figure strongly in love magic, as you can see from the popularity of necklaces made with functional locks. The idea is that one partner keeps the key while the other keeps the lock, and this maintains their relationship. Keys can bring good luck or shed bad luck, and serve the same purpose in affairs of the heart. Finding a key brings good luck and may herald a new love interest on the way. To get rid of bad luck or discourage unwanted advances, carry a key to a crossroads. As fast as you can, turn around widdershins three times and throw the key over your left shoulder, imagining what you wish to discard going with it. Then leave without looking back.

The key is an ancient symbol of knowledge and authority. Keys in mythology may represent the power to grant or refuse entry into the underworld or other realms. They also suggest enlightenment, magical prowess, knowledge of the afterlife, and interdimensional travel. You might want to keep a key on your altar as a reminder of your quest for knowledge.

THE GODDESSES OF THE LUNAR MANSIONS

BY KEN JOHNSON

How many different ways can we create a zodiac? Do we need twelve signs? Why not thirteen? Or more?

In India, there is an ancient zodiac called the Mansions of the Moon. There are twenty-seven "mansions" or "signs," and each one of them is a goddess. This is their story.

Long ago, the God of the Moon was born out of the great Cosmic Ocean. His name was Chandra, but some called him Soma, which was the name of the magical nectar of wisdom and delight. Chandra was the keeper of that nectar, and his bright Full Moon countenance in the sky was the very image of peace and joy.

In those days the creator of the world still walked among us. His name was Daksha, and he had twenty-seven goddess daughters, whom he gave to the Moon God to be his wives. Each goddess had her mansion in the sky, which appears to us earth dwellers as a bright star or, sometimes, as a constellation. Chandra visited each of his wives in turn, each in her separate mansion, as he made his progress through the sky each month. It took him twenty-seven nights to circle the sky and occupy each of the lunar mansions.

But Chandra fell madly in love with one of his wives, and he favored her above the others, lingering in her mansion for days at a time. Her name was Rohini, and her mansion is the red star we call Aldebaran.

Chandra's other wives were angry. They called upon their father, the world-maker. "Father," they complained, "this husband you gave us is just no good. He favors our sister Rohini above all the rest of us, and thereby he dishonors us, for we are all equally beautiful in our own way, and equally worthy of affection."

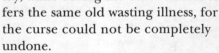

"Very well," said Daksha. "I'm sorry I put you to so much trouble. This foolish Moon God will soon fall ill and die. That is my curse."

The world-maker's sky-dancing daughters were happy, at least for a while, but as they watched Chandra lose his luster and wither away to nothing, to a mere shadow of himself, they were saddened and felt compassion for him. They regretted their anger, and they returned to their father.

"I'm sorry," said Daksha, "but when a god curses another god, the curse cannot be called back. Let me think....Well, I can modify the curse somewhat. But that is all."

So Daksha spoke another magical formula, and Chandra, who was by now a mere sliver, began to grow strong again. But his health is sustained for only half of his journey through the sky, while during the other half he suffers the same old wasting illness, for the curse could not be completely undone.

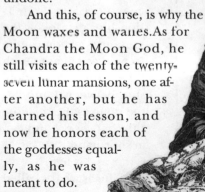

And this, of course, is why the Moon waxes and wanes. As for Chandra the Moon God, he still visits each of the twenty-seven lunar mansions, one after another, but he has learned his lesson, and now he honors each of the goddesses equally, as he was meant to do.

THE GOLDEN PROPORTION IN SACRED GEOMETRY

BY JOHN MICHAEL GREER

Most people nowadays think of geometry as a matter of lines, angles, and shapes. In traditional sacred geometry, though, another factor—proportion—has an equally important place. Proportions, and the relationships between them, provide many of the core anchors for meaning in sacred geometry. They also form the bridge between sacred geometry and the other sciences of the Quadrivium, the "Four Ways" of ancient mystical mathematics: numerology, the science of number; harmonics, the science of music; and calendrics, the science of time.

Many proportions have a place in traditional sacred geometry, but the most significant of all is the Golden Proportion, symbolized by the Greek letter Φ. To make sense of Φ and its many roles, though, it's necessary to take a very brief journey through the traditional theory of proportions.

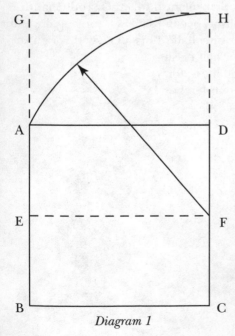

Diagram 1

A proportion is a pattern of relationship between measures. For example, the 1:2 proportion defines a relationship in which one measure is twice as large as another. Any two relationships that follow the same proportion can be treated as equal to each other; thus, the relationship between 1 and 2 is the same as the relationship between 4 and 8—in shorthand, 1:2::4:8, "1 is to 2 as 4 is to 8."

This is what's called a discontinuous proportion, because it's a proportion that relates four different measures (in this case, 1, 2, 4, and 8). A continuous proportion, on the other hand, relates three measures. Take, for example, 1:2::2:4. Here 2 is the middle or mean term, and it relates the two extreme terms 1 and 4 by way of the same 1:2 proportion. Continuous proportions allow many different measures to be related together into a harmonious pattern—one of the central goals of sacred geometry in practice.

A continuous proportion like this can be made using any proprtional relationship, whether simple (like 1:2) or more complex. The ancient sacred geometers took matters a step further, though. They sought what might be called hyper-continuous proportions, which would relate numbers by proportions that came out of the numbers themselves. Their specific goal was to relate one measure to a second the way the second relates to the sum of the first and second added together; if a is the first measure and b the second, in the usual shorthand, a:b::b:a+b, "a is to b as b is to the sum of a and b." What they discovered is that there is one and only one proportion that will do this. Like most of the other important proportions in sacred geometry, this special proportion is incommensurable—that is, it can't be expressed exactly by any number or fraction.

That proportion is Φ, the Golden Proportion. Put into numbers, it works out to 1:1.6180339... and so on for an infinite number of digits. Geometrically, on the other hand, it's easy to express exactly, as shown in Diagram 1.

What makes the Golden Proportion so special? Plenty. It has amazing mathematical and geometrical properties that are far too complex to spell out here.

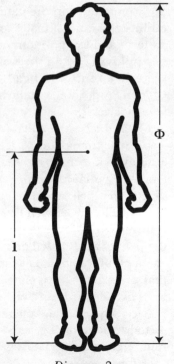

Diagram 2

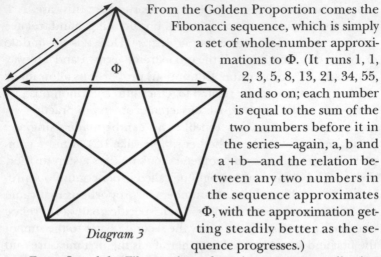

From the Golden Proportion comes the Fibonacci sequence, which is simply a set of whole-number approximations to Φ. (It runs 1, 1, 2, 3, 5, 8, 13, 21, 34, 55, and so on; each number is equal to the sum of the two numbers before it in the series—again, a, b and a + b—and the relation between any two numbers in the sequence approximates Φ, with the approximation getting steadily better as the sequence progresses.)

Diagram 3

From Φ and the Fibonacci numbers, in turn, come a dizzying array of patterns in the natural world. The breeding patterns of rabbits, the ratio of males to females in beehives, the branching patterns and leaf positions of many species of plants, the curve of a nautilus shell, and the twin spirals that govern the position of seeds in a sunflower head—all derive geometrically from the Golden Proportion. On the human body, too, if the distance from feet to navel is considered as 1, the total height from feet to the crown of the head is equal (on average) to Φ (see diagram 2).

These same patterns are to be found all through traditional art and architecture, especially from those times and places—for example, ancient Greece, medieval Europe, and the Renaissance—in which sacred geometry was honored and carefully studied. Equally, the Golden Proportion plays an important but usually unrecognized role in magical traditions. As Diagram 3 shows, the pentagram is based on the geometry of Φ. So are many other elements of traditional magical symbolism. For example, the vault that serves as the focus of the Golden Dawn's higher initiations has walls five feet wide and eight feet tall; 5 and 8 are part of the Fibonacci sequence, and the ratio between them approximates to Φ. As the ancient lore of sacred geometry becomes a part of the current renaissance of the magical arts, the Golden Proportion—the "precious jewel" of sacred geometry—is likely once again to play an increasingly important role in magical symbolism and design.

THE PAGAN CONSUMER

BY CERRIDWEN IRIS SHEA

A s consumers, with each dollar that we spend in the marketplace for goods and services, we are making a statement of approval. As Pagans, we need to bring the respect and responsibility for the Earth that we pledge when choosing this path with us when we shop. You don't need to be rich in order to make a difference.

What you do need to do is think of shopping as a political statement. How can shopping for cat litter be political? How can buying daily necessities be political?

Start by reading the labels on everything you buy. What do you know about the company? Are they reliable? Do they engage in procedures you disagree with, such as irresponsibly disposing of their waste, or animal testing? Many products now have this sort of information on the label. I realize you don't have five hours to go through the grocery store, reading every label on every jar, but try an experiment. The next time you go shopping, buy what you usually by. When you get home, read the labels as you are putting your products away. Do any of them have information on them that disturbs you? Make a note of it and do more research. You can call their consumer hotline with questions. You can look them up in the library or on the Internet. If you do get information off of the Internet, make sure you double-check it with another source. The Internet is great, but it is unregulated, and there's no guarantee that what you pull off is legitimate. If the company engages in practices with which you disagree, then switch to another product that is more in keeping with your values.

The switch itself is only one part of the process. Once you've switched product brands, write a letter to the company whose product you've discontinued, telling them why you've done so. Send a copy to your congressperson.

What about the products that you don't necessarily agree with, but have to use? If it's something that's not ingested, I charge it before I use it, so that it has a definite intent, and I ask that its environmental harm be lessened. If it's a food, I bless and consecrate it, thank it for its nourishment, and acknowledge that I am aware its circumstances were less than natural. I also write letters to the companies, letting them know that I disagree with their practices, and, while I am still using the product, I am investigating alternatives and plan to switch as soon as possible.

These principles can be used when clothes shopping, furniture shopping, appliance shopping, etc. If you are purchasing an item that will be brought into your home, you have a responsibility to know how it was created. Do you want to bring something created under painful, negative circumstances into your home? It will affect the atmosphere of the home. You may find that items break more frequently, that there are odd smells, or that something feels a bit "off." You may need to cleanse and consecrate more often than the normal lunar cleansing. I have gotten into the habit of blessing and welcoming every new item that is brought into the home. I welcome it, explain its purpose in the fabric of life here, and give it a magical intent. It takes a bit longer to unpack, but, in the long run, it's worth it.

What about paying bills? Bill paying is rarely a pleasant activity. If you have a choice of utility services, take the time to do some research and go with the company who appears to abide by principles closest to yours. If you live in a region where there is only one option, obviously, you're stuck, for the time being. I try to pay my bills at a set time each month. I light a candle, burn some prosperity incense, get out my pen, checkbook, bills, stamps, envelopes, etc. I ask one of the money deities that my dollars stretch to pay everything off (and check my balance, just to make sure). As I write out each check, I think about all the positive things that the service for which I'm paying brings me. For instance, my telephone allows me to communicate with friends all over the world. Electricity allows me to read late at night, curled up on the couch with the cats, run my computer, play music, etc. My rent check assures that my home will be reasonably secure for one more month.

If you can, support charities in whose work you believe. Yes, it's often difficult to make ends meet. I don't believe that you should starve yourself in order to send a check to a charity. One thing I've tried is a "wishing bowl." I have a pretty bowl on one of my altars. Each night, I take the largest denomination coin that I have in my wallet and drop it into the bowl, making a wish. When the bowl is full, I wrap up the change, put it in the bank, and send a check to an organization in which I believe.

Volunteer work is another way to be a creative consumer. If you can't donate money, can you donate some time? Can you lick stamps, make phone calls, donate goods to a bake sale, or drive around picking up items for a tag sale? Volunteer work can be a wonderful way to meet people with similar values and make a difference. After a volunteer experience, make sure you write a letter to the head of the organization, detailing your time there, and send a copy to your congressperson. It will help the next time the organization applies for funds.

The most important part of being a Pagan consumer is to spend your money and your time mindfully. Know where it is going, what it is doing, and what sort of impact the money and time have on those around you. Do your research, make informed decisions, and inform those who make funding decisions what you are doing and why.

I can hear you whining all the way out here: "But that's so much work! I don't have time."

You don't have time to protect the Earth? You don't have time to make the Earth a better place for your children and their children? As a Pagan, Witch, or magician, that is part of your commitment. That is part of your job as a guardian of the planet. A half hour now could make a life-changing difference later. Our path is not about asking forgiveness once a week, or paying a fee to be saved. It's about living our beliefs. Vote in every election. If you don't like any of the candidates, find one that you do, or run for office yourself. Serve jury duty when you are called. If you don't like the system, change it. Don't whine, make the time. That will make a difference.

Recipes for Potlucks

By Magenta Summerton

Pagans go to a lot of potlucks, so I am always looking for recipes for dishes that work well for groups. Kugel is excellent any time you want a hearty dish to take to a potluck. It is fairly quick and easy if you have a food processor. If you have to grate the ingredients by hand you may want to save this for special occasions. I cook this amount for my coven; I double it if I'm going to a larger group.

Potato Kugel

4   medium potatoes (approximately 4 cups grated)

2   carrots (approximately 1 cup grated)

2   onions (1–2 cups when finely chopped)

4   mushrooms, thinly sliced (optional)

1   cup grated cheddar cheese (optional)

Preheat oven to 400°F. Oil an 8 x 8-inch pan or equivalent baking dish. Coarsely grate potatoes and carrots. Chop onions very finely (use the processor only if you know it will chop rather than pulp). Mix potatoes, carrots, and onions together thoroughly. Press loosely into the baking dish. Bake for about an hour. Kugel is done when onions are transparent and completely cooked, and potatoes are soft. If you plan to use mushrooms, add them about 10 minutes before the kugel is done. If desired, top with cheese and put back in the oven for a few minutes to melt the cheese. Kugel is very forgiving, and can be left in the oven for an extra 15 minutes to half hour if you lower the heat. Makes 4–6 servings.

Spinach Polenta Pie

Polenta is a wonderful change from other starches. You can buy it already made up, but it is expensive considering what it is—corn meal mush! Why not make it up yourself? The vegetarian filling makes it

an excellent choice for large groups, and this recipe can be doubled and put in a 9 x 13-inch pan.

POLENTA

3   cups water, divided
1   cup cornmeal
½   teaspoon salt (optional)

Bring 2 cups of water to a boil. Mix the remaining cup of water with the cornmeal. Add to boiling water. Immediately turn heat to low. (If you don't do this, the polenta will be lumpy.) Simmer for 15–25 minutes until completely cooked. It's like cooking hot cereal. Allow to cool for a little while for ease of handling. Spread over the bottom of a 8 x 8 pan. Set aside to cool completely, or put in the refrigerator covered with plastic wrap. You can also buy commercial polenta and press into a pan, and fill as below.

FILLING

1   large onion, chopped
1   clove of garlic, minced
3   teaspoons olive oil
2   stalks celery, chopped
1   cup sliced mushrooms
1   (10-ounce) package frozen spinach, thawed and
      drained, or 1½ pounds fresh spinach
      Salt and pepper
½   cup mozzarella cheese

Preheat oven to 400°F. Sauté the onion and garlic in the olive oil until transparent. Add celery and mushrooms and sauté until tender. Add spinach. If frozen, stir in. If fresh, sauté until wilted, about 2 minutes. Add salt and pepper to taste. Put this mixture on top of the polenta. Top with the cheese. Bake for 20–25 minutes. Cool 10 minutes before serving. Makes 2–4 servings.

GUADALUPE

BY ELLEN DUGAN

What's a nice Pagan like me doing in a place like this? That's just what I was asking myself when a friend took me to a Catholic shrine in Illinois called "Our Lady of the Snows." My friend Paula and I have always been respectful of each others' beliefs, and when she asked me if I would like to go along with her, I thought, "sure, why not?"

She gave me the grand tour. As we were wandering around the outdoor sanctuary, I came across a large, deeply-framed display. Inside was the image of The Lady of Guadalupe painted or printed on a large section of cloth. It was beautiful—a woman in a star-covered robe standing on a crescent moon, surrounded by the rays of the Sun. I knew that Guadalupe was thought to have been associated with an Aztec goddess. I stood there a while and studied it. It gave me goosebumps. Amused at my reaction, I moved on.

Close by, there was a section full of racks and rows of different-colored votive candles. I considered it for a moment. After all, the sign at the entrance said the shrine was "A place of peace, where all faiths are welcome." Couldn't hurt, I decided. Money was tight and my husband had been looking for a better, higher-paying job. I chose a green candle. As I lit the candle, I improvised a prayer to the Goddess on the spot, and asked for her help.

The image of The Lady of Guadalupe came to my mind so strongly that I lost my train of thought and stuttered to a halt. My stomach tightened and I felt like someone was standing behind me. I looked over my shoulder, I was alone. Spooky.

I figured it was the atmosphere and quickly walked back into the sunlight where Paula had been waiting. When she suggested the gift shop, I was more than ready to get out of the petition area and walk off the mood.

In the shrine's gift shop I picked up a wallet-sized prayer card with the picture of The Lady of Guadalupe. Later, when I got home, I propped that little card up on my altar in my room and sat back and stared at it. She did seem right at home up there between my pictures of Selene and Isis. I wondered what would happen if I tried working magic with Guadalupe. I had a strong feeling that She was waiting for me to figure this out. Call me eclectic, but I wanted to try it.

Over the next several months I spent alot of time researching the subject of Our Lady of Guadalupe. The Lady of Guadalupe is a suprisingly magic-friendly subject. Tepeyac, the hill where she first appeared to Juan Deigo on December 9, 1531, was originaly the site of a healing shrine dedicated to an Aztec goddess. Before the conquest of the Spaniards, people came to the temple from all over Mexico for cures and healings. After the Virgin appeared to Juan Diego it didn't matter to the people what Her name was. This was one of their own. They could come to Her holy place and worship freely.

The Brujas, (Mexican-American Witches), have used Guadalupe and her many different aspects as a patron diety for centuries. For me it was an amazing discovery. At first I was simply trying to learn about a different aspect of the Goddess. What I discovered is a beautiful magical culture and system that I had never known before.

Want to learn something new? I bet you're wondering what an eclectic Witch would call on Guadalupe/Tonantzin for? I'd be happy to tell you—healing, children, families, pregnancy, and childbirth. She is a mother goddess, you know. She is pictured as being pregnant.

Some magical correspondences for the Lady of Guadalupe are red roses, poinsettias, white and pink colored candles, and the gemstone turquoise.

From my own personal experience, I've had success with Guadalupe when I needed help with any family situation, family finances included. By the way, my husband did get a different job, better benefits, and higher pay. Thank you, Guadalupe, very much.

So, what was a Wiccan doing in a shrine? She was getting a lesson from the Goddess. Never underestimate the power of the Lady no matter what guise She happens to be in. The Goddess truly makes herself known to us in many different ways.

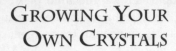

GROWING YOUR OWN CRYSTALS

By Forté Robins

In every magical supply shop there are displays of crystals and semi-precious stones. If you've ever worked with crystals, you know how useful they can be, and you may be aware that some of the crystals available for purchase in stores are man-made. What you may not realize is the crystal-growing process can be done in your own kitchen. Crystal growing kits are available in museums, hobby, and educational toy stores. The kits are designed to grow different crystal shapes, as the packaging will show you.

Why grow your own crystals? Besides being fun, crystal growing provides you with an extremely personal and flexible magical tool. A basic magic principle states that any item you create or shape is going to conduct your energy better than an impersonal item. Crystal growing gives you an opportunity to shape the creation of what is normally Earth's most solid and permanent of icons.

There is a difference, however, in the crystals you will be growing, and the naturally occurring variety. While the shape is the same, the chemical composition is different. Crystals, both the man-made and the natural ones, are formed by a tight and well-organized molecular structure. It is that structure, in addition to the chemical composition, that gives the diamond its famous hardness, and makes it such an ideal tool for focusing energy. Man-made crystals are used in lasers, watches, and computers because of their energy-focusing capabilities. Crystalline structure not only focuses power well, it is an excellent storage medium for your energy.

The instructions in crystal-growing kits are not difficult to follow, but may take some experimentation to master. The tools required in addition to the kits are readily available. For example, you will need an old saucepan and a dieter's food scale. You will also need a quiet place to leave the growing vessels, as they must remain undisturbed while the crystals are forming. The crystals are grown by dissolving the kit's chemical solution in an exact amount of hot water. Hot water will hold more of the chemical than cold water, so as the solution cools in the growing vessels, the chemicals will be forced out of the cooling water and become solid. This also happens as the water evaporates. Because of the shape of the molecules that make the chemicals, when they become solid, they will naturally form crystals.

The growth takes several days, and in itself can be done as a ritual. I grow mine on the waxing Moon, projecting my energy into the growing vessels every night. As with any item you are charging, remember not to project energy if you are tired or angry. In the case of an already-formed object, what you put in will be what you get out, but in the case of item creation, what you put in will affect the very nature of the created item.

So what can you do with your crystals? Anything you can do with a normal crystal, and more. Because you are charging them as they grow, you can attune them to a goal as they are forming. Imagine divining with a clear crystal you grew solely for that purpose! The attunement can be as complicated or simple as you like, using whatever correspondences you feel are appropriate. For example, you might project energy into a divination crystal only at night, leaving the vessels where moonlight can fall on them, and cover the window during the day. To aid in attuning your projected energy towards divination, you might drink eyebright tea, or while you project energy, burn incense that will aid in divination such as nutmeg, lilac, or bistort. On the other hand, if you desire green crystals to use for healing spells, tint the water/chemical solution with a small amount of green food coloring and consecrate the solution to the purpose of healing. Empower healing crystals during the day, and visualize your energy coming from your hands as vivid green light. You might also want to cover the growing vessels with sheer green cloth or cellophane so the crystals can absorb the power of the colored light as well.

Your crystals will also work in the deceptively simple role of power batteries. When you need extra energy for a ritual, (such as during the waning Moon), place a number of your crystals around you at the beginning of the ritual. Visualize the points shooting beams of pure energy into you. Or, place the points toward an item you wish empowered, instruct the crystals to release their energy into the item, and visualize laser-like beams performing the charge.

It is important to note that your crystals, having a different chemical composition than naturally occurring crystals, are water-soluble. This means you can't wash them, and it's not a good idea to put them in your mouth. It does, however, provide you with another way to use them. The growing process will create a few large specimens, but also a quantity of smaller pieces. Those small bits are hard to handle, but contain your energy just as the large ones do. One way to release that energy is to leave them in a bowl filled with water. The water will dissolve the crystal bits, just as a running river will wear down a mountain. As the water does its work, your energy will be released into the air to empower your spell. (Note that if you used food coloring, it will be released as well, and might stain the bowl. In any case, you shouldn't later use the same bowl for eating.)

These small crystals can also be placed into small decorative jars and then used as focal points for a spell. Runes can be drawn on the jar, herbs can be added, etc. In addition to the normal power of the spell, you'll be getting the energy the crystals absorbed while growing. Or, since oil will not dissolve your crystals, try dropping a point or two into your essential oil bottles to give the oil an extra punch.

The biggest drawback of homegrown crystals is their temporary nature. While it is true that being involved in the creation of an item personalizes it, it is also true that things done quickly don't have the staying power conveyed by slow growth. Your crystals will not last as long as those Mother Nature worked on for thousands of years. However, if you keep them away from water, they will last indefinitely until used. The trick here is to experiment and follow your intuition. Have fun, and Blessed Be!

WINTER SOLSTICE MEDITATION

BY SEDWIN

As we approach the millennium, it is important to keep in tune with our inner selves, as well as the greater web of being. Drink in the beauty of winter, the depth of your soul, and the wonder of the universe. Take time for meditation at the Solstice to ground yourself and prepare the way ahead.

Summer is a fond memory and autumn's splendor has turned dull brown and gray. The hardest part of winter lies ahead, yet the Solstice is here, and with it come lengthening days, the promise of spring, and renewal. This is the wheel of the year.

But now it is winter. This is the time of year when some animals hibernate. For us, winter is the time for turning inward to take stock of our spiritual journey in the previous twelve months and to prepare for the year ahead so that we will emerge with spring's life-force knowing where we have been and where we intend to travel. Pay attention to both inward and outward preparations for the winter holiday season.

Now is the time to prepare your winter journey—your self-work. This night is the time to seek the place within you that is pure being, where you are both student and teacher. Learn to listen to your inner voice, however it may reveal itself to you. It becomes easier to hear that voice as snow covers the ground and our world becomes a little quieter. Winter brings the power of silence. The light in our homes becomes a little softer as

we may favor candles over electric on some evenings.

The fields are empty and the earth seems dead, but the magic of this season can be seen in the evergreens. These magnificent trees are vital and strong while everything around them seems to fade. The dark needles of the yew symbolize death of the waning year and of the things in ourselves that it is time to leave behind. The bright green needles of the fir tree represent birth of the coming year and the parts of ourselves that we want to bring out or renew. The sacred holly—glorious shiny leaves protecting clusters of red berries—is fashioned into wreaths, a circle, the wheel of the year. We each live this wheel in our own way and in our own journey.

During winter, this time of darkness, the days are short and the nights long. Moonlight glitters on the frosty ground, but the air tingles with energy. The brisk air catches your breath. Think of the crystalline night sky. It may be filled with rushing snow or a few drifting flakes, or it may be sharp and clear with pinpoints of starlight. The bracing air tingles. It moves and stirs something within you.

You can feel this sky energy above your head. Reach out with your own energy to the beautiful night sky above you. Feel its energy vibrating against your scalp. As you reach out to it, you can feel your own energy vibrate with the rhythm of the universe.

Let this energy come inside you. Let it enter your head and move down your neck to your shoulders. Feel your skin and muscles come alive. The clear, crisp winter sky is part of you. Let it move down through your chest and arms—through your stomach and abdomen. As it continues to move through your hips, legs, and feet, you can feel the lightness of the energy as it now moves with your own flow of energy. There is a continuous wave of movement from the sky. Feel it circulate through you in an endless stream.

Your entire body may feel light and free, as though it could float like a snowflake. Sky energy is buoyant and can help you stay above the potential trials and tribulations of the winter months. Let it help you prepare your winter's journey. With it you will know that you can travel on whatever path you choose.

As you take this time to seek the way ahead, you may encounter animal guides who will assist you. They may speak to you or they may take you places and show you things. They will help you discover things about yourself—perhaps what you need to do in the forthcoming year or how to solve a problem.

You may feel yourself in a familiar place without any animal guides. What you see or do there will also teach or show you something that may help you in your winter's self-work. You may simply experience a feeling or have an image enter your mind that will aid you in self-discovery. These are only some of the ways that your own true spirit may reach out to your conscious mind. Follow the flow of the energy. Let it show you the way.

When you feel it is time to return from the flow of energy, thank any animal guides for their help in assisting you, and bid them farewell. As the energy winds down, you may still feel light and buoyant. Become aware of your feet on the floor. Send energy through the floor into the ground. Connect with Mother Earth by giving her your sky energy, and when you feel comfortable and grounded, stop sending energy. It's okay to keep some for yourself.

What you may have learned or encountered may not be clear to you immediately, and it may take a day or two to understand, or maybe longer. Be patient. This is part of your journey.

May the spirit of Yuletide bring you special joy and magic.

Winterlife Initiation: The Shamanic Death

By Marguerite Elsbeth

The seasonal round, turning from winter, spring, summer, fall, and back again to winter, offers us a natural metaphor for the shamanic view of the life cycle of the cosmos. Nature sleeps in her coat of hoarfrost cold. Seedlings, vegetation, and hibernating animals await the first thaw of spring, protected beneath the warmth of a crystalline blanket of snow. The creatures and things burrowed under the ground are gathering energy from the earth's fiery core. Shamans consider this state of seeming dormancy to be a power time.

Our passage through the seasonal round of physical life—from embryo to birth, adulthood, old age, and our return to the embryonic Otherworld—is also a time of empowerment, if we choose to recognize it as such. This is why shamans see winter and its pristine stillness as the actual beginning of life itself.

Change and Detachment

All human beings share the same vulnerabilities and frailties: conflicts, desires, and rites of passage such as birth, puberty, marriage, divorce, mid-life crises, old age, disease, and death. This is our common ground and bond, telling us we are all the same, no matter what our culture, race, gender, spiritual belief system, or level of consciousness might be. We all share the primal urge toward the perpetuation of life, an animal survival instinct that prevails upon us to resist detachment in all its forms to the very last. Consequently, great enlightened mystics and shamans have said that while they know by heart the spiritual and mental aspects of death, even they do not necessarily have an emotional grasp on the processes of physical dissolution.

Life experience continually draws our awareness to the fact that change is the only constant. Change is very hard to accept when we expect sameness, especially when accompanied by a sense of loss, such as when a familiar person or loved one moves or passes on. When transformation results in absence, feelings of emptiness, impermanence, surrealism, and dissociation regarding what we believed to be full, constant, real, and dependable in life permeate our emotions.

Our deep-rooted fears about death show us a mirror image reflecting our current level of emotional development, and compel us to test fate and mortality time and time again. Daredevils do this consciously, while the rest of us simply abide in the blissful ignorance of saving grace. Death has a way of sneaking up from behind when we least expect it, and eventually we all must surrender to the inevitability of apparent physical demise.

SURRENDER

Tribal and indigenous cultures steeped in shamanic mysticism recognize that when one member of the community dies, it is a death for all concerned. Grief may become the spirit inhabiting the collective soul, and so shamans of certain tribes teach their people to refrain from expressing sorrow when death comes knocking at the door. This reaction will lead us closer to merging with all creation, because heartfelt pain deepens our wisdom and understanding. However, it also indicates that we are pressing against the natural turning of the cosmic tides. The depth to which we can experience joy and gratitude in troubled times is a true measure of our ability to flow freely with Spirit.

Shamanic traditions remind us that winterlife's passage to the Otherworld carries us to reside with the gods, spirits, and relations of our cultural and familial ancestral stream. Our guardian spirits and ancestors are very much aware of our existence in this world. They hear our thoughts and prayers, reside in our hearts, and are always near. They make their presence known when they come to us in dreams, show us omens, and give us visions. Thus, the shamanic way teaches us that we need not fear. We may rest assured that the ancestors will welcome and assist us when our time comes to return to the other side.

NEAR-DEATH INITIATION

The shamanic world view holds that all creation is based on some form of destruction. Again, this idea can be seen when we look at the destruction and renewal that comes with seasonal changes and the great forces of nature.

Shamans acknowledge the power released during transformation and its chaotic aftermath, and seek to harness this energy for themselves. Therefore, when an apprentice desires full entrance into a shamanic tradition, he or she may undergo an actual near-death experience, such as an accident or illness, that serves as an initiation. When the shaman is recovered, he or she is fully transformed and renewed. Others may experience a symbolic death during a trance state or ecstatic journey, including vivid, practical knowledge concerning the dismemberment of their own body. The shamanic near-death initiation forever destroys old beliefs and the ordinary way of looking at the world. Courage in the face of death eliminates the terror of fear itself. It unlocks the mind to explore new vistas, engenders emotional flexibility and grace, and releases us to embrace the opportunities that are a gift of life. Thus awakened, we can follow our hearts, realize our dreams, and fulfill our destiny.

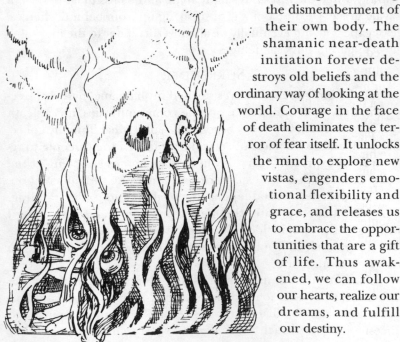

If these ideas are disturbing to you, ponder your thoughts surrounding change, detachment, and surrender a little longer before you decide to undertake the following journey to the winterlife.

THE WINTERLIFE JOURNEY

The near-death initiation is a journey ritual. Begin by seeking out a safe, quiet area in or out of doors wherein you may work undisturbed.

Lie down on your back, close your eyes, and relax your body from head to toe. Imagine that you are approaching a cave entrance, animal burrow, or any other type of doorway leading into the earth. If you have seen a natural earth-entryway during your travels, imagine it as your opening.

Once you reach the entrance, stand beside it and call on your guardian spirit, animal totem, or special ancestor. When approached, explain that you wish to go to the Otherworld place of initiation. Listen carefully to all the instructions they give you. If they refuse to take you to the Otherworld or say you aren't ready for the initiation, then stop the journey immediately, and try again another day.

Proceed by following your guardian spirit, animal, or ancestor to the Otherworld. There is no set appearance to the place of initiation, so accept wherever they bring you as being the correct area.

The initiation starts when you (or your spirit guide) begins to shred off your skin. Watch as your skin is piled up in a heap on the ground. Next, thoroughly pluck all the flesh off your bones, including your internal organs, and add these to the pile. Once you are nothing but a skeleton, dismantle your bones and place them onto the pile as well. Your consciousness remains, but your body is now gone.

Place wood on the pile of skin, flesh, organs, and bones, and set the heap on fire. Let it burn down until nothing but smoldering ash remains on the ground. Take water and mix it into the ash and dirt to create an earthen clay. Use this clay to reform and sculpt a whole new body. Replace any physical, emotional, mental, or spiritual attributes that were no longer useful or pleasing to you with ones that will suit you better, or ask your guardian spirit to do this for you.

When you are done, return with your guardian to the entrance into the earth. Thank your guardian, and notice the ways in which you feel different about yourself.

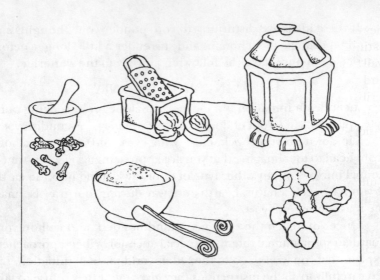

GINGERBREAD MAGIC

BY NUALA DRAGO

Gingerbread has a long and mystical history. Its seductive aroma and sensuous flavor intoxicate the senses by incorporating an enchanting blend of spices that were once more precious than jewels. Magic, food, and art combined, this ancient creation is a veritable magnet for positive energy. It was treasured by the ancient Greeks, placed in the tombs of Egyptian pharaohs, coveted as an aphrodisiac by Roman sects, given by ladies of Celtic courts as tokens of love to their knights, and used by countless races, including the Chinese, to commune with their deities. Today, it is still a powerful tool for magic.

Ancient alchemists were probably the first to notice the qualities of the spices used to flavor the fragrant confection. Although ginger, nutmeg, cinnamon, and cloves differ in physical nature from the gold and silver used in the metallurgical tradition, they were assigned the same sacred nature by ancient conjurers, who believed that the potent essences of plant extracts could influence reality in the same way as the precious metals. Like the ores, the spices came from the earth, which they perceived as their mother's womb. This view of the earth established a reverent relationship between man, nature, and the cosmos.

By the Middle Ages, society was concerned with the condition of the spirit or soul and believed that it maintained both an internal and external domain. Gingerbread addressed both realms. Baking, viewed as purification by fire, provided ritual plus aromatherapy, and eating it was believed to promote psychic and cosmic awareness as well as protect from evil influences. However, because of the precious and sacred nature of the ingredients, magicians and healers prescribed this humoral medicine only to those who could afford the luxury. Poor folk were largely excluded from partaking except for the occasional purchase from the sweet stalls at one of the seasonal fairs.

Those fair stalls were probably manned by apprentices from the Gingerbread Guild, which was a more elite entity than the Baker's Guild. Guild members had their own secret formulas and their own signature decorations for the sweet. The recipes and the molds were passed from generation to generation. Even the craftsmen, who carved the often intricate forms for the gingerbread bakers, had their own guilds.

Today, many participate in the European custom of preparing a fruited variety of gingerbread at All Hallows Eve or Samhain, when the aroma of the spices are said to protect us from malevolent spirits, while putting the "come hither" on benevolent ones. Yuletide has also has been a traditional time for gingerbread in its various forms due to the belief that it will attract prosperity in the coming year.

Modern pharmacology also makes use of the spices that flavor this delectable confection. Ginger is used to cure motion sickness and stomach upset. Ginger oil is also used topically for joint pain and spinal problems. Cloves and clove oil, which have antiseptic properties, are used for toothaches, diarrhea, and fungal infections.

Cinnamon can be added to tea or other foods to ease the discomfort of menstrual cramps, flatulence, and diarrhea, but it has some antiseptic, anti-fungal properties as well.

Spices are pleasant to use and give us a sense of well-being that aids us in positive thinking. Positive thinking is one of our most important defenses, whether we use it for medicine or magical enhancement. Please remember, though, that even something as seemingly innocuous as nutmeg can be toxic if taken in large quantities. Educate yourself about what you put into your body, or seek the help of a professional. There are also plenty of good books out there.

One title I recommend is *The Magic in Food* by Scott Cunningham. This book will be a useful reference since nuts, berries, dried fruit, oatmeal, apples, pumpkin, rose petals, and so many other good things can be added to gingerbread to enhance or alter the effect each time you prepare it. You are limited only by your imagination and intent.

Probably the hardest part of performing gingerbread magic will be to choose a recipe and shape out of the limitless numbers available. Gingerbread is an extremely versatile medium that can be molded, shaped, embossed, embellished, iced, dusted with cocoa or confectioner's sugar, painted, etched, stenciled, and even gold- or silver-leafed. Chocolate-dipped gingerbread cookies are exquisite, and chocolate is reputed to be both an aphrodisiac and a money magnet.

Whether you prefer cakes or cookies, it doesn't matter. The important thing is that you visualize your intent and bake your gingerbread with all the positive energy you can muster. Meditate, chant, pray, repeat a mantra—whatever it takes to hold a picture of the desired outcome in your mind.

Once it is baked, further enhance the effect of the finished product by decorating it with symbols such as sigils, signs of the zodiac, runes, ogham, animals or whatever you feel is appropriate for your purpose. Simple etchings done with a toothpick on the surface of your gingerbread will do, but there are even baker's catalogs that will print photographs on edible rice paper if you require something really elaborate.

Remember, too, that gingerbread is suitable for any holiday or occasion. It makes an excellent Yule log, tastes great with cream and blackberries at Imbolc, makes a great centerpiece with a dowel inserted in the center and tied with ribbons to represent the May Pole at Beltane, and the aroma will welcome ancestral spirits at Samhain.

Try to develop your own secret recipe. Use the aroma to enhance meditation. Close your eyes and think of gingerbread's powerful past, its rich history. Empower your mind with the knowledge you share with wise practitioners of ancient times; Near East, Far East, Europe to America. Exercise your creativity to make gingerbread a trustworthy old friend for the new millennium.